The Scale and Impacts of Money Laundering

The Scale and Impacts of Money Laundering

Brigitte Unger

Utrecht School of Economics,
Utrecht University, The Netherlands

With a contribution of
Elena Madalina Busuioc

Utrecht School of Governance,
Utrecht University, The Netherlands

Edward Elgar
Cheltenham, UK • Northampton, MA, USA

Published by
Edward Elgar Publishing Limited
The Lypiatts
15 Lansdown Road
Cheltenham
Glos GL50 2JA
UK

Edward Elgar Publishing, Inc.
William Pratt House
9 Dewey Court
Northampton
Massachusetts 01060
USA

Reprinted 2014

A catalogue record for this book
is available from the British Library

Library of Congress Cataloguing in Publication Data

Unger, B. (Brigitte)
   The scale and impacts of money laundering / Brigitte Unger.
      p. cm.
   Includes bibliographical references and index.
   1. Money laundering–Netherlands. I. Title.
   HV6771.N4U64 2007
   364.16'8–dc22
                                             2006035573

ISBN 978 1 84720 223 9

Contents

Tables

Figures

Abbreviations

ACFE	Association of Certified Fraud Examiners
AFP	Australian Federal Police
AML	Anti-Money Laundering
ARBIFT	Arab Bank for Investment and Foreign Trade
AUSTRAC	Australian Transaction Reports and Analysis Centre
BFI	Special Financial Office (in Dutch: Bijzondere Financiële Instelling) also called SPE or SPV
BIS	Bank of International Settlements
BSA	Bank Secrecy Act
CBS	Dutch Central Bureau of Statistics (in Dutch: Centraal Bureau voor Statistiek)
CEO	Chief Executive Officer
CFATF	Caribbean Financial Action Task Force
CFE	Certified Fraud Examiner
CFT	Countering Financing of Terrorism
CIA	Central Intelligence Agency
CPB	Dutch Central Planning Bureau (in Dutch: Centraal Plan Bureau)
DNB	Dutch National Bank
DYMIMIC	Dynamic Multiple Indicators Multiple Causes
EC	European Commission
ECJ	European Court of Justice
EG	Egmont Group member
ESD	EU's Saving Tax Directive
EU	European Union
FATF	Financial Action Task Force
FD	Financial Deposits
FDI	Foreign Direct Investment
FIOD-ECD	Dutch Fiscal Intelligence and Investigation Unit and the Economic Control Service (in Dutch: Fiscale Inlichtingen en Opsporingsdienst en de Economische Controle Dienst)
FIU	Financial Intelligence Unit
FSF	Financial Stability Forum
FTR Act	Financial Transaction Report Act
GAO	Government Accountability Office

GDP	Gross Domestic Product
GWK	Border Currency Change Office (in Dutch: Grens Wissel Kantoor)
IBC	International Business Companies
IMF	International Monetary Fund
IRS	Internal Revenue Service
MOT	Dutch FIU (in Dutch: Melding Ongebruikelijke Transacties)
NCC	Dutch Central Catalogue (in Dutch: Nederlandse Centrale Catalogus)
NCCTs	Non-Cooperative Countries and Territories
NVB	Dutch Bank Association (in Dutch: Nederlandse Vereniging van Banken)
ODA	Official Development Aid
OECD	Organization of Economic Cooperation and Development
OFAC	Office of Foreign Act
OFC	Offshore Financial Centre
SIOD	Dutch Social Intelligence and Investigation Unit (in Dutch: Sociale Inlichtingen en Opsporingsdienst)
SIRCA	Securities Industry Research Centre of Asia Pacific
SPE	Special Purpose Entity
SPV	Special Purpose Vehicle
SWIFT	Society for Worldwide Interbank Financial Telecommunication
TFP	Total Factor Productivity
TNI	Trans National Institute
UAE	United Arab Emirates
UN	United Nations
UNDCP	United Nations Drugs Control Program
UNODC	United Nations Office on Drugs and Crime
VAT	Value Added Tax
WODC	Dutch Scientific Research and Documentation Centre (in Dutch: Wetenschappelijk Onderzoek en Documentatie Centrum)
Wtt	Law on Control of Trust Offices (in Dutch: Wet op Toezicht Trustkantoren)
WVV	By the Judge estimated proceeds of a crime (in Dutch: Wederrechtelijk Verkregen Voordeel)

Foreword and Acknowledgements

This book is the outcome of a project on 'The Amount and the Effects of Money Laundering' for the Dutch Ministry of Finance, completed in February 2006 by the Utrecht School of Economics, with the support of scholars of the Australian National University in Canberra. The project participants came from five countries and four disciplines and included in alphabetic order Madalina Busuioc, Joras Ferwerda, Wouter de Kruijf, Greg Rawlings, Melissa Siegel, Brigitte Unger and Kristen Wokke. They have all participated in the project with great enthusiasm, diligence and energy. We thank Madalina Busuioc from Romania, for her knowledge of law and wonderful writing style; Joras Ferwerda from the Netherlands, who dealt with the 44,000 entries of the 220 by 220 matrices and who would not give up until he had found an answer to his research question; Wouter de Kruijf from the Netherlands, who kept control over the research output and organized everything so that the different parts of the book fitted together; Melissa Siegel, a social scientist from the US, who pioneered in unpacking the Walker model for money laundering and who had to collect, organize and deal with a huge amount of new data; Kristen Wokke, a Dutch student who wrote his bachelors thesis on the organization of money laundering policies. Greg Rawlings, an anthropologist from the Australian National University, was the consultant of this project. I, Brigitte Unger, an economist from Austria and the Utrecht School of Economics, was the project leader. Marissa van der Valk and Andrea Naylor gave administrative support. Joost Simons and his wife corrected some of the English. Titia Kloos, Willemien Vreekamp and Frans van Eck did the lay out. I thank this young and sparkling project research team, without whose preceding work, help, and support this book would not have been possible.

Many other people have helped as well. Thanks to all of them. In particular I want to mention Eric van Andel, Frank van Erp, Ben Geurts, Bernhard ter Haar, Erich Hille, Edward Kleemans, Oberinspektor J. Mahr, Piet van Reenen, Helene Schuberth, Marret Smekens, Brigitte Slot, Eva Stohanzl, and Pieter Verrest, who accompanied the project as it progressed. Furthermore, I extend my appreciation to the Dutch Central Bank (De Nederlandse Bank), The Dutch Ministry of Finance, and the Dutch Banking Association NVB.

Thanks also to the colleagues of Utrecht School of Economics, in particular to Rob Alessie, Ian Peter Engelen, Gerrit Faber, Filipa Figueira, Peter de Gijsel, Jaap Bos, Bas van Groezen, Loek Groot, Harry Garretsen, Hannah Kiiver,

Clemens Kool, Thijs Knaap and Ian Reijnders. Donato Masciandaro from Bocconi University Milano, Italy, and Raffaella Barone from the University of Lecce, Italy, also gave useful hints and comments.

I also want to mention Frans van Waarden from University College of Utrecht University, who alternated in reading parts of the manuscript and in cheering up the author.

A very special thanks goes to Greg Rawlings whom I met at the Regulatory Institutions Network (RegNet) in Australia. When he showed me his beautiful PhD on money laundering in Vanuatu, I really somehow regretted that economists when compared to anthropologists, have such a dry and limited use of language. He not only helped to shape the project from the very beginning, but also contributed substantially to the introduction of this book. It was he who analysed recent spectacular money laundering cases of Austrian and Dutch banks, it was he who first mentioned the Australian 'Walker' model to me on which the money laundering estimates in this book are based, it was he who introduced me to new data sets and literature. Greg always gave very valuable insights and comments and was very pleasant company. Thank you Greg.

Thanks to John and Valerie Braithwaite at the Regulatory Institutions Network (RegNet) at the Australian National University, and to all the colleagues there, who helped to design the original project draft.

While the research report for the ministry focused on the Netherlands solely, this book tries to incorporate a comparative perspective, by also bringing in money laundering cases from Australia and other countries. Australia is interesting because it is of about the same economic size as the Netherlands. It has a very special location because it is surrounded by a ring of islands of unrest, crime and money laundering, and therefore is an attractive transit country for launderers. Nauru, Vanuatu, Solomon Islands are some of these islands, just to name a few.

The findings of this project received widespread attention in the Dutch media. I am grateful to the Dutch journalists, whose expertise and professionalism allowed a serious public debate. I hope that this book will contribute to enhance the debate between different academic disciplines.

1. Introduction[1]

1.1. MONEY LAUNDERING, RISK MANAGEMENT AND BANK SECRECY

ABN AMRO is one of the world's largest banks. Incorporated in the Netherlands with its headquarters in Amsterdam, it has some 3000 branches and subsidiaries spread over 60 countries. It is valued at some US$830 billion. In December 2005 the US Federal Reserve Board, the New York Banking Department and the Illinois Department of Financial and Professional Regulation fined ABN AMRO, US$80 million for violating state and federal Anti Money Laundering (AML) rules and regulations (US Federal Reserve et al. 2005). US authorities, in conjunction with the Central Bank of the Netherlands, found that ABN AMRO lacked adequate risk management procedures and legal review methods; lacked effective systems of corporate governance and audit; transferred and cleared funds and issued letters of credit that contravened US laws; failed to adequately report suspicious activities; did not follow-up on negative findings from internal audits; failed to investigate enquiries referred to its New York branch and overstated its due diligence procedures when dealing with 'high-risk' correspondent banking customers (De Nederlandsche Bank NV, US Federal Reserve Board, State of Illinois and the New York Banking Department 2005, pp. 2–4). Dutch and US authorities found that ABN AMRO had engaged in 'unsafe and unsound practices' contravening the laws of both countries (De Nederlandsche Bank NV, US Federal Reserve Board, State of Illinois and the New York Banking Department 2005, p. 5).

In levying its US$80 million fine, US authorities found ABN AMRO to be in contravention of three out of the four AML compliance criteria. For example, in failing to maintain an adequate system of internal controls the bank also failed to integrate publicly available data regarding 'shell companies' into its automated monitoring systems. Between August 2002 and September 2003 the North American Regional Clearing Centre processed 20,000 wire transfers totaling US$3.2 billion for shell companies (which can be Special Purpose Entities [SPEs]) providing corporate vehicles for clients from Russia and the former Soviet Union.[2] These shell companies incorporated in the US, not some exotic offshore 'tax haven' jurisdiction, could be used to conceal the beneficial identity of their shareholders, including criminals disguised as 'investors' seeking to launder funds (US Department of the Treasury Financial Crimes Enforcement Network 2005, p. 5). US regulators observed that:

> The New York Branch of ABN AMRO failed to adequately evaluate this readily available information and implement sufficient transaction monitoring systems and controls for shell company activity. Instead, and only upon strong urging from regulators, the New York Branch of ABN AMRO commenced an analysis of the activity in August 2003 – one year after many of the transactions occurred (US Department of the Treasury Financial Crimes Enforcement Network 2005, p. 5).

The Financial Crimes Enforcement Network also reported that ABN AMRO's New York branch failed to provide an adequate number of personnel to manage compliance with the US Bank Secrecy Act (BSA)[3] and the staff that did work in this area received insufficient training. Staff 'in critical positions' appeared to 'have a lack of knowledge on the detection and reporting of suspicious transactions – a deficiency especially serious considering the substantial risk of facilitating money laundering that confronted the New York Branch of ABN AMRO' (US Department of the Treasury Financial Crimes Enforcement Network 2005, p. 6).

1.2. WIRING IRAN, SANCTION BUSTING WITH LIBYA

This volume seeks to estimate national (with case studies of the Netherlands and Australia) and global volumes of money laundering. Flows of laundered funds have definitive economic effects, particularly on growth and costs of crime. However, estimates of both the amounts and effects of money laundering need to be situated within their legal and regulatory contexts. What is money laundering in one country is not necessarily the same offence in another state. This has an impact on what and how money laundering is measured and how the amounts and effects are calculated. If anything shows more clearly the problems of defining money laundering and providing an accurate global base-line for measuring the amounts and effects of laundered funds, it was ABN AMRO's dealings with Iran and Libya. Half of the US$80 million fine levied against the bank was authorised by the Office of Foreign Assets Control (OFAC), part of the Department of the Treasury. OFAC regulates and prohibits specified transactions between the US and Iran and Libya (US Federal Reserve et al. 2005). The US Libyan Sanctions Regulations gave force to United Nations (UN) resolutions imposing economics measures against Libya in response to past involvement with international terrorism. All countries agreed to these sanctions and therefore any violation of them could give rise to allegations of money laundering that would be valid across borders. The Iranian Transactions Regulations however, by which Washington imposes sanctions unilaterally on

Iran, are specific to the US. No other major trading nation imposes such measures against Iran. Therefore, a US company dealing surreptitiously with Iran and without approval of the OFAC could be charged with money laundering. Any non-US company in a third country however, is perfectly free to trade with state-owned and private Iranian firms. Because domestic laws govern these transactions as it applies in specific third countries, and not US laws, there are no money laundering charges to be answered. In other words, what constitutes money laundering under US law may not constitute money laundering anywhere else.

ABN AMRO is defined as a foreign bank in the US, including its New York and Chicago Branches. Despite this, OFAC regulations covering Iran and Libya apply to ABN AMRO regardless of whether of not transactions are routed through the US or a third country if they involve US individuals and/or corporate entities. These regulations effectively blur the boundaries between the US and third countries. Up until August 2004 ABN AMRO's New York branch processed wire transfers remitted by Bank Meli Iran. It also honored Bank Meli's letters of credit. These transactions were sub-contracted out to ABN AMRO's third-country branches, which then obscured any reference to Bank Meli (US Federal Reserve et al. 2005, p. 5).

ABN AMRO's Chicago and New York branches were simultaneously dealing with a Libyan state chartered bank registered in the United Arab Emirates, the Arab Bank for Investment and Foreign Trade (ARBIFT). US authorities observed that

> 'Prior to August 1, 2004, the Chicago Branch of ABN AMRO cleared US dollars checks for ARBIFT. The cleared checks were submitted by one of ABN AMRO's overseas branches, which had arranged for ARBIFT to not endorse or stamp the checks' (US Federal Reserve et al. 2005, p. 6).

These dealings with Iran and Libya were found to violate US regulations, specifically transactions that have cloaking features that can be used to avoid or evade the specific compliance requirement when engaged in commercial or financial ventures with these two countries. In addition to the US$ 40 million fine (out of the total of US$ 80 million) levied against ABN AMRO for these specific infringements of the Iranian Transactions Regulations and the Libyan Sanctions Regulations, the OFAC ordered the bank to undertake independent audits. These were deemed necessary to review operations and transactions in ABN AMRO's Dubai (UAE) and Chennai (India) branches to determine the extent of US commercial relations with Iran and India. Presumably, charge information could then be used to launch investigations into specific instances of money laundering.

What is important here, is that such commercial arrangements between US individuals and firms and Iran would only constitute a money laundering offence under US law, not under the laws of India, UAE, or under the laws of The Netherlands, the location of ABN AMRO's headquarters. It demonstrates the considerable degree of variation, and disagreements between countries and companies, as to what actually constitutes money laundering and its predicate offences. Furthermore, it is crucial to emphasise that ABN AMRO was not found guilty of money laundering per se, but rather of engaging in 'unsafe and unsound practices' that increased the potential risk for criminal abuse (US Federal Reserve et al. 2005, p. 6).

Money laundering involves three key stages: *placement*, where 'dirty' money is lodged with an entity (for example a business or a bank) for 'cleaning', which occurs during the second phase of *layering* where funds are channeled through the financial system (with varying degrees of complexity). At the end of the layering phase, funds move to the final stage of *integration*. This is the last cycle of the laundering process where funds are completely cleaned and are then integrated into the economy at points of investment and/or consumption (see chapter five on techniques of money laundering for more details). Because of the speed in which the means of money can be transformed and cleansed anew through placement, layering and integration, it is a major challenge to detect and lay charges for money laundering, even though an analysis of transactions make it possible that laundering had occurred.

1.3. CARIBBEAN COMPANIES, SECURITIES FRAUD AND FAKE BONDS: THE COLLAPSE OF REFCO AND AUSTRIA'S BAWAG BANK

There is thus no uniform, consistent approach to, or definition of money laundering. The 2005 collapse of the US securities trader and the involvement of Austria's third largest bank (Bank für Arbeit und Wirtschaft) reads like a series of money laundering transactions. Refco's former CEO, Philip Bennet, has been accused in the US courts of fraudulently concealing US$430 million in losses and missing funds (Shapiro 2006). Prior to the discovery of these financial irregularities, Bennett had borrowed US$21 million from the trade-union owned BAWAG bank. Its involvement in the US derivatives and securities firms went deeper than this. BAWAG had participated in New York based Public Investment in Private Equity (PIPE) trading schemes whereby companies short of liquidity raise equity by selling stock at discount prices often through hedge funds. BAWAG used hedge funds based in Liechtenstein to facilitate its participation in the highly speculative PIPE market. In the meantime Refco had incorporated six companies on the Caribbean island of Anguilla, which were jointly owned by a company called Liquid Opportunity and

BAWAG. They in turn held US$525 million in fake bonds in an entity incorporated in Bermuda (Shapiro 2006).

In October 2005 Refco's board learned that Bennett had fraudulently hid loans from Refco to his own companies, from which he in turn borrowed again from BAWAG in an attempt to repay Refco. This was not enough to stop his suspension as CEO. The share-price plummeted. However, the collateral for BAWAG's loan to Bennett comprised of shares in the company itself. Within a few days of the scandal breaking, these were worthless leaving the bank with massive losses (Rajwade 2005). This caused a run on the bank back in Austria with depositors at one stage withdrawing as much as €100 million per day. In addition, Refco's creditors launched legal action against BAWAG claiming US$1.3 billion, 'alleging that the bank actively helped Bennett to deceive the company' (Shapiro 2006). One commentator observed that '[In] parallel with Enron, WorldCom and umpteen other companies, it is the top executives, whose compensations run into tens of millions of dollars, who seem to be perpetrating the biggest frauds' (Rajwade 2005, p. 2). However, do these transactions constitute money laundering? On one level these fraud-triggered corporate collapses exhibit classic money laundering characteristics: A crime is committed (fraud) which has a financial gain, these gains are then placed in a myriad of offshore and onshore corporate structures, they are then layered to make them appear legitimate financing and they are then reintegrated as clean property or investments such as stocks and bonds.

However, the charge of 'money laundering' has been curiously absent from the Refco case. Bennett himself has been charged with securities fraud, not money laundering, though in the US securities fraud is a predicate crime that can attach a charge of money laundering. By contrast in Austria there is no crime for 'self-laundering', that is only third parties can be charged with money laundering, not offenders who have committed an offence. There remain on the one hand substantial variations between states as to what actually constitutes money laundering and on the other hand there has been an escalating legal trend to conflate an ever-increasing number of all manner of 'crimes' and activity (both financial and non-financial) under the rubric of 'money laundering'.

This has direct consequences for attempts to measure the amounts and economic effects of money laundering. Where money laundering is defined at as broadest level to include tax evasion and fraud, it can result in a discursive and financial 'blow-out' in the very term 'money laundering' and economic estimates of the amounts of domestic and transnationally laundered funds. However, where money laundering is defined narrowly to include only the proceeds of a limited number of crimes such as drug dealing and fencing without the need for complex financial engineering, or where the layering and integration phases are not fully addressed then estimates can correspondingly be quite low. In this book, varying estimates of the volume and economic effects of money laundering are situated within these two often-competing trends (conceptualizing money laundering narrowly or expansively).

1.4. DEVELOPING DEFINITIONS AND MEASURING MONEY LAUNDERING: CONTROVERSIES AND POLITICAL CONTEXTS

Money laundering has become a growth industry involving a large number of countries and law enforcement agencies together with non-governmental, multilateral, intergovernmental and supranational organizations. The Bank of International Settlements (BIS), the Organization of Economic Cooperation and Development (OECD), the G8,[4] G20,[5] EU members' finance and justice ministers, several departments in the United Nations, the World Bank, the International Monetary Fund (IMF), and the Financial Stability Forum (FSF) are all involved in regulatory efforts designed to assess and reduce money laundering. This has led to a plethora of bilateral and multilateral rules and agreements that have made effective regulation a challenge for all Financial Intelligence Units (FIUs) that are mandated with enforcing and regulating AML provisions. It has also contributed to jurisdictional arbitrage whereby money launderers can take advantage of multiple rules and conflicting agreements.

Despite these challenges, there is growing international consensus on money laundering and the most effective ways of countering it, though these have been driven by key state actors (particularly the US). For example the G7 established the Financial Action Task Force (FATF) in 1989 to examine and investigate efforts to combat money laundering. Since that time it has become the main multilateral AML organization and its capacities to set international standards have been increasingly strengthened. For example, the FATF has issued its 40 recommendations on money laundering as a benchmark upon which countries can measure how effective their AML policies are. At the same time there remains a lack of clarity as how to best approach money laundering, due to competing national definitions and enforcement procedures. One commentator has observed that:

> Their analyses, reports and recommendations reveal a disturbing tendency to quote each other's work; since they enjoy substantially the same membership, this practice amounts to self-corroboration. Moreover, at times they offer overlapping sets of rules and best practices to deal with money laundering. It is ironic that the international community would fail to produce a single, unified set of rules to take on a criminal activity that thrives precisely on exploiting differences in laws and regulations. (Morris-Cotterill 2001, p. 22).

There is thus widespread debate and even uncertainty as to what constitutes money laundering.

Chapter two in this volume provides an overview of different definitions of money laundering. These all have distinctive meanings, but they have been appropriated without concern for these distinctions in law and in AML legal enforcement with important methodological implications when measuring the amounts and effects of money laundering.

Illegal activities can also include both civil and criminal offences. An offence that is illegal is not necessarily criminal. For example, while it is illegal to gamble in an unlicensed casino in The Netherlands it is not a criminal offence to do so. In the Australian jurisdictions of South Australia and the Australian Capital Territory it is illegal to possess cannabis but it is not a criminal offence to do so (provided possession does not exceed two grams of marijuana per person). Another striking feature is that some definitions assert that money laundering involves the attempt to hide the source of illegal or criminal income, whereas others stress the act of 'making it appear legal'. The former could include the archetypical and clichéd case of 'hiding money under a pillow', whereas the latter necessitates some degree of willful action to bring the money back into the legal economy. An active attempt to hide the source of criminal income also corresponds with analyses of money laundering that involve *placement*, *layering* and *integration*.

Despite the fact that legislation varies between countries, it is important to find a common definition of money laundering. For measuring money laundering one needs a clear definition that includes all predicate crimes. Originally, money laundering referred only to the laundering of drug money. In the last 20 years however, it has been extended to include theft, fraud and an increasing number of other offences. Today, the FATF definition includes terrorist financing. From a legal perspective this means that there has been a tremendous paradigm shift (see chapter two).

The FATF has made great efforts to define money laundering clearly. However, these efforts have been aimed at achieving an international standard that nevertheless conceals the existence of national variations in legal definitions. It seems important to have an international and interdisciplinary debate on what money laundering is, what it includes and what it excludes.

1.5. MONEY LAUNDERING: CONCEPTUAL PROBLEMS

There are several controversial points involved in conceptualizing money laundering. First, the definition of money laundering developed gradually (and was initially confined to the United States) but as it did so it began to encompass an ever-escalating number of crimes. This has affected the ability to measure the extent of money laundering in economics. Chapter 2 of the book gives an overview on definitions of money laundering in law. It opts for a broad definition that includes not only proceeds from drugs and fraud but also from tax evasion and illegal work. Chapter 3 shows how definitions of the illegal economy, the shadow economy, underground banking and money laundering are related to each other. This still leaves the question of what would be the most appropriate definition of money laundering unanswered. The choice of definition might also depend on the question posed.

Part of the controversy stems from inter-disciplinary approaches to money laundering. Criminologists opt for methods such as case studies, carefully following each dollar bill, while economists tend to use existing published data to model, forecast and predict. Some criminologists do not consider modeling an appropriate method. They simply do not believe models and find them 'luchtspiegelingen' as the Dutch say – spun out of thin air. Chapter 3 gives an overview of possible ways to measure money laundering in different disciplines and attempts to provide theoretical foundations for the economic model used in this book.

1.6. ESTIMATING THE AMOUNTS OF MONEY LAUNDERING

Another difference among disciplines is the fact that economists usually do not question the underlying data base from international organizations. In Chapter 4, these inter-disciplinary debates turn out to be of particular interest for the question whether or not global money laundering is large or small. This means that the underlying global data of international organizations are therefore also questioned.

While the diversity of definitions complicates efforts to estimate the amounts of laundered money circulating both nationally and internationally, moves to develop enhanced models that give more accurate assessments of the amount, flows and effects of money laundering may contribute resolving some of the more controversial aspects of debate in scholarship and policy. As Reuter and Greenfield (2001, p. 171) observe:

> 'knowing the value of drug exports from Mexico to the US is US$1–3 billion rather than US$10–20 billion may be very important for purposes of allocating resources for money laundering investigations or even passing money laundering regulations in Mexico'.

Therefore making estimates has important policy implications.

It is necessary to open up, critically interrogate and analyse various estimates of money laundering, which arbitrarily circulate like magic figures around the world (chapter 4). These estimates are important. International organizations, national governments, the media, NGOs and law enforcement agencies refer to them constantly. The International Monetary Fund (IMF) for example, has estimated money laundering at 2–5 percent of world Gross Domestic Product (GDP), but few others have made an attempt to quantify global money laundering. Finding the underlying model of such estimations is an important step to improve estimates of money laundering. For this we reconstruct and transparently show in chapter four a model of how to measure money laundering that closely corresponds to current estimates. This includes critiques of the assumptions made, testing the model and suggestions on ways to improve it in the future. This should allow more accurate and internationally comparable estimates of money laundering to be made.

The modeling for the estimates used in this approach adopts the methodologies used by John Walker (1995; 1999[a]; 1999[b]), an Australian economist and consultant to the country's Financial Intelligence Unit (FIU), AUSTRAC (Australian Transaction Reports and Analysis Centre). This was the first analyst to make a serious attempt at quantifying money laundering and the initial output from his model suggests that US\$2.85 trillion is laundered globally. We measured a modified Walker model with more accurate data for the Netherlands. The figure that up to US\$50 billion of funds is laundered in The Netherlands (that Walker originally calculated for the Netherlands in 1995) seems to be too high.

These new estimations exposed the strengths and weaknesses of the Walker Model. One of the main strengths in this model is that it is a pioneer study that estimates money laundering on a large scale for all countries for the first time.

Having worked for AUSTRAC, Walker also incorporated his grounded knowledge on money laundering into the modeling. Walker also had access to information, data sets and expert interviews in the field (indeed surveys of Australian police forces and criminologists were vital in the first stage of his calculations) and consequently had developed an appreciation and a 'feeling' for the extent of money laundering.

Criminological accounts of money laundering use intuition and inter-subjectivity in their methodologies, even if they are not aware of it. For example the analysis of case studies requires reflexivity and intuition about information provided in crime files.

This is not to say that the model we use is without problems. It assumes that all countries attract criminal money for the same reasons. It conflates very different countries with very different economic structures. All of these encompassing models share these problems (see for example estimates for the shadow economy by Schneider 2002). The way the Walker Model is used for the estimations made here, acknowledges these problems.

This volume incorporates national case studies of money laundering in two medium-sized industrial countries: the Netherlands and Australia. The incidences and character of money laundering in these two countries is considered emblematic for other members of the Organization for Economic Cooperation and Development (OECD). Discussions and analysis of money laundering in the Netherlands and Australia, is contextualised internationally and in relation to a number of important third countries, particularly the United States and the United Kingdom. These two country studies have allowed us to improve Walker's original money laundering model by introducing the most up-to-date data for the Netherlands and Australia, and by calibrating international measures.

Walker tends to overestimate money generated for laundering in the Netherlands, by about 40 percent, but money laundering in both the Netherlands and Australia is still sizeable. Our results indicate that there is €8 to €14 billion from crime generated in the Netherlands of which 37 to 44 percent will remain in The Netherlands to be laundered. This means that money laundering from crime in The Netherlands amounts to €3 to €6 billion per year, with the most likely estimate to be €3.8 billion. The remaining generated money for laundering will be placed somewhere else. In addition, criminal money from abroad will also flow into the Netherlands. There is also an additional €14 to €21 billion that flows into the Netherlands from the top 20 origin countries of generated money for laundering. This means that the amount of money laundering with which the Dutch have to deal accounts for about €18 to €25 billion, hence about four percent of the Dutch money demand, or about 5 percent of Dutch GDP. Findings for Australia suggest that money generated for laundering amounts to US$1–3 billion. Additional money flowing into Australia amounts toUS$12–18 billion. Money laundering is about 5 percent of Australian GDP. In both countries, money laundering is sizeable.

1.7. TECHNIQUES OF LAUNDERING

Part of the controversy about the volume and importance of money laundering is also due to the fact that different disciplines concentrate on different phases of money laundering. As discussed earlier, the first phase of money laundering occurs at placement where the proceeds of crime are deposited at a bank, smuggled over a border or infused with the turnover of a legitimate business. This phase can be called the placement or pre-wash phase. The second phase is the layering phase (the main wash) where money is circulated many times, either nationally or all over the globe to hide its illegal source. In this phase complicated financial constructions such as complicated hedging and derivative constructions can occur. The third phase is the reintegration phase, where the money is parked permanently, like in the bond market or in the real estate sector.

Do money-laundering estimates, such as those generated by Walker's model capture all possible techniques of money laundering? Does it include complex financial engineering and the risk factors that the US Federal Reserve identified in ABN AMRO's 'unsafe and unsound' banking practices that I started this chapter with? This is where legal diversity (and accompanying uncertainty), estimates of national and global volumes of laundered funds and techniques of money laundering intersect. Chapter five analyses these techniques of money laundering.

Money can be laundered archetypically through the classic style in casinos, via money exchange agencies and through under-ground banking networks. Launders can establish legitimate businesses on the one side, engage in illegal activities on the other, and pour the proceeds of their offending into their legitimate businesses laundering as turnover and profits. Smuggling cash together with wire transfers between countries can also be used to launder money, taking advantage of regulatory loopholes in banks and financial service providers such as trust companies.

Estimates of money laundering, either as a social or an economic problem, include our own face challenges when confronted by large scale laundering undertaken by companies or by criminals who create corporate structures to conceal the extent of money laundering under the guise of legitimate business activity. This also involves differences between countries in the regulation of corporate governance and wrongdoing. For example, what maybe routine corporate practice in one jurisdiction is an offence that could give rise to a charge of money laundering in another jurisdiction. This could include tax planning (which is permitted in one country, but considered criminal tax evasion in another), insider-trading (few countries now permit this, but there was a time when it was considered perfectly acceptable business practice) and dealings with third countries that are otherwise regulated (for example trading with Cuba and Iran are perfectly acceptable for European firms, but are restricted in the United States and can result in criminal charges for violations). This later case is precisely one of the reasons why ABN AMRO was fined in the United States.

Chapter three discusses ways in which money laundering could be estimated by empirical research into over and/or under invoicing exports and imports. This is potentially one way in which large firms engage in money laundering. Alternatively offenders may construct corporate vehicles that mimic the legitimate trading behavior of perfectly legitimate companies, and then turn to over/under priced invoicing together with transfer pricing as a means of laundering funds. This can be achieved using Special Purpose Entities (SPEs). SPEs are holding companies. They are shell companies. They have no minimum capital requirement, so they can be worth $1 or alternatively hold assets worth US$10 million in The British Virgin Islands, The Netherlands, Samoa, Delaware or anywhere that local legislation permits their incorporation. SPEs are often off-balance sheet, bankruptcy remote and private. They can easily be used for both legitimate and illegitimate uses. They lend themselves to money laundering by disguising loans as revenue to misstate earnings, concealment of losses, embezzlement and other accounting improprieties. Financial scandals in which SPEs were abused, include Banco Ambrosiano, the Bank of Commerce and Credit International (BCCI), Enron and Parmalat, to name only a few. The risk that SPEs pose for money laundering was another reason cited by US regulators in their decision to fine ABN AMRO. The US's own Government Accountability Office (GAO) has acknowledged that US SPE shell companies presented a potential risk for money laundering. The GAO (2006, p. i) observed that:

> Federal law enforcement officials are concerned that criminals are increasingly using US shell companies to conceal their identity and illicit activities. Though the magnitude of the problem is difficult to measure, officials said US shell companies are appearing in more investigations in the United States and other countries (United States Government Accountability Office 2006, summary page).

Austria's BAWAG bank also appears to have used SPEs for its American investments (including in its dealings with Refco) incorporated in Anguilla, Bermuda and Liechtenstein. It is the availability of SPEs in both 'onshore' and 'offshore' centers combined with their bank secrecy regimes or limited reporting requirements that have made them targets for accusations that they are conduits for money laundering. One of the findings of this book is however, that it is not just small states that launder money, but large OECD countries that produce the bulk of proceeds of crime to be laundered and whose financial systems are vital in placement, layering and integration. Large industrialised economies maintain a symbiotic relationship with small offshore tax havens, both need the other in order to remain competitive, and this applies to both lawful and criminal money at the same time.

1.8. EFFECTS OF MONEY LAUNDERING

Money laundering has significant short-term and long-term economic effects. These effects are examined in chapters six and seven. A systematic literature search has identified 25 effects of money laundering. Chapter six deals with the short term effects. These include losses to victims and society due to money laundering related crime, distortion of consumption, savings and investment and effects on output and employment. Furthermore, monetary variables such as interest rates, money demand and exchange rates can be affected. Also prices can be deterred and whole sectors affected. The latter is especially evident in the real estate sector. A considerable amount of money ends up in real estate. This sector is less transparent than financial markets, legal persons can act instead of physical persons and the value gains are high involving the placement of large volumes of wealth.

Chapter seven deals with the long term effects of money laundering such as growth effects, effects on crime together with the impact on society and politics. Interestingly there can be positive growth effects from money laundering, which is why some countries (particularly those with bank secrecy or ring-fenced financial regimes) possibly overlook the risks of money laundering as a way of attracting capital and investment. For every one billion of additional laundered currency (recorded in a major world currency such as US dollars or euro) there will be a 0.1 percent increase in annual growth. If countries have established themselves as transit entrepôts and attract both criminal and lawful financial flows then they will most likely profit rather than suffer from the consequences of money laundering. The same most likely will hold true for employment, especially in the financial services sector. The 'externalities' are likely to be felt somewhere else.

However, if money laundering attracts more crime, the growth effect will turn negative. If money laundering leads to an increase in one million more crime cases, then growth will decrease by about 0.3 percentage points per annum. Money laundering therefore poses considerable economic risks.

As long as a country takes the benefits from crime, by accepting laundered funds but keeping the crime abroad at a safe distance, it free rides on crimes committed in other countries. This may not be a particularly moral position, but economically speaking, it carries no disadvantages and may well explain why so many countries have introduced bank features and ring-fenced regimes that facilitate the incorporation of SPEs. However, other studies (see for example Masciandaro's work (with Filottto) for Italy (2001), demonstrate that criminal money will eventually attract more crime. Even if the acceptance, or tacit approval of money laundering seems like an attractive short term strategy in order to attract additional capital inflows, increased government revenues, a more buoyant business sector, employment and growth, it is a ticking time bomb in the long run.

Money laundering can also lead to corruption. In the first instance, it always needs some assistance from local third parties such as lawyers, notary publics and corrupt officials – the generous customs officer who discretely overlooks the suitcase full of cash, the friendly bank clerk who is not that diligent with proof of identity documentation or fails to report suspicious transactions. However inadvertent or tacit third party cooperation may be, there is a systemic risk that tolerating money laundering will facilitate increased levels of corruption.

To sum up: money laundering is a sizeable phenomenon in industrialized economies with undesirable effects. It is not only small islands, which launder, but rich and developed economies. Giants wash more, so to speak. It is, therefore, important to study what it is, how much it is and which effects it can have. This will be done in this book with a focus on two well developed middle-sized countries: Australia and the Netherlands. While focusing on Australia and the Netherlands, at the same time, the book is also sporadically using examples or drawing parallels with practices in other countries.

NOTES

1. This Introduction would not be what it is without the input of Greg Rawlings. In particular the case studies on banks used here I owe to him. I thank him for his generous input.
2. These 'shell companies' are specific holding vehicles with no physical presence and can be Special Purpose Entities (SPEs) or International Business Companies (IBCs).
3. In the US, the Bank Secrecy Act (31 USC 5311–5330 Bank Secrecy Act) governs key federal US AML legislation, policy and regulation. It has been incrementally strengthened since the US Congress first passed the BSA as the Currency and Foreign Transactions Reporting Act in 1970 (Biern 2004). Most notably the Money Laundering Control Act of 1986 and the International Money Laundering Abatement and Anti-Terrorist Financing Act of 2001 (part of the USA Patriot Act, Title III) have amended and extended the scope and jurisdiction of the BSA. The name Bank Secrecy Act implies that it provides US banks and financial institutions with bank secrecy when in fact its jurisdiction in the US does exactly the opposite. It requires banks and related financial institutions to maintain a paper trial of customers and transactions so that the full suite of US AML regulation and legislation, including where it is attached to predicate crimes, can be enforced. The BSA requires that banks and cognate financial service providers must provide for 1) 'a system of internal controls', 2) 'independent testing for compliance', 3) the appointment of personnel to 'coordinate and monitor compliance' and 4) to provide for their training (US Department of the Treasury Financial Crimes Enforcement Network 2005, p. 4).
4. Members of the G8 are: United Kingdom, France, Germany, Italy, Japan, United States, Canada and Russia.
5. The G20 refers to the group of countries: Argentina, Bolivia, Brazil, Chile, China, Cuba, Egypt, Guatemala, India, Indonesia, Mexico, Nigeria, Pakistan, Paraguay, Philippines, South Africa, Tanzania, Thailand, Venezuela and Zimbabwe.

2. Defining Money Laundering

Predicate Offences – The Achilles' Heel of Anti-Money Laundering Legislation

Elena Madalina Busuioc
(Utrecht School of Governance)

2.1. INTRODUCTION

Money laundering is essentially the process of disguising the unlawful source of criminally derived proceeds to make them appear legal. Anti-money laundering legislation is aimed at ensuring that 'crime does not pay' by preventing the offender from reaping the fruits of the crime. Successful money laundering makes the crime pay off and thus represents an incentive for the commission of further crimes. Therefore, anti-money laundering legislation is not only instrumental in addressing the crime of money laundering but also can be an indispensable mechanism for fighting profit-oriented crime at large. As Ringguth pointedly observes, 'if you can take the profit motive out of acquisitive crime, then that is a positive way of tackling criminality generally' (Ringguth, 2002).

However, in order to achieve the aims above, anti-money laundering measures need to be watertight and comprehensive. This chapter discusses one of the weaker points of anti-money laundering legal instruments, relating to the way money laundering is defined. With that aim in mind, first of all, a brief overview will be provided on how the conceptualization of money laundering has evolved during the past few years through a significant widening of its scope. Secondly, one of the remaining legal challenges will be pointed out and some of its negative side effects on the fight against money laundering at both the domestic and the international level will be addressed. Thirdly, some of the recent European efforts to address this challenge and the ensuing improvements will be discussed.

2.2. GENERAL BACKGROUND

The history of legislation of money laundering began with the criminalization of the proceeds of drug related offences, as provided by the 1988 UN Convention against the Illicit Traffic in Narcotic Drugs and Psychotropic Substances (i.e. Vienna Drug Convention). That is to say that initially, the only offenders that could be prosecuted for money laundering were those attempting to launder the proceeds derived from the production and sale of narcotics. However, in line with the Financial Action Task Force Recommendations (i.e. Recommendation 1) and the provisions of the 1990 Strasbourg Convention on Laundering, Search, Seizure and Confiscation of the Proceeds from Crime, many states have introduced the criminalization of laundering of proceeds derived from other sources, not only drugs. This has had a profound impact with the result that serious and highly profitable crimes such as fraud, arms trafficking, corruption etc also came under the umbrella of money laundering legislation. Although a most welcome development, this process of widening of the scope of money laundering is not deprived of weaknesses.

From a legal point of view, the Achilles' heel in defining and criminalizing money laundering relates to the so-called 'predicate offences' understood as the criminal offences which generated the proceeds thus making laundering necessary. Hiding or disguising the source of certain proceeds will of course, not amount to money laundering *unless* these proceeds were obtained from a criminal activity (i.e. predicate crime). Therefore, what exactly amounts to money laundering, which actions and who can be prosecuted is largely dependant on what constitutes a predicate crime for the purpose of money laundering. Additionally, the way in which money laundering is defined and particularly the scope of predicate offences to money laundering will have an impact, as outlined in the first chapter of this book, on the estimates of money laundering and on the assessment of the effects of the phenomenon.

2.3. THE CHALLENGE: A PATCHWORK OF PREDICATE CRIMES

Given that it was left open to states to decide exactly which crimes would qualify as predicate offences to money laundering, a veritable patchwork of national lists of predicate offences has resulted. Hence, the problem is that, despite harmonizing efforts at both European and international level, national legislations criminalizing money laundering continue to differ. Most countries have listed serious offences as predicate crimes but have nevertheless, adopted different approaches to what exactly constitutes a serious crime for the purpose of money laundering. Thus, the predicate offences vary from one country to another as follows.

In Austria, with the 1993 Amendment to the Penal Code, money laundering was criminalized and penalties were introduced for the commission of such crimes ranging from 6 months to 5 years. However, the scope of money laundering was extended only to offences of a minimum penalty threshold of three years (Silberbauer and Krilyszyn, 2003, p. 179). The United Kingdom, through the 2002 Proceeds of Crime Act, took a giant leap by introducing an 'all crimes' approach to predicate offences to money laundering. Australia was one of the first countries to criminalise money laundering in 1987 with the adoption of the Proceeds of Crime Act. At present, money laundering is criminalized in accordance with Division 400 of the 1995 Criminal Code Act. The Australian system of fighting money laundering is quite well advanced and this is also evidenced by the adoption of a relatively broad field of predicate crimes to cover the laundering of money or property from all indictable offences (i.e. offences punishable to a minimum penalty of 12 months imprisonment) (FATF, 2005 Evaluation Report, p. 4). Punishments can range from 6 months to 25 years depending on the amount laundered and the level of knowledge of the offender. The Netherlands, which explicitly criminalised money laundering in 2002 through an amendment to the Penal Code (i.e. Bill 21 565) took the approach that predicate offences refers to 'serious crimes'. The category 'serious crimes' encompasses the offences mentioned in the Dutch Penal Code, Book 2 as well as the offences punishable under the Economic Offences Act (Graaf and Jurgens, 2003, p. 472). Greece for example, has a so-called 'exclusive and restrictive' approach to money laundering in the sense that the relevant legal instrument (i.e. Law 231/95) provides a limited list of offences (16+crimes) such as drugs, theft, several categories of fraud, illegal importation etc. Laundering of proceeds of crimes not listed will not fall under the crime of money laundering. German legislation also specifically pinpoints what constitutes a predicate offence to money laundering and the German Criminal Code § 261 (1) 2 lays out a restricted list of predicate offences. The relevant Argentinean anti-money laundering legislation (i.e. Law 25, 246 § 6) is applicable only to 7 categories of offences such as: drug-related crimes, arms smuggling, conspiracy, illegal acts performed by corrupt organizations, fraud, child prostitution and pornography, crimes against the public administration (Ruiz, 2003, p. 142).

One illustration of the incoherent approach to predicate crimes outlined above is for example, the variety of national approaches to tax evasion as a predicate for money laundering. It will differ from one country to the next whether the laundering of proceeds derived from tax evasion will qualify as money laundering. For example, in the US, tax evasion is a predicate for money laundering. Similarly, in Australia anti-money laundering legislation covers the laundering of proceeds of all indictable offences and tax evasion is an indictable offence. In Germany however, tax evasion is not a predicate offence to money laundering. In Greece and Switzerland, tax evasion is not even a crime and therefore, the hiding or concealing of such proceeds does not amount to money laundering because the first requirement of the crime of money laundering, the criminal origin of the proceeds, is not met.

2.4. RELEVANCE OF THE ISSUE: DRAWBACKS ON THE FIGHT AGAINST MONEY LAUNDERING AT THE NATIONAL AND INTERNATIONAL LEVEL

The situation outlined above is indicative of considerable divergences in national definitions of money laundering. This can be extremely problematic for two reasons. First of all, it renders prosecution at the national level cumbersome. Secondly, given the trans-national character of the money laundering crime and the need for a unitary and coherent approach, it impacts negatively on the efficiency of the fight against money laundering at the international level. Each of these two drawbacks will be addressed in turn.

At the national level, a list of predicate offences, which is not all- inclusive can be problematic in practice and has been identified as one of the main reasons for extremely low prosecution and conviction rates for money laundering in countries like UK and Australia for example (Graham, 2003). This was one of the main reasons why some countries have adopted an 'all crimes' approach. As Hunter and Lawrence point out, 'in many cases it can be proven beyond reasonable doubt that the property in question is the proceeds of some form of serious criminal activity, but it is not possible to identify, let alone prove, the particular predicate offence from which the property was derived' (Hunter and Lawrence, 2003, p. 168).

Furthermore, in the case of launderers which are not the predicate offenders such as financial institutions, accountants etc they can easier defend themselves by arguing that they did not know the exact provenience of the funds. That is to say, although they suspected the criminal origin of the proceeds they had no way of knowing whether the respective proceeds were derived from a crime that is a predicate offence for money laundering or from a crime which is not listed as a predicate offence. A similar line of argumentation could also be used to justify failure to report suspicious transactions for lack of knowledge of the exact legal status of the basic crime in respect of money laundering. Moreover, as a result of limiting the application field of predicate offences:

'not only would the laundering of the proceeds of some crime activities obviously stay immune, but the limitation could also create problems of an evidential nature. Often the proceeds of various activities of organized crime are intermingled, with the result that the proceeds from drug trafficking cannot be separated from other proceeds or cannot even be calculated' (Stessens, 2002, p. 14).

At the international level, heterogeneity in the range of predicate offences can result in an additional set of challenges. The examples given above illustrate that different countries have taken expansive or restrictive approaches to the field of predicate offences. This entails for example, that what might constitute money laundering in UK might not amount to the same in Greece, given the shorter list of predicate offences in the latter. Similarly, a person that could be prosecuted for money laundering in the Netherlands might not be able to be prosecuted in Austria since the former adopts practically an all crimes approach and the latter includes only offences punishable to more than three years of imprisonment. Additionally, under the relevant provisions of the Austrian law, § 165(1) of the Penal Code (Strafgesetzbuch StGB), only the laundering of proceeds of crime committed by a third party can be prosecuted. In situations where the predicate offender attempts to launder the proceeds of his/her crime, this will not amount to money laundering. This is a significant divergence between the two countries, since the Netherlands does criminalise 'self-laundering'. Given such differences among jurisdictions, in a situation where the predicate crime (e.g. trafficking in endangered species) took place in one country but the proceeds derived thereof were laundered in another country serious problems concerning investigation and prosecution could arise. This is due to the fact that most domestic legal systems impose double criminality requirements.

The condition of double criminality means that

'the predicate activities, which generated the proceeds constitute an offence under the law of both the state where they were carried out and under the law of the state where the proceeds were eventually laundered. If state A has jurisdiction over money laundering acts that concern the proceeds from an activity in State B, most legal systems require that these predicate activities are both incriminated in State A and State B' (Stessens, 2002, p. 227).

The double criminality requirement owes its existence to two primary considerations. First of all, it makes little sense for a jurisdiction to prosecute certain behaviour as criminal if it is not regarded as such under domestic law. The second consideration flows from the legality principle (Stessens, 2002, p. 227). That is to say, it would be unacceptable and unfair for State A to punish someone for activities conducted in State B, if those activities are perfectly lawful under the law of State B. The double criminality requirement is adhered to in most European jurisdictions. For example, in the Netherlands the condition that the predicate offence must be a crime both under national jurisdiction as well as abroad is clearly stated in the Penal Code Article 5 (1) and (2). In Belgium this condition follows from established case law, whereas in Germany and

Luxembourg it is explicitly stated in the statutory definition of money laundering (Stessens, 2002, p. 228).

Thus, as long as there are differences among countries in terms of what constitutes a predicate offence to money laundering, situations could arise where one jurisdiction could not prosecute someone for money laundering due to the fact that the predicate offence was committed in another jurisdiction, which does not list the respective crime as a predicate offence to money laundering. In such a situation, one of the most important elements for the offence of money laundering will be absent, namely the *criminal* character of the proceeds. Hence, it would not give rise to prosecution. Given the double criminality requirement, as long as divergences remain in place among various states in terms of the scope of predicate offences, the efficacy of the international fight against money laundering will be seriously jeopardized. Consequently, 'the fight against money laundering should be a common effort by the international community and the laws governing money laundering crime in various countries should be as similar as possible'(Ping, 2004, p. 117).

One possible way to address the problems outlined above would be to adopt a very broad approach to predicate offences, to expand their scope as much as possible. This would increase the chances that the double criminality requirement would be satisfied, thus leading to international efficacy of law enforcement actions. Additionally, a broader list of predicate offences would also lead to increased effectiveness in the domestic legal context, in cases where the predicate offence was committed within the same state as the laundering offence. In the contrary situation, important areas relating to laundering would remain unregulated and would thus, proliferate.

In light of these arguments, it appears highly desirable that the criminalization of money laundering should not be based strictly on a limited category of offences. In order to ensure an efficient fight against money laundering through the criminal law system, two alternative solutions seem pertinent. One possibility, as suggested above, is for jurisdictions to extend the scope of predicate offences to cover all crimes. Such a solution would not only help circumvent some of the problems inherent in the double criminality requirement but would also seem more fair. From an ethical perspective, it is difficult to understand why the laundering of proceeds of crimes punishable with a maximum of more than 12 months of imprisonments should be criminalized and not for example, the proceeds of offences punishable with 5 months of imprisonment. An alternative possibility would be to adopt a more restrictive approach to predicate offences so as to cover only serious crimes. However, this approach is viable only in as long as there is international agreement on a common, expansive list of serious offences or at least, agreement on specific and clear-set criteria for determining what qualifies as such a crime.

2.5. REDEEMING EFFORTS AT THE EUROPEAN LEVEL

At the European level, significant steps have been taken to address some of the problematic aspects outlined above. The measures embarked on are two-fold. One series of efforts was undertaken under the Community pillar in the form of a series of directives meant to prevent the abuse of the financial sector from money laundering and thus, relate to the protection of the common market. The second series of efforts were carried out under the third pillar of the EU and relate to the 'criminal treatment of money laundering' and measures taken towards the so-called 'harmonization of the offence of money laundering'.[1] These measures are exemplified by a series of Council Acts and Framework Decisions building on the Council of Europe 1990 Convention. Both the former and the latter set of measures have resulted in a widening of the scope of predicate offences and will be addressed in turn below.

2.5.1. The EC Money Laundering Directives

The efforts under the first pillar began in 1991 with the adoption of the EC Money Laundering Directive on the prevention of the use of the financial system for the purpose of money laundering (91/308/EEC). The directive imposed on Member States the obligation to prohibit money laundering but similarly to the Vienna Convention defined the scope of money laundering very narrowly to encompass only the proceeds of drug trafficking. Furthermore, the directive referred primarily to financial institutions. The scope of the money laundering directive was widened with the adoption of the Second Money Laundering Directive (2001/97/EC), which extended the scope of predicate offences beyond the drugs predicate to a range of serious crimes and expanded the coverage of the directive beyond the financial sector to auditors, real estate agents, notaries, dealers in high value goods and casinos.

These first two directives were repealed with the adoption of the Third Anti-Money Laundering Directive (2005/60/EC),[2] which is the most wide-ranging of the three and represents a significant step towards a more comprehensive approach. The directive incorporates FATF's 40 Recommendations and thus, brings about a certain degree of coherence between international and European measures for fighting money laundering. The scope of the directive was extended to cover in addition to the sectors and professionals identified by the Second EC Directive also trust or company service providers and all natural and legal persons who receive payments in cash of 15,000 euro or more.[3] Further-more, for the purpose of the directive, predicate offences are serious crimes encompassing: terrorism related offences as laid out in Articles 1–4 of the Council Framework decision of 13 June 2002 on combating terrorism (2002/475/JHA), drug-related offences as put forward in Article 3(1) a of the 1988

United Nations Convention against Illicit Traffic in Narcotic Drugs and Psychotropic Substances, the activities of criminal organizations as defined in Article 1 of the 1988 Council Joint Action (98/733/JHA), fraud, corruption and all offences punishable in the Member states to detention for a maximum of more than one year or for a minimum of more than six months (i.e. for states that have a minimum threshold for offences).[4]

The directive was formally adopted in October 2005 and will have to be implemented by the EU Member States before December 15, 2007. The adoption of the directive will smooth out many of the cross-country discrepancies relating to the issue of predicate offences. It goes without saying that the obligations laid down in the directive are binding on Member States. As the guardian of the Treaties, the Commission oversees the proper implementation of the EU directive. In the case of failure or delay in implementation, the Commission will start infringement proceedings in accordance with Article 226 EC, which eventually results in proceedings before the ECJ. For example, the Greek state's failure to adequately transpose the First EC Money Laundering Directive resulted in the Commission starting infringement procedures against Greece before the ECJ for failure to transpose. Greece quickly passed Law 2331/95 thus fully implementing the EU law provisions in question. Similarly, the Commission also started infringement proceedings for failure to implement the Second Anti-Money Laundering Directive (2001/97/EC) by issuing its 'reasoned opinion' against six Member States: France, Portugal, Greece, Sweden, Luxembourg and Italy (IP/04/180).

Thus, although the new directive will conceivably suffer, as its predecessors, from similar delays in implementation or failure to implement by some Member States, this situation will conceivably be shortly remedied and Member States will bring their legislation in conformity with the provisions of Community law. Consequently, the adoption of the Third Anti-Money Laundering Directive is a most welcome addition to the EU anti-money laundering efforts and will undoubtedly bring about in the near future a most necessary homogeneity in cross-national anti-money laundering legislation concerning the financial sector.

2.5.2. The Council of Europe Convention

With regards to the incrimination of money laundering, a veritable quantum leap in this direction was made in 1990 with the Council of Europe Convention on Laundering, Search, Seizure and Confiscation of the Proceeds of Crime (hereafter the Strasbourg Convention), which entered into force in 1993. The Convention has been signed and ratified not only by all the Member States of the Council of Europe but also by non-Member States such as Australia and Montenegro. The US and Canada have failed to either sign or ratify the Convention.[5]

Article 6 of the Convention required signatory States not only to criminalize money laundering but also adopts a very wide definition of predicate offences, which covers 'all crimes'. However, as briefly mentioned in the first part of this contribution, this provision was optional. The huge impact of the Convention in terms of unifying the approach to predicate offences was watered down by a subsequent provision,[6] which allowed each contracting party to make a declaration restricting the criminalization of money laundering to a specific, limited list of predicate offences. Many countries have not hesitated to make declarations to this effect[7] thus adopting a narrower definition of money laundering by restricting the field of predicate offences. This, as observed, has resulted in a patchwork of predicate offences.

Subsequently, Council Joint Act 98/699/JHA[8] and Council Framework 2001/500/ JHA[9] restricted the reservations EU Member States can make to the Strasbourg Convention by stipulating that no reservations can be made to restrict the scope of money laundering as far as serious offences (i.e. offences punishable to detention for a maximum of more than one year or for a minimum of more than six months) are concerned. However, Member States can still exclude other offences that do not fall under the category 'serious offence' from the criminalization of money laundering. Furthermore, there is no prohibition from reservations on 'serious crimes' outside the EU, at the international level.

In 2005, the Convention was reviewed and updated. The amendments were so substantial that in the end a new Council of Europe Convention on Laundering, Search, Seizure and Confiscation of the Proceeds from Crime and on the Financing of Terrorism was opened for signing in May 2005. The Convention has been signed by 22 States including the Netherlands and Austria but so far there have been no ratifications.[10] Given that 6 ratifications are necessary for entry into force, the 2005 Council of Europe Convention has not entered into force yet.

The provision dealing with predicate offences has not resulted in a sweeping solution, which could have been achieved through the adoption of an 'all crimes approach'. Instead, the Convention provides in its appendix a list of 20 categories of predicate offences to money laundering. Provided that the definition of money laundering applies to this list of predicate offences, the Convention however, leaves it to the latitude of each state and the EC to decide upon ratification whether predicate offences for money laundering are: a. offences punishable to detention for a maximum of more than one year or for a minimum of more than six months (i.e. for states that have a minimum threshold for offences); b. only to a list of specific predicate offences; and/or c. to a category of serious offences in the national law of the state party.

Consequently, this allows for a degree of variation in the signatory countries with regards to what constitutes a predicate offence and thus, what amounts to money laundering. The Convention has clear merits given that it affords a wider definition of money laundering encompassing 20 categories of predicate offences common to all Signatory Parties. In other words

> 'in any event, the categories of offences contained in the Appendix to the Convention have to be considered as predicate offences for the purposes of money laundering and therefore cannot be excluded from the scope of application of the money laundering offence.'[11]

The convention leaves it to the latitude of each Signatory State to decide which approach to use (i.e. all crimes, penalty threshold or an enumerated list of offences) in determining predicate offences. However, relating to other crimes than those falling under the 20 categories explicitly identified in the Appendix of the Convention, states are likely to have different approaches to whether to regard them as predicate offences to money laundering or not. To this extent, trans-national prosecution of money laundering will remain cumbersome with regards to certain offences given the requirement of double criminality.

This requirement is clearly outlined in Art 9(7) of the Convention which provides that 'Each Party *shall ensure* that predicate offences for money laundering extend to conduct that occurred in another State, which constitutes an offence in that State, and which would have constituted a predicate offence had it occurred domestically'. The Convention further provides that 'each Party *may* provide that the only prerequisite is that the conduct would have constituted a predicate offence had it occurred domestically'. This provision would amount to a lift of the double criminality requirement but as it comes forth from the wording above, this part of the provision is not an obligation but it is an option left to the individual state parties. It is up to the state parties to decide whether to opt for this or maintain double criminality. Take, for example, tax evasion. It does not fall under any of the 20 categories of offences listed in the appendix and thus, prosecution will still depend on each country's approach. As seen above, some countries do not regard it as a crime. This could result in practice in the situation where for example, if money laundering was committed in France with tax evasion funds from Switzerland, France could not prosecute for money laundering unless Switzerland decides to list tax evasion as a predicate offence. This is unlikely given that under Swiss law, tax evasion is a misdemeanour and not a crime (Visini and Haflinger, 2003, p. 584).

On a side note, it is also interesting to observe that the Convention also allows for variation not only with regards to certain predicate offences but also with regards to the prosecution of predicate offenders. Article 9 (2) (b) states that 'it may be provided that the offences set forth [...] do not apply to the persons who committed the predicate offence'. In certain jurisdictions (i.e. Austria, Greece), in the case where the same offender commits the predicate offence and the laundering, it is possible to punish him/ her only for the former. The Convention does not do away with this disparity.

In summary, the measures described above, the EC Directives, the Council measures and Council of Europe Conventions, are illustrative of the realization that 'money laundering is at the very heart of organized crime. It should be rooted out wherever it occurs' and of the determination 'to ensure that concrete steps are taken to trace, freeze, seize and confiscate the proceeds of crime.'(Tampere European Council, 1999, Conclusion 51). Agreement has been reached on list of crimes as well as a set of criteria for identifying additional predicate offences (e.g. the threshold criteria). Nevertheless, variation remains with regards to offences falling outside the scope of the categories of predicate offences identified specifically in the Directive or the Annex to the Strasbourg Convention. To the extent that the threshold criteria is mentioned, this will not result in uniformity in the scope of predicate offences given that criminal penalties have not been harmonized so different countries have different penalties for the same crime. Consequently, although ground breaking and far reaching, the legal instruments discussed above still display weaknesses concerning the definition of money laundering given the fact that they fall short of imposing an 'all crimes' approach.

2.6. CONCLUSIONS

International convergence with regards to predicate offences to money laundering becomes a must if one wants to fight money laundering effectively. Even if one jurisdiction extends predicate offences so as to cover all crimes (i.e. the Netherlands), it could still encounter jurisdictional problems if the money laundering is trans-national in character and the other countries involved have not adopted an equally broad approach. Consequently, a move towards convergence would benefit not only investigation and prosecution efforts and lead to efficiency in international co-operation on criminal matters connected to money laundering but also have significant beneficial implications for the international exchange of information. A suggestion along these lines was made by the United Nations as early as 1998:

'the time may have come to end the artificial division of criminal money into categories depending on the nature of the crime. As long as criminal money can be laundered legally (...) banks and brokers who are asked to launder money will argue that they thought the money was legitimate because, although criminal in nature, it came from a non-predicate offence.' (UN, Report on Financial Havens, Banking Secrecy and Money Laundering, 1998).

A similar recommendation was also put forward by the European Parliament, which warned against the adoption of a 'variable geometry version of European criminal law', specifically referring to the issue of predicate offences (EP, Report on Criminal Procedures in the European Union, 1999).

Before concluding however, a final remark deserves consideration. There has been a relatively recent change of paradigm at the international level related to the issue of predicate offences and the relationship between money laundering and terrorism. In its Second Special Recommendation on Terrorist Financing, FATF recommends countries to list terrorism as one of the predicate offences to money laundering. This suggestion was taken up in the Third Money Laundering Directive, which includes terrorism as a predicate offence for money laundering. Similarly, in the US, through the adoption of the 2001 Patriot Act the predicate offences to money laundering were broadened to include acts of terrorism.[12]

As discussed at length throughout this chapter, predicate offences refer to the original crimes from which 'dirty' proceeds were derived and which make the laundering process necessary. Clearly, terrorism does not logically fit into this scheme. Terrorism is not a crime from which dirty proceeds are obtained and which subsequently need to be laundered. On the contrary, terrorism is usually found at the other end of the spectrum. The financing of terrorism involves money dirtying or reverse money laundering. The money is most of the times clean and by being used to finance an illegal activity (i.e. terrorism) it becomes dirty. The aim is not necessarily to separate the money from its source (i.e. the predicate offence) but rather from its destination (i.e. the terrorist act). Unlike money laundering, it does not purport to avoid detection of dirty money of past crimes but instead to primarily avoiding detection of clean money to be used for future crimes. For these reasons, listing terrorism as a predicate offence does not appear to make sense in the classical paradigm.

However, terrorism financing uses similar channels and exploits the same weaknesses in the financial system as money laundering in its aim of conceal-ment. It is in this connection that FATF listing of terrorism as a predicate crime to money laundering can be understood. FATF's approach of broadening the list of predicate offences so as to include terrorism was motivated by one primary consideration: efficiency. Given the interconnectedness of money laundering and terrorist financing in terms of the methods used, an artificial connection was created at the law enforcement level as well. In other words, since money launderers make use of similar channels, enforcement authorities could now conceivably use the same conceptual legal framework for both crimes.

To sum up, with regards to legal definitions of money laundering, we notice a push for an expansion of their scope through a broadening of the list of predicate offences for the purpose of efficient law enforcement. This drive for efficiency has been taken so far, through the inclusion of terrorism as a predicate offence, as to completely alter the traditional paradigm. To which extent this kind of change in paradigm is a desirable development remains debatable. What is indubitable however is the need that in the near future such display of political will and resourcefulness, as in the case of terrorism, be employed to bring about the much needed development of expanding the scope of predicate offences to cover 'all crimes'. Otherwise, this aspect of the incrimination of money laundering will remain the Achilles' heel of enforcement measures against profit-oriented offences by allowing certain crimes to still pay off.

NOTES

1. European Parliament, Committee on Citizens' Freedoms and Rights, Justice and Home Affairs, Money Laundering, <http://www.europarl.europa.eu/comparl/libe/elsj/zoom_in/26_en.htm>.
2. Directive 2005/60/EC of the European Parliament and of the Council of 26 October 2005 on the prevention of the use of the financial system for the purpose of money laundering and terrorist financing.
3. See Art 2(1).
4. Article 3 (5).
5. For additional information concerning signatures and ratifications see <http://conventions. coe.int/Treaty/Commun/ChercheSig.asp?NT=141&CM=11&DF=7/10/2006&CL=ENG>.
6. Article 6 (4) of the Directive.
7. See reservations to the Convention. <http://conventions.coe.int/Treaty/Commun/ListeDeclarations.asp?NT=141&CV=1&NA= 6&PO=999&CN=999&VL=1&CM=9&CL=ENG>. Eighteen of the Signatory Countries have made reservations to narrow the scope of Art 6.
8. Joint Action of 3 December 1998 adopted by the Council on the basis of Article K.3 of the Treaty on European Union, on money laundering, the identification, tracing, freezing, seizing and confiscation of instrumentalities and the proceeds from crime.
9. Council Framework Decision of 26 June 2001 on money laundering, the identification, tracing, freezing, seizing and confiscation of instrumentalities and the proceeds of crime.
10. For additional information concerning signatures and ratifications see <http://conventions. coe.int/Treaty/Commun/ChercheSig.asp?NT=198&CM=11&DF=7/10/2006&CL=ENG>.
11. Council of Europe Convention on Laundering, Search, Seizure and Confiscation of the Proceeds of Crime and on the Financing of Terrorism – Explanatory Report, <http://www. coe.int/t/dcr/summit/conventions_en.asp>.
12. The US Patriot Act, 2001, Title III, s 376.

3. Ways of Quantifying Money Laundering

3.1. MEASURING THE IMMEASURABLE

Money laundering is a largely secretive phenomenon. The exact number of launderers that operate every year, how much money they launder in which countries and sectors, and which money laundering techniques they use is not known. Apart from recent spectacular media coverage, such as an US$80 million fine levied against ABN AMRO by US regulators, the involvement of the Austrian BAWAG bank in money laundering through the Caribbean, or the charges against Jean-Cyril Spinetta, the president of Air France–KLM, for money laundering and fraud in connection with the bankrupt company Pretory (see Financieel Dagblad 13th July 2006, p. 2), money laundering remains largely in the dark. It only comes to light when it is detected.

Are these spectacular events the entire story or are they just the tip of the iceberg? Are they random samples of a small or large underlying population? Does the media overreact to scandals and overestimate money laundering as some criminologists believe (see for example, van Duyne 2006) or is the problem larger than one could possibly imagine, amounting to several trillion US dollars per year (Walker 1999[a])?

In order to examine the money-laundering problem, one has to measure it according to country as well as globally. But estimating money laundering means measuring the immeasurable.

Nevertheless, courageous attempts have been made to at least estimate the ranges and magnitudes of money laundering. Calculating the amount of money laundering will introduce problems similar to measuring the shadow economy, the amount of capital flight, the number of 'illegal' workers, the extent of illegal weapons, the amount of drugs and the number of drug users: one simply cannot observe and measure the variable.

Money laundering can occur in many forms and, therefore, can appear in different economic transactions. Some examples include official figures and statistics such as in the capital balance as capital transfer, in the trade balance as over- or underpriced exports and imports using transfer-pricing methodologies, 'offbook balance sheets' as cash smuggled across borders, as non-traceable intra- and intercompany transfers, in the real estate sector as a sudden increase of real estate purchases and sales in a fluctuation of house prices, in the precious gemstone (particularly diamonds) industry, in the natural resources sector (especially timber) as a sudden increase in demand. It can appear as unusual movements regarding bank transactions, or as phone calls made between an underground banker in country A and an underground banker in country B who pays the money out in cash without it having to physically cross the border. It can be in the shadow of the hidden economy and it can be disguised as fake transactions in the formal economy. Given the huge variety of ways in which money laundering can occur, it is even more difficult to trace and measure it.

Therefore, it is difficult to determine exactly where laundered money actually is. When measuring the informal or shadow economy, Schneider and Enste (2000) partition the economy into two formal and three informal sectors. The formal sector comprises industry and households. The informal sector comprises regular, irregular and criminal activities. Money laundering includes most of the criminal underground activities and parts of the irregular sector like tax evasion and social fraud. Shadow work is mostly not part of laundering. Added to these categories were the formal sector white collar cross border crime, which typically hides itself in the formal sector and produces legal outcomes but uses illegal or sometimes even criminal procedures. One example is an exporter who ships very expensive watches at a very low price to an importer who sells them for a high price abroad. This can be represented diagrammatically (see Figure 3.1).

John Walker (1995, 1999[a], 1999[b], 2003) was the first to make a serious attempt at quantifying money laundering and initial output. His model suggests that US$2.85 trillion are laundered globally. This estimate indicated that the amount of money laundering is quite sizeable. Since then, the debate whether or not money laundering can be measured globally has continued. Some, like the Financial Action Task Force (FATF) in its 2005 report, suggest that the variety of money laundering techniques makes it impossible to estimate. Other institutions, particularly national Financial Intelligence Units (FIUs) such as the Australian Transaction Reports and Analysis Centre (AUSTRAC), have made efforts to estimate the volume of both domestic and transnational money laundering.

However, these efforts at estimating volumes of laundered funds have not been confined only to national regulators. Multilateral organizations have also been engaged in determining ways to measure money laundering, despite the FATF's reservations about the validity of the measurement. For example, the International Monetary Fund (IMF) has estimated money laundering at 2–5 percent of world GDP or about US$1.5 trillion circulating around the globe (see IMF 2004). This is much less than Walker had estimated originally, but is still sizeable: 1,500,000,000,000 US dollars.

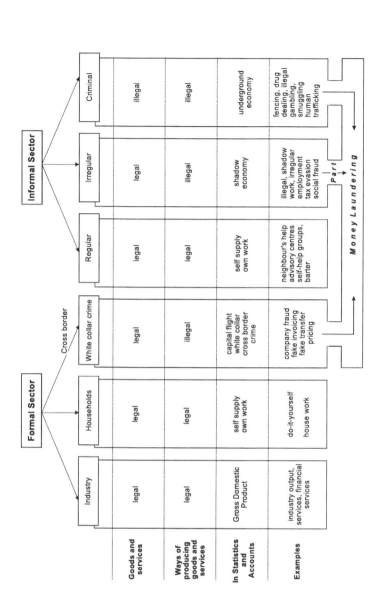

| | Formal Sector | | | Informal Sector | | |
	Industry	Households	White collar crime	Regular	Irregular	Criminal
Goods and services	legal	legal	legal	legal	legal	illegal
Ways of producing goods and services	legal	legal	illegal	legal	illegal	illegal
In Statistics and Accounts	Gross Domestic Product	self supply own work	capital flight white collar cross border crime	self supply own work	shadow economy	underground economy
Examples	industry output, services, financial services	do-it-yourself house work	company fraud fake invoicing fake transfer pricing	neighbour's help advisory centres self-help groups, barter	illegal, shadow work, irregular employment tax evasion social fraud	fencing, drug dealing, illegal gambling, smuggling human trafficking

Cross border

Money Laundering

Part

Source: Schneider and Enste (2000), own translation and with some modifications.

Figure 3.1 Money laundering and the shadow economy

3.2. MEASUREMENT WITHOUT THEORY

Measuring money laundering has become a controversy between the purists, people who want to measure and model precisely, and the innovators – those who try to measure the immeasurable, even if they run the risk of being criticized. They attempt to measure a *fata morgana*, a reflection of air that gives the illusion of being water (van Duyne 2006). It has also become a controversy between those who measure by muddling through with ad hoc assumptions and those who urge for a proper theory which can then be tested. Thomas (1999), for example, criticized the empirical approaches used for measuring the black economy (of which money laundering is a part) as 'measurement without theory'. Not much has changed since then.

Indeed, a comprehensive economic theory regarding money laundering is still missing. The different approaches to measuring money laundering that exist so far can be classified as being based on case studies, on surveys and expert interviews, on measuring indirect variables related to money laundering and on statistical and econometric models.

The remainder of this chapter will provide an overview of potential ways to measure money laundering in economics. Depending on the broadness of the definition of money laundering, it can include all categories of crime, including tax evasion. In this case, the measurement of money laundering begins to approximate the measurement of the shadow economy. It is therefore also necessary to discuss approaches to measuring the shadow economy. Money laundering, however, also involves moving out of the shadows.

3.2.1. Ethnography and the Economics of Measurements: Anthropological Perspectives

These economic measurements reinforce parallel ethnographic efforts to 'research into the shadows' (Nordstrom 2004). They demonstrate that money laundering is not only a distinctive sphere of criminological activity that can be partitioned off from the rest of the body-politic, but is rather integrated into the domestic and transnational conduits of contemporary capitalism. There is an emerging anthropological approach to money laundering that draws on critical insights based on the relationship between representation and power and is using the disciplines defining methodology of ethnographic fieldwork and participant observation increasingly (see for example, the discussion on 'research into the shadows' on the relationship between war and profiteering, Nordstrom 2004; see also Haller and Shore et al. 2005).[1]

3.2.2. Case Studies

One way of finding out about what money launderers do, how much they launder, how they spend their money and whether they keep it in one country or transfer it abroad is to study prosecutions and cases of criminal convictions.

In the Netherlands, criminologists Meloen et al. (2003) analysed 52 criminal cases wherein property had been confiscated (*ontnemingszaken* in Dutch). Unlawful advantages in these cases had been estimated at more than one million Dutch guilders (about €430,000) per case. In other words, the courts handed down sentences on the assumption that the unlawful advantage must have exceeded one million guilders. These 52 'million cases' totalled €100 million in laundered funds. The problem with this kind of approach is that it is unclear how representative the data are. Do the 52 money launderers who were caught stand for 0.5 percent, 5 percent, 10 percent or 50 percent of the money launderers in the Netherlands? Are the money launderers caught representative of all money launderers, or are only specific offenders caught?

Case studies provide a good indication of the extent of money laundering at the smaller end of the scale. The amounts estimated form the bottom line of what can possibly be laundered. They are also very helpful in our understanding the behaviour of launderers, what they consume, where they launder, how they launder and so on. However, in order to be more than just descriptions of 52 cases, they must make some assumptions about the underlying population of money launderers. For example, is the behaviour of the '52 launderers' representative of other launderers throughout the Netherlands or elsewhere? While interpretations based on these case studies are compelling in their own right, they also exclude the full range of money laundering practices, networks and behavioural assumptions. It is these assumptions about representative behaviour and cooperation patterns that have to be incorporated into theories that are as yet still missing.

It is very likely that the 52 cases of Meloen et al. (2003), for example, suffer from a selection bias. Only criminals who get caught are in the selection. This can lead to an over- or underestimation. On the one hand, criminal organizations who are successful and do not get caught could be larger and make more profit from the crimes they commit than the criminals who get caught. On the other hand, if a criminal organization grows in size, this might increase the chances of detection, which would mean that big criminals get caught. The conclusion from this is that it is unclear if these 52 cases represent an overestimation or an underestimation of the amounts and types of money laundered.

3.2.3. Surveys and Expert Interviews

Another way to measure the amounts of money laundering is to interview business people and experts from police and government departments and ministries.

In 1992 John Walker (1995) was commissioned by AUSTRAC to undertake the first-ever survey of expert opinion on the volume of money laundering. Walker wanted to find out what the average proceeds for each type of crime were. When multiplying reported proceeds with the total amount of crime for each type of crime, it is possible to calculate the *total proceeds of crime*. From this a certain percentage will be laundered. The percentages laundered from each type of crime Walker found through expert interviews done in 1992.

In order to do so, the survey was designed to obtain up-to-date data on Known Proceeds of Crime and estimates of the ratio of Total Money Laundering to Total Proceeds of Crime for each type of offence. From the latter, an average amount of money laundered from each crime could be calculated.

The questionnaire was circulated by AUSTRAC to each state and territory police service, each branch of the Australian Federal Police (AFP), and a number of independent researchers. From these police and expert responses, Walker (1995, see chapter 4 for more details) estimated the total amount of money laundered in Australia to be valued between A\$3,520 and A\$4,227 billion per year.

As with all surveys, this approach is limited by diverse biases. The sample might not been representative and the people interviewed or questioned might have had their own perception biases. To give an example, there might be an overestimation of money laundering by those authorities responsible for combating money laundering. At the same time, there might also be an underestimation by the same people if they feel that they fulfil their task of fighting crime efficiently and do their job well. Perception biases, interpretation biases, biases from non-respondence and sample biases might be in these data.

3.2.4. Reports of Unusual Transactions

Another method of estimating money laundering is by analysing suspicious or unusual transactions reported to Financial Intelligence Units (FIUs), which have been established in most countries to control money laundering. There are variations between countries regarding reporting requirements, particularly thresholds that will trigger a report and the extent to which non-monetary payment instructions (such as bearer instruments) should be included. Moreover, information overload can lead to delays in follow-up investigations into suspicious transactions. The Netherlands, for example, has one of the highest reporting intensities, but one of the lowest rates of prosecution for money laundering in the world. Banks and other financial institutions are required to report any transaction that exceeds €15,000 to the Dutch FIU, the *Melding Ongebruikelijke Transacties*, the Office for the Disclosure of Unusual Transactions (the MOT), but these reports can often not be acted upon since the FIU is overwhelmed with information. Moreover, the police are preoccupied with prosecuting other crimes such as drug dealing and theft.

Despite this overload, in 2004 the total value of executed suspicious transactions was €3.2 billion in the Netherlands. If one would add up all reports of unusual transactions in all FATF countries (these are the countries that report), that are determined to be instances of money laundering, one could at least arrive at an estimate for the lower section of money laundering. However, there is significant variation between reporting intensities and prosecution between FATF member states. For example, in 2004, the Caribbean Financial Action Task Force (CFATF 2005), found that in Suriname, only 6 out of the 114 reporting units filed their reports to the country's FIU. In some countries there might also be the tendency to report transactions from specific countries no matter whether these transactions are related to money laundering or not. In this case the amount and value of suspicious transactions from and to this specific country might be overestimated.

3.2.5. Measuring Proxy Variables

One way to begin to measure the immeasurable is by finding a good proxy variable that can be used in place of the original variable. In order to measure the (unobservable) total amount of illegal workers in Rotterdam, van der Leun, Engbersen and van der Heijden (1998) measured the amount of bread sold in districts where undocumented workers were likely to live. One person consumes, on average, one loaf of bread in a certain period of time. The total amount of bread sold in these districts was, hence, taken as a proxy for the amount of workers living there. This can be problematic due to the fact that some ethnic groups comprising this work force that labours 'in the shadows' cannot afford bread, do not like Dutch bread, are used to baking their own bread or are not consuming bread at all, biasing the indicator. However, it transpired that the sale of bread in the districts of Rotterdam selected for research was significantly higher than the population registered there could possibly eat. This difference was used to estimate the number of undocumented workers.

Lackó (2000) used this same method to measure the shadow economy with electricity consumption as a proxy. She assumed that a certain part of the shadow economy is associated with household consumption of electricity. This includes so-called household production, do-it-yourself activities, and other non-registered production and services. Lackó further assumed that in countries where the portion of the shadow economy associated with household electricity consumption is high, the rest of the hidden economy (the part Lackó couldn't measure) would also be high. From this, she estimated the whole shadow economy. The shadow economy was, therefore, measured by the consumption of electricity.

For money laundering, the indirect variable is drugs or other forms of crime and proceeds from it. Walker (1999[a]) approached money laundering in this way. He tried to calculate the proceeds of crime per crime category and assumed that a certain percentage of these proceeds had to be laundered, with that percentage of laundered funds based on surveying police forces and criminological experts. The problem with this proxy variable for money laundering is that proceeds of the crimes themselves are only estimates. Money laundering is, therefore, estimated from an estimate of the proceeds of crime and an estimate of the percentage that will be laundered.

The problem with all proxy variables is that one does not know how close the proxy variable gets to the underlying variable that it tries to measure. And if money laundering is measured from an estimated proxy, this certainly does not make things easier, unless two errors just happen to cancel out one another.

3.2.6. Observing Discrepancies in Statistics

Another way of measuring money laundering is to use statistical discrepancies or unusual statistical movements as an indicator of money laundering. The shadow economy is often calculated by the difference of income and expenditure in the National Account figures. If expenditure exceeds the income of the population, this excess must have been earned on the black market. This is because officially, by definition, in the aggregate people cannot spend more than they earn.

One way of determining illegal work is to calculate the discrepancy between the officially employed and the total working age population between 15 and 64. A decreasing official rate of labour participation can be seen as an indicator of an increase in the activities in the shadow economy, ceteris paribus (see Thomas 1999). The shadow economy is measured herein as the difference between the total working age population and the officially employed.

For money laundering, the following discrepancies in statistics are relevant: Errors and Omissions in the Balance of Payments, differences in capital inflows and outflows, differences in money supply and money demand, unusual changes in money demand, unusual price fluctuations in the real estate sector and unilateral transfer pricing agreements.

3.2.6.1.   Errors and omissions – the hot money method
One way of measuring money laundering is to link it to capital flight. One can hypothesize that capital flight can be comprised of either money laundering or

tax evasion (or that tax evasion is part of money laundering) and to measure capital flight accordingly. The 'hot money approach', for example, calculates private capital flows by using the errors and omissions in private short-term capital accounts from the balance of payments. The assumption is that errors and omissions arise primarily because of failure to measure certain movements of private short-term capital, and that it is appropriate to add them to the recorded flows of short-term capital in order to get an estimate of total flows of 'hot money' (see Schneider 2006).

The errors and omissions term accounts for unusual discrepancies in the balance of payment, reporting mistakes, delays between merchandise delivery and payment etc. It is the post for all mistakes and errors done. Furthermore, some countries do no longer calculate their balance of payment by adding all transactions. The Dutch, for example, switched to a survey system in 2003, from which they calculate the underlying population for the posts of the current account. This also affects the error and omission post.

3.2.6.2.   Capital inflows and outflows – the residual approach
Another approach, the residual approach, measures capital flight by looking at the difference between inflows (sources) of funds, including net official inflows and net inflow of Foreign Direct Investment (FDI), and the outflows (uses) of funds (evident in the current account deficit and additions to reserves) of a country. The residual of the difference between the sources and uses, which is unrecorded, is considered to be the amount of capital flight (see Boyrie et al., 2005[a] and 2005[b], see also under transfer pricing). As with all other proxies, the question here is how well the residual reflects capital flight and does not include other discrepancies such as time lags and different calculation conventions.

3.2.7.   The Currency Demand Approach

The currency demand approach measures the discrepancy between the regular and excess demand for currency. Tanzi (1996 and 1997) used this approach to demonstrate both the shadow economy and money laundering. For the shadow economy, he assumed that hidden transactions are undertaken using cash in order to avoid observable traces for the authorities. An increase in the shadow economy will therefore necessitate more cash, and hence increase the demand for currency. Tanzi (1996) adjusted for the factors usually determining demand for money, such as income, price level, payment habits and interest rates. The increase in money demand that cannot be explained by these factors was attributed to the growth of the shadow economy.

Tanzi (1997) used the same approach in order to measure money laundering. By comparing the amount of money printed and the amount of money circulating in the US in 1984, Tanzi calculated that 5 billion US dollars per annum was appropriated in cash through the illegal drug trade. This amount was attributed to money laundering from drugs. Whether this is money laundering or not depends highly on the definition of money laundering chosen. Parts of this cash money are certainly never presented at a bank. So, narrow money laundering definitions would not apply to this.

A major problem with this approach is that it cannot be applied to countries within the Eurozone. Though central banks in countries of the Eurozone still publish the money supply per country, it is impossible to distinguish the money demand per country. Therefore, it is no longer known how much of each country's money supply is circulating in which Eurozone country. The currency demand approach cannot be applied, therefore, to individual countries within the Eurozone. This means it cannot be applied to Austria, Belgium, Finland, France, Germany, Greece, Ireland, Italy, Luxembourg, The Netherlands, Portugal, Spain and Slovenia, the members of the Eurozone in 2007. The fact that money cannot be measured for each country separately, also means that all monetary issues related to money laundering are much more difficult to identify.

The same argument applies to Quirk (1997) who attempted to estimate the correlation between money laundering and the demand for money for the IMF. He suggested that money laundering, through its effects on demand, affects interest rates and exchange rates. An increase in the money demand for reasons of needing cash to buying drugs, will make money more expensive. This means that the price for money, the interest rate, will go up. Higher interest rates will attract foreign investors and can lead to more capital inflow and hence an appreciation of the exchange rate. But, again, this approach cannot be applied to single EU countries anymore.

3.2.8. Observing Abnormal Prices – Real Estate and Transfer Pricing

A promising way to estimate money laundering, at least in some sub-sectors, is to observe abnormal price movements. Real estate prices fluctuate quite substantially in some countries like the Netherlands. By measuring land register prices one can identify those objects that quickly change hands between owners, while displaying unusual price increases. Like this, real estate objects used for money laundering can be defined or identified as those that have large price increases or fluctuations. One has to be aware, however, that price increases or fluctuations can also be due to pure speculation, or to the splitting of apartments or office spaces that result in higher housing or real estate prices. Siegmann (2006) did an interesting first investigation that involved looking at land register prices in the city of Amsterdam. He identified several hundred objects which changed owners several times within days and which showed unusual changes in prices. Some objects had a price that was eight times higher than the day before. He found out that most of the unusual price increases could not be linked with money laundering but included several transactions at the same time. In a newer version he corrected for this and only showed the price changes for individual transactions. Figure 3.2 below shows a map of Amsterdam and the price difference between two consecutive sales of an apartment or house that take place within 30 days. Most of the points plotted represent a resale on the very same day. Between 2004 and 2005 351 houses experienced unusual price increases. In Figure 3.2 Siegmann only plotted the 169 ones that were not multiple transactions. A bar of 100K means that the price difference was €100.000. 200K means that the price difference was €200.000. The higher the bar, the bigger the price difference. This is a promising area that is recommended for further research. In particular business objects should be analysed in the same way, since it is there that big money laundering is supposed to happen.

Source: Arjen Siegmann (2006), Department of Finance, Free University of Amsterdam.

Figure 3.2   Unusual housing price increases in the city of Amsterdam in 2004–2005[2]

Import and export businesses are another sector that is also susceptible to money laundering. Launderers can create fake invoices for high amounts and ship merchandise of low value or reverse this procedure as a way of concealing ill-gotten gains. This can be very difficult to detect. For example, if an exporter ships watches worth €1 million to a third country, but invoices the 'customer' (who may be a subsidiary of the supplier) only €100,000 for low-value watches, and the importer sells the expensive watches for €1 million in her/his country, then €900,000 are laundered by fake invoicing.

The exporter, who has spent his illegal cash on watches in his own country, has thus 'frozen the money into watches' and has shipped it to the other country with the help of the importer. The importer makes honest earnings from selling expensive watches and in his country puts the money on an account for the exporter. In the exporting country (mostly also the one with high taxes) the exporter only declares low income from the export of cheap watches.

Unusual price movements, suspicion regarding under- or over-invoicing, is one reason why the United States and some other countries have issued interquartile ranges for specific transaction prices. Every four months, price ranges are set and prices are not supposed to exceed these limits. In 1994, the US Internal Revenue Service issued 482 transfer pricing regulations. Prices that were not within the interquartile range were considered abnormal (Boyrie et al. 2005[a]). Transfer pricing and under- or over-invoicing can be used for money laundering, but are not money laundering per se. One can use this indicator for money laundering only if there is some stable relationship between the use of transfer pricing for laundering and for other purposes of capital flight.

Zdanowicz et al. (1999) have analysed transfer pricing between Brazil and the US, and Boyrie et al. (2005[a]) analysed transfer prices between Switzerland and the US. Every import and export transaction between Switzerland and the US for every month in the years 1995 to 2000 was analysed. Transactions that exceeded the transfer pricing range were considered abnormal. They found overvalued Swiss imports from the US and undervalued Swiss exports to the US. Between 1995 and 2000, the resulting capital outflows from Switzerland totalled some 31 billion US dollars. They also found a significant increase in the amounts of capital outflows from Switzerland after the country passed AML legislation in 1998. One explanation is that stricter AML regulations encouraged launderers to switch from channelling the proceeds of crime through banks to invoicing.

The same method of transfer pricing was used to investigate discrepancies in Russian and US trade (Boyrie et al. 2005[b]). The amount of capital flight from Russia to the US through abnormally priced trade between 1995 and 1999 was valued at US$8.92 billion, comprising 7.24 billion in under-invoiced exports to the US and 1.68 billion in over-invoiced imports into Russia (Boyrie et al. 2005, p. 259). Analysing transfer pricing is one of the most promising methods of measuring money laundering. Though extremely labour intensive, similar work would be very useful for Australia and the Netherlands as it could give empirical back-up to the existing aggregate money laundering estimates.

3.2.9. Statistical and Econometric Analysis

The DYMIMIC (dynamic multiple-indicators multiple causes) model uses two sets of observable variables and links them as a proxy to the unobservable variable. One set of variables is the causes (for the shadow economy or for money laundering) such as regulations, taxation and prosecutions. The other set is called indicators, which measure the 'effects' of the shadow economy or money laundering. These observable variables parallel money laundering and include the growing demand for money, less official growth and/or increases in crime rates. Schneider (2006) uses this approach to estimate the shadow economy for 145 countries. One problem with this approach is that the choice of cause and indicator variables is arbitrary and not reinforced theoretically. The DYMIMIC model uses factor analysis to determine how well the different cause variables explain the unobservable variable and those that can be grouped together. The same is then done for the indicator variables. This means statistics decide which indicators form the relevant bundle for causes of the shadow economy (or money laundering) and which are relevant for the effects of a shadow economy (or money laundering). Indicators are classified into sub-groups that are supposed to represent parts of the unobservable variable. But, again, statistics cannot replace theory. Nevertheless, the method allows demonstrating the variables that are highly correlated and measure the same part of the proxy variable and reducing redundancies in the choice of proxy variables.

Figure 3.3   Measuring unobservable variables

Tedds and Giles (2000) and Schneider (2006) give a description of this model for the underground economy. A MIMIC model is formulated mathematically as follows: ML is the scalar (unobservable) 'latent' variable (the size of money laundering; $y' = (y1, y2, ..., yp)$ is a vector of 'effects' or 'indicators' for ML; $x' = (x1, x2, ..., xq)$ is a vector of 'causes' of ML.

Under the assumption that all of the elements are normally distributed and uncorrelated, one can estimate money laundering by regressing the observable causes on the observable effects.

The MIMIC model can be expressed as:

$$y = aML + e \qquad (1)$$
$$ML = b'x + c \qquad (2)$$

Substituting (2) into (1), the MIMIC model can be written as:

$$y = ab'x + (c+e) \qquad (3)$$

DYMIMIC then refers to a change in these variables. For a further explanation and description of the model, see Tedds and Giles (2000).

3.3. THE WALKER MODEL

3.3.1. A Pioneer Study

Walker (1995 and 1999[a]) was a pioneer who attempted to measure money laundering worldwide, using an ad hoc equation. His model still looks like the most promising one. Though heavily criticized as 'ad hoc', as lacking a solid theoretical or methodological background, and as overestimating the amount of money laundered, it still provides a relevant point of departure for further improving the measurement of money laundering.

The Walker Model examines two different aspects of the money laundering process. First, it scrutinizes money generated for laundering per country. Second, it examines flows of generated money from one country to another. Money can be laundered in the country in which it was generated or sent to another country for laundering. An important point within this model is that as soon as money has travelled (flowed) at least once, it is 'white washed', or laundered. This model only counts this first transaction involving the placement of funds. Although 'hot money' can be moved on multiple occasions in efforts to disguise its criminal origins, this model does not count each of these transactions, or movement of funds.

As we will see in the next chapter regarding the amounts of money laundering, it seems as if Walker only takes into consideration the first phase of money laundering, the placement phase. On the other hand, he also assumes some kind of layering. He uses prices for drugs and other crimes from Australia, which means he assumes that the money comes from or has at least passed by some of the rich countries before it is sent from a poor drug producing country to another destination. One can imagine his model working in the following way. The drug producing country, Pakistan for example, sells drugs to rich countries. The high mark up between poor countries' producer prices and sales prices in rich countries leads to high proceeds that first have to flow back in all sorts of layering to the poor country before they are sent to another country, the Netherlands for example. If the model is interpreted this way, the fact that Walker uses high proceeds can be justified. If he applied the high sale prices of rich developed countries to the drugs produced in and sold from Pakistan directly, this would overestimate Pakistan's drug proceeds. For criticism on using the retail prices of rich countries for estimating crime and proceeds of crime in poor countries, see Reuter and Greenfield (2001).

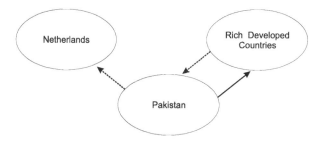

Figure 3.4   Flows of money captured in the Walker model

The strength of this approach, however, is that it is a pioneer study which estimates money laundering on a large scale for all countries for the first time. Furthermore, Walker, in consultation with AUSTRAC, used his partly tacit knowledge on money laundering that he had gathered through experience. Walker also had access to a vast amount of information and expert interviews in the field and developed an appreciation, or 'feeling', for the extent of money laundering. It appears that he used this 'tacit knowledge' and 'feeling' to calibrate his model. I believe that when Walker suddenly ends up with some cryptic sounding formulas, such as three times Bank Secrecy plus 15, this is the outcome of trial and error estimation. He tried to narrow down the potential outcomes according to some accurate estimates, which he might have had in his head before creating the model. One could call this a very rough form of calibration of his model. The advantage of developing a global model is paralleled by the deficiencies of such a procedure. The model lacks detailed information about each country. It relies on the same variables for all countries, such as SWIFT code membership, bank secrecy and strictness of anti-money laundering policy. However, it provides a good starting point for improving estimations by using more detailed information about each country, such as peculiarities of specific channels used for laundering or specific routes taken for distributing drugs.

3.3.2.   The Seven Steps of the Walker Model

Step 1: Dirty money – the proceeds of crime

Walker takes the proceeds of crime as a proxy for money laundering. How much dirty money is generated in a country? If data for crime rates is available and this can be measured in kilograms of heroin, numbers of ecstasy pills and the sale of illegal weapons multiplied by average sales price per kilo of heroin, ecstasy tablet and/or a weapon, then it is possible to estimate the proceeds of crime.

AMOUNT OF CRIME multiplied by the AVERAGE PRICE OF CRIME = PROCEEDS OF CRIME

The amount of crime can be measured by the number of victims, the number of people prosecuted or by the amounts confiscated. The amount of drugs can be measured by the amount of drugs seized or the number of drug addicts (see diverse UNDCP reports).

Step 2: Domestically generated money for laundering

The proceeds of crime – the dirty money – comprise the amount that can be potentially laundered. However, not all types of crime generate the same amount of laundering. Some crimes, such as proceeds from homicide, do not usually generate large revenue streams that need to be laundered; if someone kills their husband without being caught and inherits his fortune, then this is automatically clean money. Criminal activities that do generate earnings, however, such as proceeds from drug dealing, do need to be laundered in order to make use of them. This could take the form of rent or other regular payments that have to be paid from bank accounts making them inconspicuous. For each type of crime it is necessary to determine the percentage of proceeds that will be laundered. This information can be gathered and estimated from surveys and case studies in each country. By calculating all money laundered from different types of crime, based on surveys of expert witnesses, it is possible to approximate the total amount of money generated for laundering per country. Alternatively, the proceeds of crime and the proportion laundered can be calculated by establishing the average amounts of money laundered per type of crime. Multiplying this with the number of crimes also gives the total amount of money laundered.

> PROCEEDS OF CRIME multiplied by PERCENTAGE LAUNDERED =
> MONEY LAUNDERED
> NUMBER OF CRIMES multiplied by MONEY LAUNDERED PER
> RECORDED CRIME = MONEY LAUNDERED

Step 3: Worldwide laundering

In principle, the same calculations would have to be made as per steps one and two for all the countries in the world in order to calculate worldwide money laundering and to determine the amount of money remitted per country to all other countries in the world.

> SUM UP MONEY GENERATED FOR LAUNDERING OF ALL
> COUNTRIES

Step 4: Laundered funds flowing into a country from abroad – the index of attractiveness

A country's attractiveness for laundering and its relative distance to third countries influences the percentage of worldwide money available for laundering that it takes. For the calculation of cross-border flows of laundered money, Walker introduces two indices, the attractiveness and the distance deterrence indicator.

> ATTRACTIVENESS INDEX =
> (GNP per capita) multiplied by (3 times BS +GA+SWIFT-3timesCF-
> CR+15)

A country can be more attractive to money launderers due to its higher gross national product per capita (GNP), Bank Secrecy (BS), the tolerant attitude of the government towards money laundering (GA), SWIFT membership (Society for Worldwide Interbank Financial Telecommunication), low levels and a low risk of conflict (CF) and lower incidences of corruption (CR). The constant 15 guarantees that all attractiveness scores are positive (see Walker 1999[a]).

This index has to be calculated for all countries, ascribing each of them attractiveness scores. The higher the score, the more attractive the country is for money launderers.

Step 5: Dirty money flowing into a country from abroad – the distance deterrence index

The amount that will be laundered depends not only on the attractiveness of a country, but also on how close it is to other potential laundering countries. For this, a distance deterrence index is included in the calculation. In his original model, Walker used the distance squared. He observed that '[T]he use of the distances squared as a measure of deterrence uses empirically-based regional economic analysis conventions, by which interactions between communities reduce according to the square of the distance between them' (Walker 1999[a]). More recent literature on international trade theory confirms this (see under gravity model below).

CALCULATE SQUARED DISTANCES BETWEEN COUNTRY j AND COUNTRY i
DO SO FOR ALL PAIRS OF COUNTRIES

These distances have to be calculated bilaterally between all pairs of countries in the world.

Step 6: The percentage of dirty money flowing into a country
In order to calculate the percentage of dirty money that flows from one country i into country j (originally Walker defines this for outgoing money, but the reverse also holds when seen worldwide), one has to divide the attractiveness rank of country j by the squared distance between the two countries. A higher proportion of money will be laundered in country j if it is attractive for money launderers and if it is close to the other country i.

| PROPORTION OF MONEY LAUNDERING FLOWING FROM COUNTRY i TO COUNTRY j | = ATTRACTIVENESS OF j/ (DISTANCE BETWEEN i AND j)^2 |

If j is the country of interest, only the attractiveness score of country j has to be calculated with the squared distances between all countries and country j. This gives the percentage of the dirty money that will flow from each country of the world to country j.

It is also possible to make these estimates by calculating the proportions for the top 20 money laundering countries that Walker has identified and to observe what these 20 top countries send to the specific country of interest.

Step 7: Total amount of money laundered in a country
The percentage of dirty money that flows from country i to country j has to be multiplied by the money generated for laundering in the sending country. All countries' flows to country j have to be added. This gives the influx of money for laundering from all other countries to country j. Furthermore, the money

generated in country *j* itself has to be added in order to arrive at the total amount of money laundered in country *j*.

MONEY GENERATED IN THE COUNTRY FOR LAUNDERING plus
MONEY FLOWING INTO THE COUNTRY FROM ABROAD =
TOTAL AMOUNT OF MONEY LAUNDERING

Following these seven steps, Walker (1995) arrived at estimates of money laundering for each country of the world, of which e.g. US$50 billion were laundered in the Netherlands, US$48 billion were laundered in Austria, and US$5–10 billion were laundered in Australia. Worldwide he arrived at US$2.85 trillion laundered. This was the first worldwide number ever given regarding the amount of money laundering. How much can one trust this number? Which theory supports it?

3.4. SUGGESTIONS FOR IMPROVING MEASUREMENTS OF MONEY LAUNDERING

So far all empirical approaches lack a theoretical underpinning. Walker's (1999[a]) attractiveness and distance deterrence index lack a theoretical model; at least he does not refer to any. The equation given should be the reduced form of an underlying model. One way would be to find a model that produces this equation as the reduced form that can be used for estimation.

A second way would be to explore existing theoretical models for the legal economy and use them to find an allocation model for international investment or financial flows, which then could be modified for the illegal economy.

A third way is to develop a new model of money laundering. It would have to start by modelling the behaviour of money launderers, describe their utility function and maximizing problem, the constraints under which they maximize their utility and derive an equation that can be used to make estimations.

The principle problem of using (neoclassical) economic theory is that it considers capital to be neutral and that money is simply a veil that does not affect the real economy, at least not in the long run. However, I argue that money laundering is a monetary phenomenon that does have real effects (see chapter 6 and 7 on effects of money laundering). Laundered money after reintegration is capital, which affects the economy; it is not neutral. Most modern economic approaches can, therefore, not be applied.

In the following section, the first suggestion is explored further: finding the underlying theory for the Walker model.

3.4.1. Searching for the Model behind Walker's ad hoc Formula

I am looking for a model of money laundering that should conclude that the proportion of laundered money sent from country i to country j (Pi,j) equals the attractiveness of country j (GNP per capita multiplied by BS, SWIFT, GA, CR and CF) divided by the square distance between the two countries.

$P(i,j)$ = ATTRACTIVENESS of j/ (Distance between country i and country j)^2

where the ATTRACTIVENESS INDEX =
(GNP per capita) times (3 times BS +GA+SWIFT-3timesCF-CR+15)

When looking for an appropriate theory one sees that Tinbergen and modern trade theory have produced these types of equations already, when applying Newton's laws of physics and gravity to economics. Over the centuries the gravity formula slowly developed into an empirical ad hoc equation and finally into a complex theoretically underpinned reduced form equation of modern trade theory.[3]

3.4.1.1. Newton's Law of Universal Gravitation
A look at the gravity models used in international trade theory reveals that the Walker formula comes close to Newton's Apple. In 1687, Newton proposed the 'Law of Universal Gravity', which held that the attractive force between two objects i and j depends on their masses, the square distance between these objects and a gravitational constant which depends on the units of measurement for mass and attractive force (see Head 2003).

Attractive Force Fij = G* Mi*Mj/ (Dij)^2

Fij...Attractive Force between object i and j
Mi...Mass of object i
Mj...Mass of object j
Dij...Distance between object i and object j
G...Gravitational constant

3.4.1.2. Tinbergen's ad hoc formula
In 1962, the Dutch Nobel prize winner Tinbergen transformed the understanding of the newly established economics of international trade by applying Newton's formula to bilateral trade flows. The trade from country i to country j depends on the economic mass of the two countries (measured by GDP) and the distance between the two locations (see Head 2003).

$$Fij = G* Mi^{\alpha} * Mj^{\beta} / (Dij)^{\theta}$$

The export flows from country i to country j depend on the GDP of both the exporting and importing country and the distance between them.

Note that if α, β = 1 and θ =2, then this is the same as the original Newton formula.

For a long time, this formula was criticized as being a- theoretical and ad hoc (see Gauws 2005, chapter 6). Despite its use in many early studies of international trade, the equation was particularly suspect, considered in so far as that it could not easily be shown to be consistent with the dominant paradigm of international trade theory, the Heckscher–Ohlin model which explained net trade flows in terms of differential factor endowments (see Head 2003). According to the predominant economic paradigm it was the amounts of labour and capital that determined the comparative advantage of countries that in turn determined which goods countries traded with each other.

Tinbergen's formula, however, had one convincing advantage: it predicted international trade flows very well (Head 2003, p. 9). 'Measurement without theory' turned out to perform better than measuring from existing trade theories. Tinbergen's use of the Newton's model of physics in economics can be applied to other fields, such as migration. Migration flows can be seen as the product of the population between two countries divided by distance. The Tinbergen gravity model can be applied to a whole range of social interactions, such as trade, the inflow of migrants, the inflow of tourists into a country, and foreign direct investment. So why not also to money laundering flows?

3.4.1.3. Theoretical underpinning of the ad hoc gravity formula

Since the Tinbergen formula worked so well but lacked theoretical justification, many scholars attempted to develop an adequate economic theory that was commensurate with the gravity formula. The first to develop such a theory was Anderson (1979), who showed that the gravity model was evident in expenditure share equations assuming commodities to be distinguished by place of production. Anderson also included remoteness measures in order to be fully consistent with the generalized expenditure share model. Helpman (1984) and Bergstrand (1985) demonstrated that the gravity model could also be derived from models of trade in differentiated products. Deardorff (1998) showed that a suitable modelling of transport costs produces the gravity equation as an estimation, even for the Heckscher–Ohlin model (for an overview, see Helliwell 2000). The theoretical basis for the Tinbergen formula as applied to trade can be seen in following (Head 2003, p. 4).

The trade flows from country i to country j

$$Fij = sij*Mj$$

Where sij is the share of country j's income spent for goods from country i. This share lies between 0 and 1, increases if country i produces a greater variety of goods (ni) or a higher quality of goods (larger mi). This share also should decrease due to trade barriers such as distance.

One can write this as:

$$sij = g(mi, ni, Dij) / \Sigma\ g\ (ml, nl, Dlj)$$

Depending on the trade theory used, either mi=1 (which means all products from a country have the same average quality) or ni=1 (each country exports only one single good).

Under the assumption that mi=1 and that all firms q are of the same firm size, the number of products ni = Mi/q. The higher the income of the country, the more products will be produced, and the larger the firms size in the country, the less variety will be produced (this follows from monopolistic trade models a la Dixit–Stiglitz, see Head 2003, p. 4, which show that monopolists produce less variety than firms under perfect competition [see Head 2003, 4f]).

From these assumptions and after some modification, it follows that:

$$sij = Mi\ Dij^{-\theta} Rj \quad \text{where } Rj = 1/\Sigma\ 1\ (Ml, Dlj^{-\theta})$$

From this follows Newton's–Tinbergen's formula:

$$Fij = Rj * Mi*Mj / Dij^{\theta}$$

Now, Rj replaced the constant factor G of the old gravity formula. For a long time it was interpreted as a constant across countries. In more recent literature, it is the remoteness factor. Rj stands for each importer's set of alternatives. Countries that have many nearby sources of goods themselves will have a low value of Rj and, therefore, import less. This factor of 'remoteness' explains why country groups that have the same distance from each other might still have different trade flows. The remoteness measure also includes Mi/Dii, the distance of the country from itself. Head (2003) suggests taking the square root of the country's area multiplied by about 0.4 as an approximation for this internal distance. Other authors (Helliwell 2000) just use a value of 1 instead.

If one takes the logarithm of the newly derived economic Newton equation, one finds a linear reduced form equation that can be estimated with ordinary regression if the left-hand variable is observable or a proxy that can be observed.

1) $\ln F_{ij} = a_0 + a_1 \ln M_i + a_2 \ln M_j - a_3 \ln(DIST_{ij}) + a_4 \ln Rj + e_{ij}$

where F_{ij} is some measure of transaction between i and j, with any movement being from i to j, M_i and M_j are the masses of units i and j, $DIST_{ij}$ is the distance between them, Rj is a remoteness and e_{ij} is a random error term usually taken to be normally distributed.

Why is distance so important for trade flows?

- it is a proxy for transport costs
- it indicates the time elapsed between shipment
  - damage or loss of the good (ship sinks in the storm)
  - spoiling of the good
  - loss of the market (purchaser unable to pay once it arrives)
- communication costs, proxy for the possibilities of personal contact between managers, customers, i.e. for informal contacts which cannot be sent over a wire
- transaction costs (searching for trading opportunities, establishment of trust between partners)
- cultural distance (clashes in negotiation style, language) (Head 2003 p. 8)

The distance indicator used by Walker (1999[a]) assumes a similar importance for money laundering flows. Though physical distance is less important for money flows, since money cannot perish, and transportation costs are negligible given that money can be sent around the globe at the click of a mouse, the communication costs, transaction costs and cultural barriers might still be important.

Income per capita The gravity model has been augmented by income per capita. This takes into account that richer countries tend to trade more. Walker assumes the same for money laundering. Richer countries attract more money laundering funds from poorer countries.

Borders McCallum (1995) claimed in his seminal paper in the *American Economic Review* that borders still matter as far as it concerns trade. He compares trade between two Canadian provinces to trade between Canadian provinces and US States and shows that borders are a barrier to trade.

Countries trade more if they have no border than if they have one. But when borders exist, it is better for trade to share a border than to be further apart. Trade is about 65 percent higher if countries share the same border than if they do not have a common border (Head 2003). So the Netherlands, for example, will trade more with Belgium than with France, even if one corrected for the difference in distance, just because they share a border. This means that if one takes coordinates of capitals and their distance to each other (as I and Walker do), one might overestimate the effective distance, because neighbouring countries often engage in large volume border trade.[4]

Common language and colonial links   Speaking a common language and sharing a common history and cultural background can lower transaction costs. 'Two countries that speak the same language will trade twice to three times as much as pairs that do not share a common language' (Head 2003, see especially the works of Helliwell, e.g. Helliwell 2000).

3.5. MODELLING MONEY LAUNDERING: LESSONS LEARNED FROM INTERNATIONAL TRADE THEORY – A REVISED WALKER MODEL

The formula that Walker suggested in his seminal 1995 paper is very similar to the gravity model. It shares the beginner's fate regarding this kind of model: namely, to be called ad hoc and a-theoretical. International trade theory, from the Heckscher Ohlin to the Dixit–Stiglitz model, shares important theoretical synergies with the Walker model. One can also hope that the theoretical underpinning of the Walker model will not take as long as the microeconomic theoretical underpinning of the gravity formula by international trade theory. While the Tinbergen formula could always take the credit for predicting trade flows so accurately, the Walker model has, thus far, not received the same degree of acknowledgement. This is for the simple reason that the flows of money laundering stay in the dark and are unobservable. This means that it is not possible to assess the quality of the formula, the effectiveness of the fit and of forecasting. However, there are many parallels between flows of laundered money and FDI, and the gravity model has been shown to be valid and theoretically sound in these contexts.

Walker's gravity formula assumes the following:

$$\text{Fij/Mi} = \text{Attractiveness j / Distance ij}^{2}$$

where:

$$\text{Fij/Mi} = (\text{GNP/capita})j * (3\text{BSj} + \text{GAj} + \text{SWIFTj} - 3\text{CFj} - \text{CRj} + 15) / \text{Distance ij}^{2}$$

Where *GNP/capita* is GNP per capita, *BS* is Banking Secrecy, *GA* is Government Attitude, *SWIFT* is SWIFT member, *CF* is Conflict, *CR* is Corruption.

If one compares this to the original gravity model, Walker assumes, Rj=(3BSj+GAj+SWIFTj–3CFj–CRj+15) and Mj=(GNP/capita)j. He has divided the flow formula by Mi. The GNP per capita of the sending country is not included in the percentages of laundering flows that he calculates. It is included later, when the percentages are multiplied by the total amount of money that each country launders. Mi represents the proceeds of crime multiplied by crime multiplied by the percentage that is laundered. It is the total money generated for laundering in the sending country. The 'mass' indicator between the sending and receiving country varies and this variation accounts for the economic and criminal size of countries. All the variables relevant for money laundering have been captured in the remoteness variable. The gravitational 'masses' of the two objects country i and country j have been assumed to be GNP per capita and money generated for laundering, respectively.

This formula has been modified for the estimates below. With regard to the attractiveness indicator it is very similar to Walker; it accepts that the size of the financial market might be an important factor for attracting money for laundering in rich countries. Furthermore, it takes a variable for combating money laundering into account explicitly, namely, whether or not the country is a member of the Egmont group, a group of countries which devote themselves to money laundering (see next chapter). Leaving the index j out for the moment, the formula used in our empirical part for attractiveness becomes:

Revised Attractiveness = (GDP/capita)* (3BS + GA + SWIFT + FD – 3CF – CR – EG +10)

Where *GDP/capita* is gross domestic product per capita, *BS* is Banking Secrecy, *GA* is Government Attitude towards money laundering, *SWIFT* is being a SWIFT member or not, *FD* is Financial Deposits, *CF* is Conflict, *CR* is Corruption, and *EG* is Egmont Group membership.

The model used in this volume is thus very similar to the original Walker model and also assumes a remoteness variable that includes all kinds of variables relevant for money laundering such as the size of financial markets and being a member of the Egmont group.

For the distance indicator Dij $^\theta$ Walker assumed Θ =2 and used the squared kilometre distance between capitals. As mentioned above, this can overestimate the effective distance due to intense cross border trade.

Walker (1999[a]) suggested that variables measuring 'social distance' should be included in the model. Taking developments in international trade theory and Walker's suggestion to include indicators of 'social distance', the model used here includes not only physical distance but also language, the colonial background, and trading status.

The new distance deterrence indicator is now:

Revised Distance = DIST= language+3*colonial background+3*trade+physical distance

Here I opt for $\Theta = 1$, using linear and not squared distance. This is backed up by the fact that many trade gravity equations come up with this coefficient as well

(Helliwell 2000).[5] For estimating the proportions of hot money sent from each country i to country j, one can either divide the two indicators by each other, as Walker suggests, or take the logarithmic form, used more often in international trade theory:

$$\ln F_{ij} = a_0 + a_1 \ln M_i + a_2 \ln M_j - a_3 \ln(DIST_{ij}) + a_4 \ln R_j + e_{ij}$$

Since our $\ln Mi = \ln 1 =$ the constant e, one can include $a_1 \ln Mi$ in the constant term a_0 of the equation and call it $c_0 = a_0 + a_1 \ln Mi$.

$$\ln Fij = c_0 + a_2 \ln M_j - a_3 \ln(DIST_{ij}) + a_4 R_j + e_{ij}$$

where $\ln Mj$ is the logarithm of the per capita GDP of country j, $\ln DIST$ is the logarithm of the distance deterrence indicator plus the attractiveness index (without GDP per capita), hence plus $(3BS + GA + SWIFT + FD - 3CF - CR - EF + 10)$.

Adding the indicators (due to the lack of knowledge about the coefficients) means to assume that $c_0 = e_{ij} = 0$ and that the coefficients a_2, a_3, and $a_4 = 1$.

$$\ln Fij = \ln (GNP/capita)j + \ln Rj - \ln DISTij$$

$$\ln Fij = \ln (GNP/capita)j + \ln(3BS + GA + SWIFT + FD - 3CF - CR - EF + 10) - \ln (language + 3*colonial\ background + 3*trade + physical\ distance)ij$$

Besides modifying the attractiveness index and incorporating cultural distance into the distance deterrence index, I also revised the formula for calculating the percentages. In the original model, Walker used the following formula to calculate the proportion of laundered money flowing from one country to another:

$$P (X, Y) = Attractiveness\ Score\ Y\ /\ (Distance\ X\ to\ Y)^2$$

There is nothing built into this model to ensure that the values of the proportions of money flowing from the country to other countries and to itself (money laundered locally) do no exceed 1, or 100 percent. For this reason, it seems important to calibrate part of the formula to ensure that values do not exceed 1. The formula that follows seems to be a better choice:

$$P(X, y_i) = \frac{1}{\sum\limits_{i=1}^{n} \left[\dfrac{attractiveness(y_i)}{dist(X, y_i)} \right]} \times \frac{attractiveness(y_i)}{dist(X, y_i)}$$

where P is the proportion of money flowing from country X to country y_i.

For example, X is a specific country (the Netherlands), y_i is another country (Aruba). Then, the proportion of money flowing from country X (Netherlands) to country y_i (Aruba) equals the attractiveness of Aruba, weighted by the distance between the Netherlands and Aruba. In order to make sure that shares add up to 1, this weighted attractiveness for money laundering is corrected for the total weighted attractiveness scores throughout all countries.

The three modifications to the Walker model and incorporating international trade theory have to be seen as a first step to open up the Walker model and identify its theoretical underpinning. As the next step, the assumptions of international trade theory have to be compared to the assumptions of money laundering. What do traders and FDI actors have in common with money launderers, and what not? There is still some modelling necessary in order to move from the gravity model to a money laundering model, but given the progress that international trade theory has made, there is optimism that this can happen soon. The money laundering debate can draw on a long history of developments and findings in economic trade theory.

For the time being, due to the lack of better models, I will continue to work with the Walker model. I will, on one hand, measure it with the modified model as outlined above, and on the other hand improve the calculations for one specific country, the Netherlands. If each country would perform similar improvements, the overall estimates of worldwide money laundering could be substantially improved.

What is still not captured in this and Walker's model of money laundering is the full layering phase of money laundering (money laundering is measured at the first phase, at placement, when it is generated and invested domestically or sent abroad). But the second phase of money laundering, when money is transferred all over the globe in order to hide its origin, is much higher in volume and much more prone to all kinds of financial tricks and sophisticated constructions, but is only sporadically treated. This second phase will be discussed in more detail in chapter five regarding the techniques of money laundering. The third phase of laundering, the reintegration phase, where money is invested in real estate, diamonds or assets for fixed periods of accumulation is also not accounted for in this model. This phase will be discussed in further detail in chapters five, six and seven, examining the techniques and effects of money laundering on the economy.

NOTES

1. I owe this point to anthropologist Greg Rawlings.
2. I thank Arjen Siegmann for sending me this figure on 10th of July 2006 and allowing me to publish it.

3. Many thanks to Thijs Knaap and Harry Garretsen, both at the Utrecht School of Economics, for this hint.
4. I owe this point to Thijs Knaap.
5. I owe this point to Thijs Knaap.

4. Measuring Money Laundering for Australia and the Netherlands[1]

With Melissa Siegel and Joras Ferwerda

4.1. THE CONTROVERSY ON GLOBAL MONEY LAUNDERING – IS IT BIG OR SMALL?

Before measuring money laundering for specific countries, one has to face the principle question of whether it can be measured on a large scale at all. The calculations of international flows of money laundered streaming into a country depend on worldwide money laundering, which again depends on the amount of worldwide crime and the proceeds of crime. So, one must rely on some of the international estimates regarding the global proceeds of crime and money laundering in order to say something about specific countries.

The question is, how much can one trust the global estimates? Global money laundering estimates are based on estimates of global crime and its proceeds. There seems to be a controversy going on between those who believe that the proceeds of crime and money laundering are small compared to other sectors of the economy, and those who believe that they are huge. This chapter supports the view that money laundering is sizeable.

This view conforms to International Organizations such as the United Nations and the International Monetary Fund (IMF), which see global crime and global money laundering as a huge problem. The UNDP (1996, p. 3) showed that the estimated annual illicit drug turnover in the 1990s was about US$400 billion, 6 times higher than official development aid (US$69 billion in 1995). The drug sector accounts for about 8 percent of international trade. It is larger than the global iron and steel industry, the motor vehicle industry or the textile and clothing industry and is about the same size as worldwide tourism (UNDP 1996, p.3 UNDP 1999, p. 103).

The latest report created by the UNODC (2006) shows that illicit drug use is stable if not increasing. The total number of drug users in the world is now estimated at some 200 million people, equivalent to about 5 percent of the global population aged 15–64. Cannabis, ecstasy and heroin use are increasing, whereas the use of cocaine, opiates and amphetamines stays constant or shows a slight decline (UNODC, 2006).

The amount of drug seizures has also increased. The largest seizures amongst Western European countries were made by the authorities in the United Kingdom (in 2003), Italy, The Netherlands, Germany and France. They accounted for close to 85 percent of all opiate seizures in Europe in 2004. The United Kingdom is Europe's main opiate market and a final destination country. Italy is Europe's second largest market for opiates as well as an important transit country for opium coming from Albania and Turkey. The Netherlands is primarily an important transhipment location for opiates en route to other countries in Western Europe, primarily France, Belgium, The United Kingdom and Germany. It is the world's largest producer of ecstasy pills (UNODC, 2006).

According to the UN, annual worldwide illegal drug sales are 0.9 percent of the world's GDP and greater than the gross domestic product of 88 percent of the countries in the world. The UN report, issued in Stockholm, said the global drug trade generated an estimated US$321.6 billion in 2003, the latest year for which figures were available. The bulk of the money, US$214 billion, was produced at the retail level; drugs sold on the street and back alleys. Most of the buying took place in North America, with 44 percent of all estimated sales, followed by Europe with 33 percent. Africa was in last place with only 4 percent (Pollard, 2005).

Estimated numbers for fraud exceed even drug numbers. For the US, the Association of Certified Fraud Examiners (ACFE) estimated that 5 percent of annual revenues were due to fraud in 2006. Based on the US Gross Domestic Product in 2006 – US$13.037 trillion – this percentage indicates a staggering estimate of losses around US$652 billion amongst organizations (Association of Certified Fraud Examiners, ACFE 2006). In 2002, their estimate was about the same amount (US$625 billion) with 6 percent of GDP based on the Gross Domestic Product of US$10 trillion (see TNI 2003 and Chapter 5).

The IMF has stated that the aggregate size of money laundering in the world could be somewhere between 2 and 5 percent of the world's Gross Domestic Product. Using statistics from 1996, these percentages would indicate that money laundering ranged between US$590 billion and US$1.5 trillion (FATF-OECD, 1999). Walker (1995) estimated worldwide money laundering at $2.85 trillion.

All these numbers indicate that the proceeds from drugs crime and money laundering are very large and pose a serious threat to the economy, society and to politics. They are, therefore, phenomena that have to be studied and politically dealt with.

Opponents think that these numbers are highly exaggerated and that the global crime and money-laundering problem is largely overstated. According to their view, politicians and the press exaggerate the amount of drug crime and fraud as well as the amount of money laundering. According to Thoumi (2003), data on the size of the illegal drugs industry are used by different groups for different purposes. Journalists want to impress their public, policy makers want to measure the success or failure of drug policies, analysts want to identify the beneficiaries of criminal activities and anti-drug movements and advocates of peasants want to highlight coca and opium price injustice.

Most users of the data cite figures without first studying the methodologies used or reading the studies that produced them. They want the 'facts' but they do not want to be bothered by the devil in the details (TNI, 2003).

The TNI (2003) participants highly criticized the UN estimate that drug trade is equal to around 8 percent of global trade. The US$400 billion figure is turnover at retail level expenditures, which is much greater than the value of the illicit international drug trade. Any serious estimate should study the difference between wholesale export and import prices, which are about 1,000 percent, compared to about 5 percent in licit trade.

Reuter and Greenfield (2001) dismissed the UN comparison of the illicit drug industry with other industries. 'The UN claim that global trade in illegal drugs exceeds that for iron and steel is a gross exaggeration; it is only one fifth the size of that industry's trade flow. Drugs are a modest contributor to total world trade.' They came up with US$25 billion rather than US$500 billion!

For worldwide money laundering Reuter came up with an estimated range between US$45 and US$280 billion instead of the US$1.5 trillion of the IMF and Human Development Report 1999 (see TNI 2003). The wide range of the estimates reflects the diversity in possible assumptions required at several stages in the production, smuggling and marketing chain. In particular, assumptions on mark-up between wholesale and retail prices, on the difference between export and import prices and on the differences between turnover and income.

Clearly, one of the biggest differences in the distribution of value added in the illicit drug industry is in cross-border shipping ... the difference between export and import values for world agricultural trade amounted to about 6 percent of the export value; absent data for a particular product or market, the Food and Agricultural Organization typically applies a standard 'add factor' of 12 percent. In glaring contrast, the cross-border mark-up on Pakistani–US heroin shipments is about 2,700 percent; the mark-up on Colombian–US cocaine shipments is about 2,100 percent (Reuter in TNI 2003).

Peter Reuter also criticized the American fraud data. In the seminar given by the TNI (2003), the fact that the Association of Certified Fraud Examiners surveyed 10,000 members of which only less than 10 percent responded was objected to. Respondents were asked to estimate the percentage of revenues that will be lost in 2002 as a result of occupational fraud and abuse. The median figure was 6 percent; using an estimate for US GDP of US$10.4 trillion in 2002, this led to their estimate of US$625 billion.

> No effort was made to adjust for non-response or to ask whether respondents were in fact qualified to make such estimates. Nor did the study consider whether or not Gross Domestic Product was the correct base for these calculations. If each examiner had estimated the share of the flow through the corporation, then the right base would have been much larger, namely the total volume of transactions through the corporations. (TNI 2003).

All TNI (2003) participants seem to share the same opinion, namely that drug crime, fraud and money laundering are of minor importance. But out of all of them, only Reuter has done recalculations. The two groups – those who think that money laundering is major and those who think that it is minor – seem to make some effort to meet in the middle. If one looks at Walker's 2003 data revision, he has downsized his estimates for Australia. If one looks at Reuter's and Greenfield's estimates for money laundering, he has upsized his findings from 2001. The two groups can certainly learn a lot from each other, and maybe one day come together.

The following study uses the data of international organizations, the big data. So far they still seem more convincing than the downsizing of the crime and money laundering problem. But one has to be aware of the fact that any estimate is also a guestimate. And some of the suggestions, such as looking more carefully at the retail sales prices used when doing global estimates, are certainly valuable.

The next section estimates a revised Walker model for Australia and the Netherlands. It follows the seven steps of the model, which have been explained in the preceding chapter.[2]

4.2. THE SEVEN STEPS OF THE WALKER MODEL

4.2.1. The First Step: Domestic Dirty Money – the Proceeds of Crime

How much dirty money is generated in Australia and in the Netherlands? Where crime involves illicit goods and services (such as drug dealing and people trafficking) that have a monetary value then the costs from such criminal activity can be measured. For example, where crime is measured in kilograms of heroin, numbers of ecstasy tablets or the sale of illegal weapon multiplied by the average price per kilogram of heroin, ecstasy tablet or weapon, then this equals proceeds of crime per category of crime. Alternatively or in conjunction with this method, surveys of law enforcement agencies can also provide estimates of the total costs of crime. Proceeds can be calculated as a percentage of these estimated total costs. Proceeds are then seen as a kind of mark-up on total costs. This is what Walker did for Australia.

When we replicated his model to calculate figures for the Netherlands, we took the amount of crime and average price of crime instead of crime costs.

CRIME COSTS multiplied by PERCENTAGE OF TOTAL COSTS =
PROCEEDS OF CRIME for Australia

CRIME multiplied by AVERAGE PRICE OF CRIME = PROCEEDS OF
CRIME for the Netherlands

To obtain estimates for the amount of money generated for money laundering in Australia, Walker started with a survey of crime experts. He circulated a questionnaire to each of the state and territory police services and each branch of the Australian Federal Police (AFP) (including criminologists and police analysts), all police commissioners, and a number of independent researchers. In the questionnaire, experts were specifically asked about proceeds from crime (financial gain for the criminal) and the proportion of proceeds laundered. To further confirm the survey figures, Walker also looked at proceeds from crime based on restraining orders, estimates based on underestimated income, estimates based on reports of suspect financial transactions, and estimates based on flows of finance through Australian banks and international transfers (Walker 1995).

Walker also estimated the total costs of crime in a paper for the Australian Institute of Criminology (AIC), which he updated in 1999 (shown in Table 4.1). These estimates come from several agencies, whose statistics were aggregated to provide an overall estimate.

In a presentation in Bangkok in 2003, Walker revised or slightly modified some of the data and assumptions made. This is indicated in italics in Table 4.1. In principle, one can say that Walker downsized his model. In particular, data on fraud are much lower in this new version, whereas the costs of drugs almost doubled. Furthermore, theft was reconsidered in more detail and the revised estimates suggested that it generated greater proceeds from crime than previously expected. Breaking and entering, on the other hand (as distinguished from straight-forward theft) resulted in lower proceeds than in the original. For the rest, the table stayed quite stable with regard to judgments on the mark-up of proceeds on costs.

Overall, Walker estimated the costs of crime to be between A$ 10.9–12.8 billion in 2003. This corresponds to about US$ 8–9.5 billion. These figures are presented in the table below in the first three columns, which show the crime categories, the costs of crime and the proceeds of crime (calculated as percentage mark-up on costs). The other two columns refer to the percentage and amounts of laundering and will be explained in step two.

Table 4.1   The proceeds of crime and money laundering in Australia in A$ (millions)

Crime Category	Best available estimate of costs (mil A$)	Proceeds of crime (% of total costs)	Portion laundered (% of proceeds)	Amount being laundered (mil A$)
Homicide	275 *max 323*	Low (1%)	Medium (10%) *Low*	0.275 *0.0323*
Assault (including sexual assault)	331 *min 979*	Low (1%)	Low (1%)	0.0331 *0.0979*
Robbery and extortion	93 *37*	High (80%)	Medium (10%)	7.44 *2.96*
Breaking and Entering	893 *1193*	High (80%) *Medium*	Medium (10%)	71.44 *11.93*
Fraud/forgery/false pretences	6710-13770 *3000-3500*	High (80%)	High (80%) *Medium*	4294-8812 *1920-2240*
Theft	1232-2712	High (80%)	Medium (10%)	98.56-216.96 *138.3-253.5*
Car Theft **Shoplifting** **Stealing from persons** **Other Theft**	*654* *1020-2460* *545* *659*	*Medium* *High* *High* *Medium*		*6.54* *82.6-196.8* *43.6* *6.59*
Property/ Environmental damage	525-1645 *min 510*	Low (1%)	Medium (10%)	.0525-1.65 *0.51*
Drug Offences	1200 *2000*	High (80%)	High (80%) *Medium*	768 *160*
Total in 1998 **Total revised in 2003**	11259-20719 *10920-12860*	- 	- 	5240-9878 *2133-2669*

Source: Data from Walker 1995, 1999[a] and 2003 plus own calculations of the italic numbers in the last column. This was done under the assumption that Walker has not changed the percentages attributed to low, medium and high. We changed the terminology of the categories of *very small*, *small*, and *considerable* from Walker (1995) where he assigned percentage values to these categories: very small= 1 percent, small=10 percent, considerable=80 percent. We adjusted the terminology he used in 2003, in order to compare the changes he made. *Very small* (Walker 1995) became *low*, *small* (Walker 1995) became *medium* and *considerable* (Walker 1995) became *high*.

The rationale for classification is based on expert interviews and surveys (Walker 1999[a]). The majority of homicides do not financially benefit the offender. Only rare crimes such as contract killings and homicides committed in order to benefit from insurance payment or inheritances would be financially beneficial. However, most homicide occurs within families or between close friends. Most assaults are not committed for financial gain. Assaults committed for financial gain are usually classified as robberies. Property and environmental damage are also crimes rarely committed for financial gain. Drug and fraud offences generate large proceeds. Fraud, on the other hand, can be quite different and complex. There is tax fraud, social security fraud and corporate fraud. Whether or not legal systems distinguish these different types of fraud varies between countries. For measuring purposes these types are frequently distinguished. Theft can also take many forms ranging from car theft to shop lifting and stealing from another person. It usually has medium to high returns.[3]

For the Netherlands, and for all other countries except Australia, Walker estimated money laundering by taking the number of crimes and multiplying it with the fixed amounts (proceeds) that those offences generate. He immediately started with step two. Similarly, our calculations made for the Netherlands also started with step two.

4.2.2.   The Second Step: Domestic Money Generated for Laundering

The proceeds from crime – the dirty money – form the potential amount that can be laundered. However, not all types of crime necessitate the same amount of laundering. Some crimes, such as proceeds from homicide, usually do not require much laundering, whereas proceeds from drugs need substantial laundering. Drug dealers need laundered money in order to create facades of legal income for their businesses and thus enjoy the profits from their illegal activities. Robberies are quite costly to the community but the amount of money gained from each robbery is usually a small enough amount that it has no need of being laundered. Ordinary theft is similar to robbery (in fact can be the same in some jurisdictions) in so far as there is little need for laundering. Offenders are much more likely to spend any money earned from theft rather than undertake the often complex transactions required to first 'clean' their gains through laundering. Drugs and fraud offences, however, are usually associated with money laundering. Large amounts of money are involved (earnings exceed those amounts that could be reasonably spent without detection) which creates an incentive for laundering. Walker revised the percentage that is likely to be laundered for drug proceeds by lowering it. Before, he assumed that 80 percent or 'considerable amounts' of drug proceeds were laundered. In his latest revision (Walker, 2003), he speaks of 'medium laundering intensity' without giving a figure.

Additional income that results from tax evasion can either be immediately spent (as with ordinary theft) or laundered, depending on the amount of money involved. Company fraud can be 100 percent laundered. Social security fraud, wherein social benefits are paid out under false pretences can *either* be spent immediately *or* laundered, depending on the amounts involved or the techniques used to achieve the fraud. Overall, Walker's revision is that proceeds from fraud are medium intense laundered, whereas previously he had assumed that they are considerably or highly laundered.

For each type of crime, it is necessary to determine the percentage of proceeds that are laundered. By attributing a percentage value of money laundered per crime type it is possible to estimate the amounts of money generated for laundering for each crime type in a country. By summing up all money laundered from different types of crime, one gets the total amount of money generated for laundering in the country.

PROCEEDS OF CRIME multiplied by PERCENTAGE LAUNDERED = MONEY LAUNDERED

4.2.2.1. Calculating domestically generated money for laundering in Australia

For Australia, Table 4.1 shows that in 2003 the amount of money laundered, calculated this way, ranges between A$2.1 and A$2.6 billion, which amounts to about US$1.8–2.3 billion. Compared to the earlier results from Walker this is about half or one third of what he originally calculated (A$5–10 billion or US$3.5–7 billion). However, he might also have changed the weight he attaches to the term 'medium' in Table 4.1, which would result in higher total amounts than calculated for 2003.

Table 4.2 compares all Australian estimates on domestic Australian money laundering available.

Table 4.2 Australian domestically generated money for laundering

Based on expert criminologists	A$0.4–A$4.5 billion
suspect transactions	A$52 million
proceeds of crime seizures	A$20–A$40 million
based on other polices research and statistics	A$0.3–A$3.8 billion
based on Australian Federal Police estimates including drugs and major frauds	A$3.5–A$4.2 billion
based on understatement of income	A$3–A$5 billion
based on mismatch between foreign trade and overseas flows of funds	A$6.3–A$8.7 billion
Walker 1992–2003	A$2–A$7 billion

Source: Walker (2003) and own calculations.

4.2.2.2.   Calculating domestically generated money for laundering in the Netherlands

For the Netherlands, we first calculated the proceeds of crime for different offences. The Dutch Statistical Office, the Centraal Bureau voor de Statistiek (CBS), recently published a study by Smekens and Verbruggen (2004) in which they estimated the illegal economy in the Netherlands. The activities of drugs, prostitution, illegal workers, illegal gambling, fencing and copyright infringements are all areas that generate money for laundering in the Netherlands. The proceeds from these activities can then be calculated. Table 4.3 provides a breakdown of illegal activities by crime category and their proceeds. The proceeds are then multiplied by the estimated percentage laundered for each activity to obtain the total amount generated for laundering. From this CBS study, we find €2.3 billion generated for laundering in the Netherlands.

Second, the estimated damage for businesses and institutions has also been included in the table. Direct damage is defined as the amount of money earned by an offender with respect to crimes like burglary, theft and cyber crime, as opposed to indirect damage such as higher insurance costs or the outlay required when installing security systems. These direct damages resulted in €94 million worth of laundering (see WODC 2003 p. 60 and Table 2.8. in Unger et al. 2006).

Third, we added data regarding fraud. Fraud is an extremely important area to consider when measuring money laundering, since most money generated for laundering comes from drugs and fraud. According to the Annual Report from the fraud department of the Dutch ministry of Social Affairs and Work SIOD (Sociale Inlichtingen- en Opsporingsdienst, 2004), €84 million worth of social security fraud was identified in 67 investigations. The annual report done by the fraud department for fiscal and economic matters of the Ministry of Finance and Ministry of Economic Affairs (FIOD-ECD, Fiscale Inlichtingen- en Opsporingsdienst en De Economische Controledienst 2003), showed that approximately €689 million of tax revenue loss had been discovered that was related to tax fraud. Interviews with experts revealed that they discover only approximately 5–10 percent of fraud. This means that the amount of fraud detected should be multiplied 10–20 times to obtain the total figure for fraud committed. We take 10 percent of fraud being discovered as the most likely scenario. Given these assumptions, we calculated the range of fraud proceeds for laundering shown in the last rows in Table 4.3.

The estimates that Dutch experts had provided of the percentages of proceeds of crime per offence were compared with the figures cited in Meloen's (et al. 2003) case studies. In these case studies, the behaviour of money launderers caught is being studied (see chapter 3 under case studies). The percentages concur with Walker's (1995) original observations as well.

Table 4.3   Proceeds of crime and money laundering in the Netherlands

Offence	Proceeds (million €)	% Laundered	Total amount generated for laundering (million €)
Drugs (Heroine, Cocaine, XTC, Cannabis)	1,960	80	1,568
Prostitution	460	80	368
Illegal Workers	490	10	49
Illegal Gambling	130	80	104
Fencing	190	80	152
Illegal copying	90	80	72
Total	**3,320**		**2,313**
Offence against business			
Burglary	340	10	34
Theft	345	10	34,5
Vandalism	140	0	0
Computer crime	26	80	20,8
Violent offences	6	0	0
Other offences	47	10	4,7
Total direct damage against business	**1,044**	-	**94**
FIOD-ECD (2003) (Tax fraud and financial fraud)	689	-	-
SIOD (2004) (Premiums, fiscal, social fraud)	84,6	-	-
total fraud if 10% get caught best case	**7,735**	80	**6,189**
total fraud if 5% get caught worst case	**15,450**	80	**12,376**
Amounts generated for laundering	-	-	**8,596-14,783**

Source: Smekens and Verbruggen (2004). Van der Heide and Eggen (2003, p. 60); taken from NIPO (2002). Fraud data are from the FIOD and SIOD. For the FIOD data we assumed that 40 percent tax is due on average on the amounts of income not reported to the tax authorities. The SIOD data give the amount of social security fraud; according to FIOD experts approximately 5–10 percent of fraud is caught.

The last row of the table shows the sum of the amounts of money generated for laundering. Based on the available information, between €8.5 and €14.7 billion is generated in the Netherlands for laundering each year.

A second way of ascertaining the volume of money generated for laundering domestically is to extract estimates for proceeds of crime from the Australian survey data and the proportions and amounts laundered. Walker used these numbers to arrive at money laundered per recorded crime shown in column three (Table 4.4). He applied these figures to all countries, including the Netherlands. We tried to replicate his model for the Netherlands, by using more recent crime statistics but applying the proceeds of crime data that Walker recommends. To use the same proceeds of crime data all over the world has often been disputed (see Reuter and Greenfield at the beginning of this chapter). Walker himself suggested some corrections by adjusting the proceeds for rich and poor countries (see under GNP pro-rating below). When using this alternative method of calculating domestic money laundering, the average money laundering amounts per recorded crime have to be multiplied with the number of recorded criminal offence.

We followed Walker's assumption that crime pays more in corrupt countries and that it returns higher proceeds in rich countries. For this, each type of crime is multiplied by the estimated profitability of each crime, with fraud being factored up by the corruption index on a scale of 1 to 5. The numbers are then multiplied by a pro-rated GNP per capita figure which takes into account the differences in profitability between countries (Walker, 1995; Unger et al., 2006).

NUMBER OF CRIME multiplied by MONEY LAUNDERED PER RECORDED CRIME = TOTAL AMOUNT OF MONEY GENERATED FOR LAUNDERING

The Netherlands generates approximately A$14.4 billion or US$12 billion per annum for money laundering according to crime statistics from 2000–2004 (see Table 4.4). Variations between the US$12 billion calculated here and the approximately US$18 billion that Walker had calculated for the Netherlands in 1995 can be explained by differences in crime statistics by year. Table 4.5 shows how sensitive the outcomes are due to the use of different crime statistics. There can be great volatility in figures produced according to which crime statistics are used. Table 4.5 shows a comparison of different crime statistics for the Netherlands. The main difference here is between statistics from police records and from victim surveys. It is logical that statistics from victims' surveys will be higher than those recorded in police statistics since not all crimes are reported (Unger et al., 2006).

It is clear that a vast amount of money is generated in the Netherlands for laundering. Earlier findings (Schaap, 1998) show that EU fraud only was estimated at between €3.2 and €16 million in the Netherlands in 1991. In the same year, however, proceeds from drugs, weapons and illegal gambling houses amounted to approximately €4.5 billion.

Table 4.4   The Dutch money generated for laundering (Walker model recalculated)

Crime	Number of crimes[a]	A$ laundered per crime	Total A$ for laundering (millions)
Fraud	241,600	50,000*1[b]	12,080.0
Drugs	7,474	100,000	747.4
Theft	1,776,000	400	710.4
Burglary	288,000	600	172.8
Robbery	480,000	1,400	672.0
Homicide	183	225	0.04
Assault/sexual assault	960,000	2.23	2.14
Total	-	-	14,384.78

Notes
a.   Source: The International Crime Victims Survey 2000, Seventh United Nations Survey on Crime Trends and Operation of Criminal Justice Systems 2000, and the Statistical Yearbook of the Netherlands (2004).
b.   1 is the corruption index by which fraud data is multiplied. It would be a maximum of 5 if the country were very corrupt. Source of this column is Walker (1995).

Table 4.6 shows the different estimates of money generated in the Netherlands for laundering. Walker (1999[a]) estimated this at US$18 billion. Recalculating this model with more recent data and with some slight modifications results in lower figures of US$12 billion. Earlier findings for the Netherlands show €4.5 billion. Our estimates for proceeds from different types of crimes range between €8 and 14 billion. This means that the domestic part of money laundering in the Netherlands is about 1–2.5 percent of the Dutch GDP.

In adapting the model for money generated within the Netherlands, it is important to take as many factors as possible into account to get a more accurate estimate. Originally, Walker (1999[b]) only used those statistics that he could obtain from the United Nations Survey of Crime Trends and Operations of Criminal Justice Systems, which included only fraud, drugs, theft, burglary, robbery, homicide, and assault/sexual assault. These are not the only crimes from which money can be laundered. The Centraal Bureau voor de Statistiek (CBS) recently published the report *De illegale economie in Nederland* in which it examines drugs, prostitution, illegal workers, illegal gambling, fencing and illegal copying (copy-right infringements). To gain more informed estimates of money generated for laundering, we use both groups of illegal activity and any subcategories that are relevant.

Table 4.5   Differences in numbers of crimes in the Netherlands according to source

Crime	Victim Surveys (2000)	Seventh UN Survey on Crime Trends (2000)	European Source-book (2003) offences	European Source-book (2003) offenders	Statistical Yearbook Netherlands (2004)
Fraud	241,600	19,698	-	-	15,100[a]
Embezzlement		7,805			8,900[a]
Drugs		7,474	7,694	11,899	12,700[a]
Theft	1,776,000	728,261	880,689	98,615	1,809,300[b]
Burglary	288,000	91,946	509,750	47,433	293,400[b]
Robbery	480,000	18,630	19,071	7,172	-
Homicide		183	2,804	2,771	-
Assault	960,000	44,129	45,233	30,644	978,000[b]
Sexual Assault		1,648	1,695	978	
Prostitution	-	-	-	-	-
Illegal gambling	-	-	-	-	-
Illegal workers	-	-	-	-	-
Fencing	-	-	-	-	2,200
Illegal Copying	-	-	-	-	-

Notes
a.   from police records
b.   from victim surveys

Source: Unger et al. (2006).

Table 4.6   Different estimates of generated money for the Netherlands

Source	Estimate of generated money (billions)
Walker (1999)	US$18.4 = €15 billion
Recalculated Walker (2005)	US$12.0 = €8.4 billion
Schaap (1998)	€4.5 billion
Our estimates from proceeds 2005	Between €8 and €14 billion

Table 4.7　Generated money from criminal activities in the Netherlands

Types of crime	FATF Recommenda-tions (2002)	Walker (1995)	Van der Werf (1997)	CBS (2004)	Meloen et al. (2003)*	Unger et al. (2006)
Drugs	X	X	X	X	X	X
Prostitution	X		X	X		X
Public Order (against persons)						
- Theft and Fencing (& burglary and robbery)	X	X	X	X	X	X
- Homicide	X	X			X	X
- Assault and sexual assault	X	X			X	X
- Participating in criminal org.	X				X	
- Possession of arms	X				X	
- Terrorism	X					
- Environmental crime	X					
- Kidnapping	X					
- Extortion	X					
Smuggling						
- Smuggling goods	X					
- Trafficking in human beings	X			X	X	X
Financial Economic crime						
- Illegal activities in the labour market				X	X	X
- Fraud and deception	X	X			X	X
- Terrorist financing	X					
- Counterfeiting currency	X					
- Insider trading and market manipulation	X					
Illegal Gambling			X	X		X
Illegal Copying	X		X	X		X
Corruption (bribery)	X		X			

*　These categories are used with the 52 selected cases (1 million guilders and higher). For the calculation of the total proceeds of crime in the Netherlands the following categories are used: theft, drugs, economic crime, fraud and deception, public safety, sexual assault and participating in a criminal organization.

Source:　Unger et al. (2006) with some modifications.

Table 4.7 shows the types of activities included in diverse empirical studies. If one looks at empirical studies done so far that relate to crime, costs of crime, money laundered or the effects of money laundered one can see that these studies do not only differ with regard to the definition of their research subject but also with regard to the types of crime they analyse.

The above table gives an overview of the types of crime listed in the *Basic Facts of Money Laundering* of the FATF (2002), the types of crime used in the Walker (1995) model on the amount and effects of money laundering, the study of Van der Werf (1997), the study done by the Smekens and Verbruggen (2004) and by Meloen et al. (2003). While the FATF recommendations list a great variety of types of crime that can lead to money laundering, Walker (1995) restricts himself to drugs, theft, homicide, assault and fraud. Van der Werf (1997) deals with drugs, prostitution (illegal, but not a crime in the Netherlands), theft, illegal gambling, illegal copying and corruption. The study of the CBS has the goal of defining the size of the illegal economy and not of money laundering or effects of money laundering. It includes drugs, prostitution, theft, smuggling, illegal workers, illegal gambling and copying. The micro case study *Buit en Besteding* by Meloen et al. (2003) deals with drugs, theft, homicide, assault, participating criminal activities, possession of arms, smuggling, fraud, and illegal labour exchange (*koppelbazerij*).

If one compares the original Walker model estimates with the results of the Dutch CBS and our own earlier study, one can see that the studies refer to different types of crime. The CBS calculates the added value of the illegal economy and comes up with €3.3 billion, from which we conclude that money laundering amounts to €2.3 billion. The only overlap with the Walker model is for drugs. For the rest, Walker includes sexual assault, homicide, robbery, burglary, theft, and fraud. Our calculation includes all types of crime that either the CBS or Walker mention. I do not think that all of them are necessarily related to money laundering. It is meant to give everybody the opportunity to deduct those components that he does not consider relevant for money laundering. I have opted for too much rather than too little information here.

4.2.3. The Third Step: Worldwide Money Laundering

Walker (1999) not only made calculations for the Netherlands and Australia, but also for all other countries. The table below ranks the top 20 origins of laundered money, which make up more than 90 percent of the total origins of laundered money. As mentioned before, it is estimated that US$18 billion is laundered in the Netherlands. Walker estimates that US$2.85 trillion is laundered globally. Australia does not appear in the list of the top 20.

A criticism that could be applied to the Walker model is that the amounts of money for laundering generated in specific countries are too large. Austria, for

Table 4.8   Top 20 origins of laundered money (Walker 1999[b])

Rank	Origin	Amount ($US million per year)	% of Total
1	United States	1320228	46.3
2	Italy	150054	5.3
3	Russia	147187	5.2
4	China	131360	4.6
5	Germany	128266	4.5
6	France	124748	4.4
7	Romania	115585	4.1
8	Canada	82374	2.9
9	United Kingdom	68740	2.4
10	Hong Kong	62856	2.2
11	Spain	56287	2.0
12	Thailand	32834	1.2
13	South Korea	21240	0.4
14	Mexico	21119	0.7
15	Austria	20231	0.7
16	Poland	19714	0.7
17	Philippines	18867	0.7
18	**Netherlands**	18362	0.6
19	Japan	16975	0.6
20	Brazil	16786	0.6
Total	All countries	2850470	100

example, is a country with low crime rates and half of the population of the Netherlands. It seems very unlikely that it should have higher proceeds from domestic crime than the Netherlands. Specifically, there are concerns that the numbers for the United States may be inflated (though it concurs with other reports, see Napoleoni 2003). If this is the case, then the inflated numbers would have a large influence on other countries since, according to the Walker Model, 46.3 percent of all money generated in the world for laundering comes from the US.

In the original Walker model, it was estimated that the United States generates $1.3 trillion per year for money laundering. Concerns were raised, not without justification, that these figures are too high. For example, taking into account the amount of money generated by drugs and some forms of fraud, the total proceeds of crime approach about half of the Walker figure. If 80 percent of these proceeds get laundered, the US would launder US$686 billion, about half of the amount that Walker originally estimated (see Table 4.9).

Table 4.9   Proceeds from crime in the US

Crime	US$ Generated (billions)	% Laundered	US$ Money Laundered (billions)
Drugs	65	80	52
Occupational Fraud	660	-	-
Insurance Fraud	30	-	-
Telemarketing Fraud	40	-	-
Check Fraud	10	-	-
Identity Fraud	53	-	-
Total	**858**	80	**686**

Source: Unger et al. (2006) and revised calculations.

To conclude, the original Walker (1999) model has overestimated domestic money laundering by about 30–50 percent. Walker revised his own data for Australia. Recalculating Dutch and US data points in the same direction. While Walker's original estimates for money laundering for large countries such as the US may have been overestimated, they remain sizeable even with the revised calculations. They expose the myth that it is small microstate tax havens – islands and alpine enclaves – that are primarily responsible for money laundering. By contrast it is medium-sized to large economies that are the main centres for worldwide money laundering.

In order to proceed to the subsequent steps of the Walker model, it is necessary to estimate domestic money laundering per country, or at least for the top 20 money laundering producing countries in the world.

Trusting Walker's percentage allocation of money laundered worldwide, these could be multiplied by the percentages of worldwide money that each country produces. More recent IMF estimates of global laundering could then be applied to this allocation. The last IMF estimate for money laundering was US$1.5 trillion (compared to the US$2.85 trillion estimated by Walker) given that each country would have about 40 percent less volume of money laundering than Walker calculated in his original model.

4.2.4. The Fourth Step: Dirty Money Flowing into a Country from Abroad – the Index of Attractiveness

In order to calculate the percentage of each country's domestic criminal money flow into each third country for laundering, the gravity model is particularly useful. One has to understand how attractive each country appears for money launderers and how accessible it is. For the calculation of cross-border flows of laundered money, Walker introduced two indices: the attractiveness and the distance deterrence indicator.

Important assumptions for the index of attractiveness are:

- Foreign countries with a tolerant attitude towards money laundering will attract a greater proportion of the money than more intolerant countries: tolerant countries are those with banking secrecy laws or uncooperative government attitudes towards money laundering.
- High levels of corruption and/or conflict in a country will deter money launderers from laundering money in that country because of the added risk of losing their funds.
- Countries with high levels of GNP per capita will be preferred by money launderers, since it is easier to 'hide' their transactions (Walker 1999[a]).

If one compares the ranking of countries of the original Walker attractiveness index (for the formula see chapter three) with our own modified formula, it is evident that Australia scores lower in the latter ranking. In order to compare both rankings, we have listed the Walker ranking for attractiveness in the footnote below our own attractiveness score, in Table 4.11.

Our modified formula for attractiveness is, as outlined in chapter three:

$$Attractiveness = (GDP)*(3 * BS + GA + SWIFT + FD - 3 * CF - CR - EG + 10)$$

Where *GDP* is GDP per capita, *BS* is Banking Secrecy, *GA* is Government Attitude, *SWIFT* is SWIFT member, *FD* is Financial Deposits, *CF* is Conflict, *CR* is Corruption, and *EG* is Egmont Group member.

4.2.4.1. Explanation of the variables used

Two new variables have been added to the original Walker formula: Financial Deposits and Egmont Group membership. Financial Deposits were added in order to account for the size of the financial market as a proxy for the financial attractiveness of a country. The variable Egmont Group member was added or left out in order to give more weight to countries' attitude towards money laundering by taking into account international AML cooperation efforts and the presence of an FIU. For the rest, we followed Walker (1999[a]) and his scales and statistical sources quite closely.

GDP per capita is measured in US dollars for the most recent year possible and prorated against the Netherlands. GDP per capita of the Netherlands = 1. Data was drawn from the CIA World Factbook.

Bank Secrecy is from a scale of 1 (no secrecy laws) to 4 (bank secrecy laws enforced). Source: OECD (2000). Countries are given a 1 if they have no secrecy laws and are civil law countries, and a 2 if they have no secrecy laws and are common law countries. The idea behind this is that civil law countries have no built-in legislated bank secrecy. Common law countries have a certain measure of confidentiality, by default, given the tradition of client legal privilege in such jurisdictions. Countries that have specifically legislated regarding bank secrecy provisions are accorded a score of 3 and countries are given a 4 if they are on FATF, FSF or OECD country lists.

Government Attitude is from a scale of 0 (government hostile to laundering) to 4 (tolerant of laundering). Countries that are part of the Financial Action Task Force (FATF) are given a value of 0, while those countries that are currently on the FATF 'Non-Cooperative list' are given a 4. The calculations were done using the numbers from 2003 and 2004. In 2006, there was only one country left on this list, Myanmar (Burma); Nigeria was removed shortly beforehand. Countries that were previously on this list are given a value of 3. Countries that are part of an anti-money laundering group other than the FATF are given a 1 and countries that are part of no group or used to be on the non-cooperative list but are now part of a group are given a 2.

SWIFT member is 0 for non-member countries and 1 for members of the SWIFT (Society for Worldwide Interbank Financial Telecommunication). In the future, this indicator could be removed, since currently there are only 17 countries worldwide that are not SWIFT members.

Financial Deposits are financial system deposits to GDP. This figure is demand, time and saving deposits in deposit money banks and other financial institutions as a share of GDP, calculated using the following deflation method: $\{(0.5)*[F_t/P_{et} + F_{t-1}/P_{et-1}]\}/[GDP_t/P_{at}]$ where F is demand and time and saving deposits, P_e is end-of period CPI, and P_a is the average annual CPI (see Beck et al. 1999). Raw data are from the electronic version of the IMF's International Financial Statistics (IFS lines 24, 25, and 45). Data on GDP in local currency (lines 99B..ZF or, if not available, line 99B.CZF), end-of period CPI (line 64M..ZF or, if not available, 64Q..ZF), and annual CPI (line 64..ZF) are from the electronic version of the IFS.

Egmont Group is a 0 (non member) or 1 (member). The Egmont group is a group of FIUs established to coordinate international efforts to combat money laundering.

Conflict is from a scale of 0 (no conflict) to 4 (conflict situation exists). 0 is given when there has been no conflict since 1989. 1 is given if there was conflict at a minor level that has now ended. 2 is given if there was a serious conflict that has now ended. 3 is given if there is a conflict situation at present. 4 is given if there is an ongoing war situation (Source: Uppsala Conflict Data Project http://www.pcr.uu.se/database/index.php).

Corruption is the transposed Transparency International index (1=low, 5=high).

The Constant 10 is included ensuring that all scores are above 0. For a further description of how to calculate the variables, see Unger et al. (2006).

4.2.4.2. The correlation matrix of the attractiveness indicator variables

As a simple test of the credibility of the choice of indicators we did a correlation test. If the correlation between indicators is high, they measure basically the same part of the unobservable variable money laundering, and they could be reduced to a single one. As the correlation matrix shows, correlation is about 0.4, thus, moderately high between Government Attitude towards money laundering and membership of the Egmont Group and between corruption and government attitude. Correlation between Egmont group membership and corruption is relatively high as well. For future work it might be advisable to cluster Egmont group membership, Government Attitude towards money laundering and corruption into one joined variable. The rest of the variables measure different aspects of the variable money laundering.

The new attractiveness index ranks Australia and Belgium higher and the Netherlands, the US and the UK lower than Walker (1999[a]). Luxembourg, Switzerland and the Cayman Islands rank highest in both scores. Some countries, such as Angola seem underestimated in both rankings.

Table 4.10   The correlation matrix of the attractiveness variables

	BS	SWIFT	GA	Conflict	Corruption	Egmont	FD
BS	1	-	-	-	-	-	-
SWIFT	-0.077	1	-	-	-	-	-
GA	0.069	-0.205	1	-	-	-	-
Conflict	-0.131	0.019	0.159	1	-	-	-
Corruption	-0.133	-0.005	0.462	0.280	1	-	-
Egmont	0.357	0.179	-0.436	-0.170	-0.425	1	-
FD	0.171	0.169	-0.384	-0.106	-0.404	0.328	1

Table 4.11   New index of attractiveness (The higher the score, the greater the attractiveness to money launderers)

Country	Score
Luxembourg	55.4
Bermuda	26.4
Switzerland	25.7
Cayman Islands, Norway, Hong Kong, Austria, Liechtenstein	21–20
Belgium, Aruba, Jersey	19–18
Iceland, Canada, Ireland, Singapore, **Australia**, Isle of Man, Vatican City (Holy See)	17–15
France, San Marino, Guernsey/Alderney/Sark, Germany, **Netherlands**	15–13
United Arab Emirates, Bahrain, Gibraltar, Italy, US Virgin Islands, Cyprus (Greek), Falkland Islands, Finland, Bahamas, Greece	13–12
Malta, New Zealand, Japan, Barbados, Guam, Sweden, **United States**	12–11
Greenland, Hungary, Denmark, Israel, British Virgin Islands	11–10
Taiwan, French Polynesian, Qatar, **United Kingdom**, Spain, Macau, South Korea, Brunei	10–9
Puerto Rico, Slovenia, Oman, Portugal, New Caledonia, Pitcairn Islands, Antigua, Northern Mariana Islands, Mauritius, Turks and Caicos, Czech Republic, Saint Kitts and Nevis, Botswana, Martinique, Uruguay	9–6
Seychelles, Malaysia, Anguilla, Slovakia, Kuwait, South Africa, Namibia, Lithuania, Palau, Chile, American Samoa, Trinidad and To-bago, Samoa, Saint Pierre and Miquelon, Poland, Cook Islands, Nauru	6–4
Latvia, Panama, Saint Lucia, Dominica, Croatia, Ukraine, Grenada, Guadeloupe, Belize, Tunisia, Bulgaria, Fiji, Thailand, Russia, Libya, Argentina, Kazakhstan, Costa Rica, Reunion, Niue, Belarus, Jordan, Lebanon, Maldives, Turkmenistan, Brazil, Montserrat, Jamaica, Philippines, Gabon, Egypt, Guyana, Guatemala, Saint Vincent and the Grenadines, Vanuatu, El Salvador	4–2
Monaco, Mexico, Romania, Suriname, Macedonia, Albania, Swaziland, Iran, Dominican Republic, Mayotte, Estonia, Syria, Lesotho, Armenia, Andorra, Tonga, Cuba, Venezuela, Colombia, Ghana, Honduras, Marshall Islands, Vietnam, Bosnia and Herzegovina, Federated States of Micronesia, Paraguay, Zimbabwe	2–1
Ecuador, Mongolia, Papua New Guinea, Peru, Morocco, Bolivia, Solomon Islands, The Gambia, Turkey, Mauritania, Netherlands Antilles, Myanmar, Sri Lanka, Nicaragua, Algeria, Kyrgyzstan, Guinea, Bhutan, Nigeria, Azerbaijan, Cape Verde, Djibouti, Cameroon, China, Equatorial Guinea, India, North Korea, Laos, Uzbekistan, Moldova, Saudi Arabia, Kenya, Indonesia, Bangladesh, Togo, Benin, Burkina Faso, Chad, Sao Tome and Principe, Tuvalu, Ivory Coast, Zambia, Angola, Haiti, Cambo-	1–0

Country	Score
dia, Pakistan, Kiribati, Georgia, Madagascar, Serbia and Montenegro, Liberia, Ethiopia, Malawi, Congo, Eritrea, Tanzania, Mali, Rwanda, Iraq, Niger, Uganda, Central African Republic, Mozambique, Tajikistan, Sudan, Yemen, Senegal, Sierra Leone, Democratic Republic of Congo, Comoros, Guinea Bissau, Nepal, Western Sahara, Somalia, West Bank/ Gaza Strip, Afghanistan, Burundi	

Source: Unger et al. (2006).
For a comparison with the original Walker ranking see endnote 4.

4.2.5.   Step 5: Dirty Money Flowing from Abroad – the Distance Deterrence Index

It is not only the attractiveness of a country but also the distance between the sending and receiving country that affects money laundering. Distance can be a barrier to trade flows as well as money laundering flows. The closer the countries, the higher the proportion of money laundered. In the original Walker model, distance deterrence is measured as the square of physical distance between countries' capitals (see Walker 1999[a]). In our modified indicator we follow Walker's proposal for further research and assume that:

- All other things being equal, geographic distance, linguistic and cultural differences are deterrents to money launderers.
- Being a top trading partner of a country makes a country more probable to engage in money laundering (Walker 1999[a], p. 15).

Distance = language +3 trade + 3 colonial background + physical distance

Distance deterrence assigns a value to countries in relation to their relative distance with other countries depending on language, colonial background, trade and geographical distance. Countries have more distance between them if they speak different languages, have different historical backgrounds, do not trade with each other and/or have a large geographical distance separating them. We modified the weights given to the four indicators in the sensitivity analysis and found the formula above, with 3 multiplied by trade and colonial background to give the most realistic fit.

4.2.5.1.   Explanation of variables
We used three dummy variables for cultural and social distance and kilometres for physical distance.

Language is 0 if countries have the same official language or the same widely used language and it is 1 if a different language is spoken. A score of 0 means that there is less distance between the countries than a score of 1. Data were taken from the CIA World Fact Book.

Colonial Background is 0 if countries share the same colonial background and it is 1 if they have a different background. Colonial background has to do with whether or not a country was or is a colony or territory. Data were taken from the CIA World Fact Book.

Trade is 0 if the sending country is a top trading partner of the receiving country and this is ascribed by examining each county's trading partners. Zero indicates that there is less distance between them due to their trading experience with each other. It is 1 if the sending country is not a top trading partner of the receiving country. Data was taken from the World Trade Organization (WTO).

Physical distance = distance in kilometres between the capitals of each country. As a source we took a spreadsheet from 1995, which lists the capitals in coordinates (Knaap 2006).

4.2.6.   Step 6: The Percentage of Criminal Money Flowing into a Country

Walker (1999[a]) calculated flows of money been sent between all countries. First, he calculated the percentage of money laundering flows that each country sends to another country by using the gravity formula (see chapter 3):

$$\text{Proportion of Money Laundering} = \text{attractiveness of j}/(\text{Distance between i and j})^2$$

As can be seen in Table 4.12 the US attracts 18 percent of worldwide money laundering and the Netherlands 1.7 percent. Australia is not on the list of top 20 receiving countries. Its share is smaller than 1 percent of worldwide money laundering.

Our calculation with the modified formula including language, colonial background and trade relations in the distance formula resulted in proportions shown in the table below for the top 20 countries sending money for laundering to the Netherlands.

4.2.7.   Step 7: Total Amount of Money Laundered in a Country – Giants Wash More

The percentage of the dirty money that flows from country i to country j has to be multiplied by the money generated for laundering in country i. All countries' money flows to country j have to be included. This gives the inflows from money for laundering from all other countries to country j. In addition, the money generated in country j itself has to be added.

Table 4.12   Top 20 destinations of laundered money

Rank	Destination	% of worldwide money laundering	Walker originally 2.85 trillion US$ Amount in million US$	Using IMF estimate of 1.5 trillion world-wide Amount in million US$
1	**United States**	**18.9%**	**538,145**	**283,500**
2	Cayman Islands	4.9%	138,329	73,500
3	Russia	4.2%	120,493	63,000
4	Italy	3.7%	105,688	55,500
5	China	3.3%	94,726	49,500
6	Romania	3.1%	89,595	46,500
7	Canada	3.0%	85,444	45,000
8	Vatican City	2.8%	80,596	42,000
9	Luxembourg	2.8%	78,468	42,000
10	France	2.4%	68,471	36,000
11	Bahamas	2.3%	66,398	34,500
12	Germany	2.2%	61,315	33,000
13	Switzerland	2.1%	58,993	31,500
14	Bermuda	1.9%	52,887	28,500
15	**Netherlands**	**1.7%**	**49,591**	**25,500**
16	Liechtenstein	1.7%	48,949	25,500
17	Austria	1.7%	48,376	25,500
18	Hong Kong	1.6%	44,519	24,000
19	United Kingdom	1.6%	44,478	24,000
20	Spain	1.2%	35,461	18,000

Source: Walker (1999[a]) and own calculations.

The top 20 countries receiving money (both because of their attractiveness and taking into account the physical distance of the sending countries) are listed in Table 4.12. The right column recalculates the amounts when adjusting for the estimate of the IMF for global money laundering.

Two thirds of worldwide money laundering was sent to the top 20 countries listed above. Note that most of these countries are well-established, well developed, and quite sizeable countries, and that there are only a few microstate OFCs and tax havens amongst them (Cayman Islands, Vatican City, Bermuda and Liechtenstein). The majority of countries that attract money-laundering flows are economic giants, not dwarfs. Giants seem to wash more.

The US has the largest worldwide share of money laundering, but there are a number of EU countries that also appear on the list. For the Netherlands, the numbers adjusted for the latest IMF forecast appear more reasonable. According to this table, the Netherlands receives (including its own generated money for laundering) US$ 25 billion, or about €19 billion. This comes close to our own findings after having introduced step 5. Also the Austrian data appear more reasonable. Walker had originally estimated US$48 billion for Austria, a country half as big as the Netherlands. Austria's GDP in 2005 was US$267.6 billion, so Walker's original calculation would have indicated that Austria launders almost 20 percent of its GDP! Though Austria, due to its higher bank secrecy, is certainly an attractive country for money launderers, 20 percent of GDP seems too high and the 10 percent calculated by the IMF appears more reasonable, though it is still very sizeable. For the UK, we come up with 9 percent of GDP laundered as opposed to the 20 percent with which Walker came up with.

4.2.7.1.   Total amount of money laundered in Australia

Australia is not in the list of the top 20 countries for money launderers. However, as Walker observes:

> There is consistency across the different estimates if one chooses the following quanta. Firstly, one concludes that between $1000 million and $4500 million of Australian proceeds of crime are laundered within Australia or sent overseas. Next, one takes the International Finance-based estimates as showing the potential for incoming money laundering and for laundering of money through Australia. This suggests as much as $5500 million may be being sent out of Australia to overseas tax havens (some of which would be from Australian crime and some being from overseas crime laundering via Australia), and as much as $7700 million brought to Australia for laundering (Walker 1999[a]).

When we recalculated the money flowing into Australia with the same model we applied to the Netherlands, we get at higher amounts. Ferwerda estimated money generated in Australia and flowing into Australia for laundering at US$19 billion. This amounts to about 5 percent of the Australian GDP. Late reports of the FATF (2005) confirm that Australia is a country more and more popular for money launderers. The FATF (2005, 2.8) complains that there is the low number of money laundering prosecutions at the Commonwealth level (ten dealt with summarily and three on indictment since 2003, with five convictions), indicating that the anti money laundering regime is not being effectively implemented. 'Overall, the evaluation team did not find the implementation of the AML/CFT supervisory system to be effective in terms of the standards required by the revised 40 Recommendations' (FATF 2005, 3.39).

*Table 4.13   Inflows of money and domestic laundering in Australia in
million US$*

	Walker (1999)	Ferwerda (2006)	
	total generated money for laundering per country	Percentage and amount of each country's money for laundering flowing to Australia	
Country	amount	%	amount
Germany	128,266	0.5%	645
Austria	20,231	0.4%	82
Spain	56,287	0.5%	294
UK	68,740	0.5%	347
Romania	115,585	0.8%	892
Italy	150,054	0.5%	750
Poland	19,714	0.7%	134
France	124,748	0.5%	574
US	1,320,228	0.7%	9,285
Mexico	21,119	1.0%	210
Canada	82,374	0.5%	424
Russia	147,187	0.8%	1,141
China	131,360	1.2%	1,601
Hong Kong	62,856	0.8%	479
Thailand	32,834	1.4%	458
Japan	21,240	0.8%	168
Philippines	18,867	1.6%	298
South Korea	21,240	0.9%	185
Brazil	16,786	1.0%	161
Sub-total	-	-	18,127
Australia	1,764	53.0%	935
Total			**19,062**

Source: Ferwerda (2006).

The figures provided in Table 4.14 are based on the original 'generated'
money that Walker (1999) estimated multiplied by revised proportions that equal
the volume of money that flows into the Netherlands. For the Netherlands the
own estimated data have been filled in. The countries in Table 4.14 are the top
20 origins of laundered money and comprise 90 percent of the total money
generated for laundering. Although only 0.8 percent of the total money
generated in the US flows to the Netherlands, it is for the Netherlands the largest

amount of incoming funds (US$11 billion) that are flowing into the country for laundering purposes (Unger et al. 2006). The last two columns show the results of Ferwerda (2006), who has recalculated the model. He improved the distance indicator. In Unger et al. (2006), Siegel had calculated distance by world regions. For this she had attributed numbers between 0 and 7 depending on how far one country was from the other. Ferwerda used kilometre distances between capitals. Another improvement was that Ferwerda used, for each country, the percentage of its total exports sent to its top trading partners. Before, there were only 0–1 variables used to indicate whether there were more or less intense trade relations between countries. Further improvements will necessitate a look at top import partners. To give an example: Suriname is a top importer of Dutch products but does not export much to the Netherlands. For the Netherlands, exports to Suriname are too small to make it appear as a top export country. This is why both indicators should be included. Siegel (in Unger et al. 2006) did have top import and export partners as listed by the CIA World Factbook, but only as dummy variables.

In their report on money laundering in the Netherlands, Unger et al. (2006) observed that it was:

> A very unrealistic conclusion of the original Walker model was that only 20 percent of the money generated for laundering in the Netherlands would stay in the Netherlands. Doubts were raised as to why a country, which seems so attractive for other countries to whitewash their money, should not be attractive for its own criminals. The low percentage of the Walker model was due to the fact that he assumed laundering in the own country based on corruption in that country. We modified the model by using a country's attractiveness to itself and distance to itself with a minimum distance to ensure correct calculations (Unger et al. 2006).

According to these calculations, 44 percent of the money generated for laundering from the proceeds of crime in the Netherlands will stay in the Netherlands. This means that about US$4.7 billion or about €3.8 billion of criminal money generated in the Netherlands will also stay in the Netherlands. Furthermore, US$26 billion or about €20 billion will flow into the Netherlands from crime abroad.

Ferwerda (2006) tried to improve the distance deterrence indicator. He showed that with a more accurate distance indicator, the numbers become smaller. Altogether US$24.7 billion will flow to the Netherlands, of which US$4 billion are from own generated money for laundering and the rest from crime abroad. The percentage of money staying in the Netherlands is 37 percent. The percentages sent from each country to the Netherlands are smaller once one introduces the assumption that each country will have a larger share of domestic laundering. Ferwerda (2006) and Siegel (in Unger et al. 2006) did this by assuming that the distance of a country to itself is 0.1. This brings us to the next point, the robustness of the estimates.

Table 4.14   Inflows of money and domestic laundering in the Netherlands in million US$

Country	Walker (1999) total generated money for laundering per country amount	Siegel in Unger et al. 2006 percentage and amount of each country's money for laundering flowing to the Netherlands %	amount	Ferwerda 2006 percentage and amount of each country's money for laundering flowing to the Netherlands %	amount
Germany	128,266	1.6%	2,113	0.8%	1,027
Austria	20,231	0.9%	187	0.7%	149
Spain	56,287	1.1%	617	1.0%	542
UK	68,740	1.6%	1,127	0.8%	584
Romania	115,585	1.3%	1,461	1.3%	1,472
Italy	150,054	1.1%	1,580	0.9%	1,286
Poland	19,714	2.0%	399	1.2%	238
France	124,748	1.0%	1,267	0.8%	1,050
US	1,320,228	0.8%	11,099	0.7%	9,271
Mexico	21,119	1.1%	228	1.0%	205
Canada	82,374	0.8%	650	0.6%	503
Russia	147,187	1.5%	2,179	1.2%	1,788
China	131,360	1.0%	1,367	1.1%	1,447
Hong Kong	62,856	1.0%	630	0.5%	302
Thailand	32,834	0.9%	307	0.9%	292
Japan	21,240	0.8%	143	0.7%	139
Philippines	18,867	1.3%	242	0.9%	166
South Korea	21,240	0.9%	189	0.7%	156
Brazil	16,786	1.4%	229	1.0%	164
Flowing to NL			26,014		20,779
Netherlands	10,750	44.2%	4,750	37.0%	3,978
Total			**30,764**		**24,757**

Source: Unger et al. (2006) plus new calculations by Ferwerda (2006).

4.2.8. Robustness of Estimates

As shown in Unger et al. (2006), our findings for the Netherlands might underestimate money laundering from smaller countries, especially for Aruba, Suriname and the Netherlands Antilles, which have very close links to the Netherlands. In the case of Aruba and the Netherlands Antilles this might be even more problematic as these two are also substantial offshore centres. George Soros used Aruba-based entities to 'break' the Bank of England in 1992, forcing the UK to withdraw from the European Exchange Rate Mechanism. Sizeable amounts of money flow through Aruba and the Netherlands Antilles each day. Soros won about £1 billion with this operation (see Downes 2004).

In our study we suggested that the model could be calibrated by including indicators on special ties between countries that are not captured in the regular measurement indices. Since there is little variation in the data from the top 20 countries sending money to the Netherlands (they are not colonies, they do not speak the same language, they are mainly border countries) the volume of funds remitted from small states for laundering might be underestimated.

In order to test whether our results – in particular that the proportions of money for laundering flowing into each country – are robust, we re-estimated the model with different weights given to the variables of the attractiveness and distance indicator (see Unger et al. 2006). We found, that given the fragility of the topic, our results are fairly robust. The proportion attributed to the Netherlands can change by 10–15 percent. In other words, our results can be under- or overestimated by 10–15 percent (see Unger et al. 2006).

Ferwerda (2006) showed that the results of Unger et al. (2006) were indeed robust with regard to the attractiveness indicator. However, the results become much more sensitive once one modifies the distance deterrence index. He pointed out that the proportions sent from each country i to a country j (not the total amounts sent to country j) are very sensitive to assumptions about the distance of the country to itself. The Walker formula includes the distance of a country to all countries, and therefore, the distance of a country to itself also. If one sets this distance equal to 1, then distance does not matter in the formula anymore. One cannot set it to zero, which would be the most logical number, because mathematics does not allow the division of a fraction by zero, at least not if one wants to stay in the domain of real numbers. If one sets it to 0.1, close to zero, as Siegel (in Unger et al. 2006) did, the proportions become much larger than if one sets it to 0.4, the number that Helliwell (2000) suggested. The findings of Ferwerda (2006) suggest that the distance deterrence indicator must still be improved in order to make the model outcomes more robust.

Since Walker's calculations of which specific countries send what amount of money to the Netherlands were not available to us, we could not compare our findings with his. Walker identifies those countries that send and how much they send, but does not provide specific details for the Netherlands. In testing the applicability of our model, we require an alternative data-set which could give us some indication on whether or not the top countries following from our modified gravity model are in fact the most important states for the Netherlands. For this, we took reports of suspicious transactions at the Dutch FIU, the MOT. These do not necessarily lead to prosecution but they do give an indication of serious doubt and suspicion regarding the destiny and origin of transactions.

According to the MOT, in 2004 suspicious transactions totalled €3.2 billion. Of the executed suspicious transactions, 510 came from the Netherlands itself. This means these transactions were sent from one Dutch account to another Dutch account. We have indication that, on average, these were much larger amounts than those sent from abroad. Executed suspicious transactions account for about 90 percent of suspicious transactions. The other top countries of origin of executed suspicious transactions were the UK, the US, Italy, Germany, Spain, Austria and France. The last two, Portugal and Turkey, are countries which seem to be more important for sending money to the Netherlands than the gravity model would estimate, since Portugal and Turkey do not appear on our list of the top 20 countries of Netherlands bound remitting countries. For the rest, the findings of the gravity model largely correspond to the ranking of MOT suspicious transactions as shown in Figure 4.1.

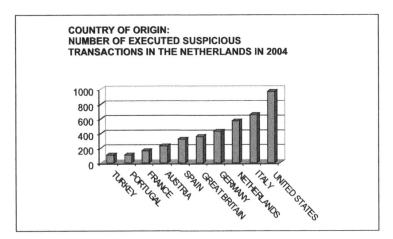

Source: data from Table 2.18 in Unger et al. (2006).

Figure 4.1   Netherlands: Number of executed suspicious transactions by country of origin

Figure 4.2 shows the top 10 countries of destination of executed suspicious transactions. The MOT lists the Netherlands Antilles, Columbia, Turkey, Surinam, the Dominican Republic, Nigeria, the Netherlands to itself, Spain, Brazil and Morocco as the top 10 countries.

From our findings it can be concluded that money laundering is sizeable. Money flows to the Netherlands from large countries. Funds are then remitted out of the Netherlands, destined for third states and the post-colonial world.

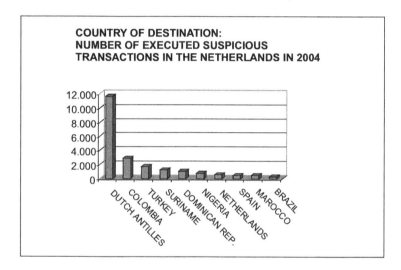

Source: data from Table 2.19 in Unger et al. (2006).

Figure 4.2   *Netherlands: Number of executed suspicious transactions by country of destination*

NOTES

1. This chapter uses the calculations of Dutch money laundering from Unger et al. (2006). The original calculations of Unger et al. (2006) were made by Melissa Siegel. Her attractiveness indicator calculations are used here. For this version, Joras Ferwerda has recalculated the model for the Netherlands and Australia by modifying the distance deterrence index. Furthermore, he made the correlation matrix calculations of the proxy variables.
2. This chapter takes the following exchange rate: A$1 = US$ 0.7348 and €1 = US$ 0.79, as in June 2006.
3. I changed the terminology of the categories of *very small*, *small*, and *considerable* from Walker (1995) where he assigned percentage values to these categories: very small=1 percent, small=10 percent, considerable=80 percent. I adjusted the terminology to the terminology he used in 2003, in order to compare the changes he made. Very small from Walker (1995) is transformed into low, small from Walker (1995) into medium and considerable from Walker

(1995) is transformed into the category high. It is very likely that I underestimate drug laundering when doing so.

4.   The original scores of Walker (1999[a]) were Luxembourg 686, United States 634, Switzerland 617, Cayman Islands 600, Austria 497, Netherlands 476 ,Liechtenstein 466, Vatican City 449, United Kingdom 439, Singapore 429, Hong Kong 397, Ireland 356, Bermuda 313, Bahamas, Andorra, Brunei, Norway, Iceland, Canada 250-299, Portugal, Denmark, Sweden, Monaco, Japan, Finland, Germany, New Zealand, Australia, Belgium 200-249 Bahrain, Qatar, Italy, Taiwan, United Arab Emirates, Barbados, Malta, France, Cyprus 150-199, Gibraltar, Azores (Portugal), Canary Islands, Greenland, Belarus, Spain, Israel 100-149, Czech Rep, Latvia, St Vincent, Malaysia, Estonia, Oman, Lithuania, N. Mariana Isls, Greece, South Korea, Seychelles, Azerbaijan, Anguilla, Aruba (Neth.), Kuwait, Hungary, Saudi Arabia, British Virgin Islands, Guam, Brazil, Panama, Russia, Costa Rica, Mauritius, Gabon, Armenia, Thailand, Macedonia, Grenada 50-99, Poland, Slovakia, Georgia, St. Kitts-Nevis, Dominica, St. Lucia, Belize, Guadeloupe, Martinique, Puerto Rico, U.S. Virgin Islands, Argentina, Croatia, Uruguay, Midway Islands, Barbuda, Slovenia, Suriname, Botswana, Romania, Chile, Bulgaria, French Polynesia, New Caledonia, Yugoslavia, Trinidad and Tobago, Libya, Turkey, Albania, Lebanon, Guatemala, Ecuador, Moldova, South Africa, French Guiana 25-49, Falkland Islands, Vanuatu, Venezuela, Ukraine, Cook Islands, Philippines, Turks and Caicos Islands, Fiji, Marshall Islands, Mexico, Nauru, Algeria, Antigua, Bolivia, Uzbekistan, Syria, Western Samoa, Morocco, Indonesia, Colombia, Cuba, Bosnia and Herzegovina, Tunisia, Jordan, Paraguay, Jamaica, San Marino, Mayotte, Palau Islands, Honduras, Niue, Reunion, Namibia, Somalia, Congo, Tonga, Iraq, Swaziland, Dominican Republic, Kazakhstan, Kyrgyzstan, Turkmenistan, El Salvador 10-24, Cameroon, Bhutan, North Korea, Ivory Coast, Fed States Micronesia, Kiribati, Tuvalu, Papua New Guinea, Zimbabwe, Western Sahara, Iran, Cape Verde, Senegal, Egypt, Peru, Sri Lanka, Djibouti, Mongolia, Solomon Islands, Zambia, Lesotho, Yemen, Comoros, Sao Tome, Maldives, Benin, Nicaragua, Pakistan, Guyana, Burkina, Nigeria, Equatorial Guinea, Mauritania, Gambia, Myanmar, Guinea, China, Ghana, Haiti, Vietnam, Madagascar, Kenya, Togo, Tajikistan, India, Central African Republic, Sudan, Tanzania, Mali, Laos, Niger, Malawi, Uganda, Guinea Bissau, Nepal, Angola, Bangladesh, Liberia, Zaire, Kampuchea, Rwanda, Mozambique, Ethiopia, Afghanistan, Burundi, Sierra Leone, Chad, Antarctica, Europa Island 0-9.

5. How Money is Being Laundered

With Madalina Busuioc

As mentioned in earlier chapters, money laundering can take place in different phases. In the first phase the criminal money that was collected, for example, through drug sales on the street is placed in a financial institution. This first phase, of bringing cash to some financial institution, is called the placement phase (or the pre-wash phase). After the dirty money is integrated into the financial system, the second phase, the layering or main wash, starts. The money gets transferred to the bank account of company X, is then sent via wire transfer to an offshore centre correspondent bank at, say, the Seychelles. The Seychelles bank gives company Y a loan, which pays for a false invoice from company X. Company X now has a legal receipt from company Y. So now the origin of this money, namely company X itself, is not traceable anymore. The more often the money gets transferred around the globe in the layering phase, the less traceable its criminal origins are. The third phase consists of integrating the now clean money. This after wash phase includes purchasing of luxury commodities, assets, making financial investments or buying companies (see Figure 5.1).

In the following discussion, a variety of techniques used during these three phases will be described. We describe the techniques and give empirical examples from different countries for them. Quite a lot of techniques are not easily attributed to one laundering phase alone. They might be used in different phases of laundering. If this is the case, it will be indicated in the description of the techniques.

5.1. LAUNDERING TECHNIQUES IN THE PLACEMENT PHASE

Smurfing and Structuring   As a first phase, Smurfing and Structuring (breaking up a large deposit into smaller deposits which helps avoid the currency transaction reporting requirements) takes place. Since many countries now have reporting requirements for unusual transactions, launderers will try to stay slightly below the benchmark for reporting. The Australian limit is A$10,000, the Dutch limit is €15,000.

Launderers who do not want to risk reporting will smurf, that means put amounts up to A\$9,990 or €14,990 on their accounts. By doing so, they stay slightly under the reporting mark. The problem of over-reporting by banks was addressed recently in the Netherlands and the US (see Takacs 2006). Dutchmen's cash withdrawals for buying a new car costing €15,000 or more would have to be reported as an unusual transaction. Lately, the regulatory trend is going in the direction of avoiding information dilution through too much reporting. According to this trend, banks should rely more on subjective, rather than objective criteria for suspicious characteristics or behaviour of their clients.

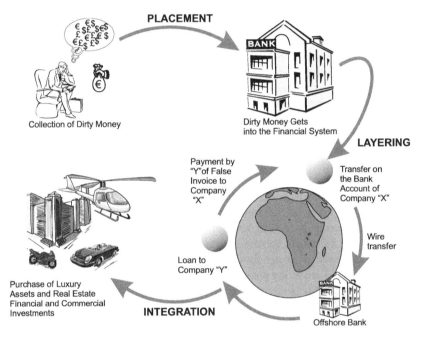

Source: Own graphic. For a similar graph see UNODC (2006), http://www.unodc.org/unodc/money_laundering_cycle.html.

Figure 5.1   The three phases of laundering

Currency smuggling   This method refers to the physical movement of bulk currency across borders in order to disguise its source and ownership. A launderer smuggles ill-gotten cash into a country with lax or nonexistent money laundering laws. He then places it in a bank there. Very often it is deposited in an offshore bank account and eventually wired back, say, to the United States at a later date. Smuggled cash has been found in bowling balls, coffins and scuba diving oxygen tanks of supposed tourists.

Smuggling cash out of a country to another country with minimal AML standards and then sending it back via official bank transfers is a popular method. For example, the latest FATF evaluation report on Australia identifies cash smuggling as one of the more common typologies (FATF Third Mutual Evaluation Report, Australia, October 2005). However, there are two drawbacks inherent to this money laundering method. First, cash is heavy and thus more difficult to transport inconspicuously and second, there is the danger of getting caught at the border.

The US government estimated that if two-thirds of illegal drug money (estimated to be 120 billion US dollars per year) were placed in US banks, traffickers would have to place currency weighing about 1,685,000 pounds in $20 bills. If a drug trafficker sells heroin for $1 million, he or she must transport 22 pounds of heroin, but then end up with 250 pounds of currency (if there is an equal mix of 5, 10 and 20 dollar bills) (see Cuéllar 2003, p. 13). This means that there is great incentive to place money into the financial system or to use the cover of an existing cash-intensive business.

Second, smuggled cash is at risk of confiscation. In 1998, Dutch customs caught 231 people who tried to smuggle cash over the border, totalling 34 million guilders, which amounts to €15 million. Often it was more than half a million guilders (Kleemans et al. 2002 p. 107–108). In a recent television report on money laundering, the Dutch journalist Dirk Kageman (Witwassen, in Zembla, Nederland 3 in September 2006) interviewed a courier who transports 250,000 Euros every week in his car from Amsterdam to Hungary. The bills fit exactly under his seat, he showed proudly. In comparison, the latest reports on drug confiscation show that the value of drugs confiscated at customs in the Netherlands is much higher than cash confiscation and amounted to about €1 billion (Unger et al. 2006, Figure 3.1).

Travellers' cheques   The purchase of travellers's cheques with 'dirty money' is quite a lucrative laundering technique. The FATF has reported cases of purchase of large quantities of cheques for cash in several of the FATF member states (FATF *Report on Money Laundering Typologies*, February, 2002). The 'advantage'of the method is due to the fact that the checks are easier to move across borders given to lack of reporting requirements. Moreover, given the fact that this type of cheques are issued by respectable companies, they are easily convertible into cash and will not easily give rise to suspicion (FATF *Report on Money Laundering Typologies*, February, 2002).

Gambling, casinos   Casinos can be used for the first and third phase of money laundering. A launderer can clean cash by converting it into chips at a casino, and then exchanging it back into cash to deposit at a bank and have a cheque from the casino showing a legitimate transaction. In the third phase of laundering, the launderer can buy a casino. Casinos are a highly cash intensive business. The launderer can own a casino and claim that the large amounts of cash held are profits from the casino. This requires taxes to be paid but gives launderers a legal cover for their illegal activities. One of us was recently in Suriname, a country suspected of being a trading port for cocaine from Columbia and ecstasy from the Netherlands, where casinos pop out like mushrooms. At the moment there are 27 casinos in its capital, Paramaribo, for a population of about 400,000 people (see Unger and Siegel 2006). This makes one casino per 15,000 inhabitants. In comparison, there are 13 casinos in Australia for approximately 20 million people and 12 casinos in the Netherlands for 16 million people, which brings it down to one casino per 1.3 million inhabitants.

In Australia, casinos are a lucrative enterprise which contributed A$5.9 billion to Australia's GDP in 2003 and brought A$8.6 in industry sales (FATF, *Third Mutual Evaluation Report*, 2005). The Australian casino industry has been identified as being susceptible to money laundering (Graham, p. 157, 2003). In the Netherlands, gambling is a sizeable enterprise with about 4500 employees, 12 casinos and a turnover of about €672 million in 2002. Six million visitors spend on average €111 per year (see Holland Casino, 2003). In the 1990s the Dutch Council of Casino gambling[1] wrote, in a report to parliament, that there were about 25–30 illegal casinos in the Netherlands who realized an estimated turnover of 50 percent from the legal turnover (Donker et al. (2001), van Dijck and R. Koning (2003) 't Veer, A. van (1998)). The amount of illegal casinos seems to have dropped drastically. By 2007 there should be none.

Recently there has been much media speculation that Holland Casino was a major money laundering institution. The casino in Amsterdam alone was said to whitewash several million euro per year. It was estimated that about 80 percent of the money gambled in casinos is criminal money. This was particularly juicy news, because Holland Casino is a quasi-public enterprise. It is a foundation with the Council of Commissioners[2] appointed by the Minister of Justice.

However, if one takes a closer look at how casinos operate, this does not seem realistic. Holland Casino falls under the Wet MOT and must, therefore, report suspicious transactions (above €10,000). This leads to the preference of customers to stay slightly underneath this limit (Paauw, 2005). In 2003, 1576 transactions were reported of which 509 were reported to the Ministry of Justice.

Large winnings are not paid out in cash but are transferred to a bank account. Holland Casino deposited €17.5 million directly to winner's bank accounts in 2003. From this, €7.5 million came from unregistered activities at gambling tables from 132 guests. This means that, on average, €27,000 are being deposited directly into clients' bank accounts (the other €10 million was from gambling machines and jackpots won by 149 guests). The tax authorities are informed, customers are registered at the entrance, a photograph is taken, and more than 150 cameras record activities in the gambling hall. Paauw (2005) estimates that not more than €1.5 million can be whitewashed by means of bank transfers through Holland Casino per year.

The estimates for money laundering through casinos range between €1.5 million and €480 million (80 percent of turnover). Most experts interviewed think that money laundering through Dutch casinos is negligible and highly exaggerated in the media. A new loophole for money laundering is gambling via the internet. Legal enforcement in this regard is still very difficult (see Kaspersen, 2005). Other countries' casinos might be more prone to laundering.

5.2. LAUNDERING TECHNIQUES IN THE LAYERING PHASE

Correspondent banking   Correspondent banking amounts to one bank (the 'correspondent bank') carrying out financial services for another bank (the 'respondent bank'). By establishing networks of a multitude of correspondent relationships at the international level, banks are able to undertake international financial transactions in jurisdictions where they do not have offices. For example, there is no Dutch bank in its former colony, Suriname, since 2003. In order to send money from the Netherlands to Suriname, a Dutch bank works with one or more of the Surinamese banks. The respondent bank of the Dutch Rabobank is, for example, the Surinamese Landbouwbank. Both banks specialize in agricultural business. ABN AMRO, who were active in Suriname until 2003, have several respondent banks. One is RBTT, the Royal Bank of Togo and Trinidad, which took over ABN AMRO in Suriname in 2004 (see Unger and Siegel 2006). The respondent bank can also be at some offshore centre, such as Cayman Islands or Seychelles, which are historically known for lax anti-money laundering regulations.

Correspondent banks can carry out a variety of services for the respondent bank ranging from cash management to payable – through accounts, international transfer of funds, exchange services etc. (FATF, *Report on Money Laundering Typologies*, February, 2002). Evidently, these relationships are vulnerable to misuse for money laundering. The reason for this is the indirect character of this type of banking where the correspondent bank will carry out services for clients of another bank, the integrity of which it has not had verified beforehand by the correspondent bank. Thus, it is forced to rely on the respondent bank to perform all the necessary monitoring and checking procedures. This can pose serious problems with regards to 'know your customer' policies and the reporting of suspicious transactions. Additionally, this is problematic since in some jurisdictions these procedures will be more lax than in others and as a consequence, correspondent banking can be a gateway for illegal funds into the regular banking system. Thus, 'shell banks, certain offshore financial institutions and banks from non-cooperative countries and territories (NCCTs) are of particular risk to legitimate correspondent banking relationships' (FATF, *Report on Money Laundering Typologies*, February, 2002). For example, Al Qaeda used the correspondent network of a Sudanese bank for cross border dealings. These cross border dealings included France's Credit Lyonnais, Germany's Kommerzbank and the Saudi Bank in Jeddah in which ABN AMRO of the Netherlands has a 40 percent stake (Nawaz et al. 2002, *Journal of Money Laundering Control*). Once ill-gotten funds have leaked into the regular system, they are nearly impossible to detect.

Bank cheques and bank drafts   According to FATF, the use of bank cheques and one of its more specific form, bank drafts, which allows for funds to be transferred between persons or jurisdictions, is usually not reportable and there are no identification requirements unless the transferred amount is in cash and it surpasses a certain threshold (e.g. €10,000 or €15,000). The use of this instruments as a technique for money laundering has been frequently identified in cases of money laundering (FATF *Report on Money Laundering Typologies*, February, 2001–2002).

Collective accounts   Dishonest professionals can use *collective accounts* as a way to launder money. Because the professional will have a reputable standing with the financial institution, they can pay in large amounts of cash and pay it out to a variety of different people. These people will, of course, be associates of the launderer. This method is a more advanced form of smurfing.

Payable-through accounts   This process requires the launderer to have a bank account with a foreign bank that has a payable-through account system with a bank in a different country, such as the US. These accounts give the launderer the ability to conduct business in the second country as if they had a bank account in that country, without having to submit to those countries' banking regulations. For example, a launderer from Colombia can bank in the US if the Colombian bank has a payable-through account with a US institution without having to notify the US financial authorities, which may require a greater degree of evidence of the origin of funds. These types of accounts are set up in the context of correspondent banking relationships.

Loan at low or no interest rates   A very easy method is to give interest-free loans. This allows the launderer to transfer large amounts of cash to other people and so avoid having to deposit the money into a bank or other institution. These loans will be paid back slowly, which avoids deposits hitting the reporting threshold. The receiver of the loan is likely to be aware of the dubious nature of the money, but will be put off from reporting it due to the benefits he receives from the preferential loan rates.

Sometimes these loans are given for special purposes. For example, in Suriname one can buy second hand cars without any savings and pay the lease rent back every month. In this case, the loan is given in the form of a car, which the money launderer pays for in cash with US dollars. The car market in Suriname is entirely in US currency and cash. He then slowly gets clean money back from the lease.

Back-to-back loans   Back-to-back loans are a construction used for currency hedging. They involve an arrangement in which two companies in different countries borrow each other's currency for a given period of time, in order to reduce foreign exchange risk for both of them (http://www.investorwords.com/1240/currency.html). For example, a US company loans US$1000 to a British company in the US which in turn loans the equivalent amount in Pounds Sterling at the spot market exchange rate to the US company in the UK. This saves both from going to the foreign exchange market and running an exchange risk.

This hedging construction can also be used for laundering purposes. In the Netherlands, it is sometimes used when launderers want to buy real estate, which needs a Dutch bank guarantee. For example, a person takes cash to Paraguay and deposits it in a bank account there. This money is then transferred to Switzerland. The person then purchases real estate in the Netherlands using the bank deposit in Switzerland as a guarantee.

Money Exchange Offices   Money exchange offices are a legal way of exchanging money into the currency of choice. But they can also be used for money laundering. In the first phase of laundering, this usually requires a corrupt exchange bureau as the levels of cash would raise suspicion. In the third phase of laundering, the launderer can operate an exchange bureau and thus incorporate the illegal cash as profits. Whilst the launderer would pay tax on these 'profits', it gives the launderer a simple explanation on the high levels of cash held. The paid taxes also give an added layer of legitimacy to the funds.

Money exchange offices[3] have been highly suspect of money laundering in the Netherlands. They perform not only money exchange but also coupon cashing. Security coupons issued abroad (effectively, this includes bonds, shares and money certificates), mostly issued in Belgium and Luxembourg, are exchanged at the Dutch border. The money exchange offices cash these coupons. Later, the coupons are in turn cashed back in Luxembourg and Belgium. The total money flow here is €350 million. The EU's savings tax directive (ESD) should reduce this problem in the future. However, the ESD preserves bank secrecy arrangements for Luxembourg and Austria in the EU and Switzerland is outside this jurisdiction.

Money exchange offices can also be abused regarding unauthorized money transfers. Most of the Surinamese Cambios, for example, are only authorized to do money exchange but not international money transfers. However, many of them do (see Unger and Siegel 2006). The drug dealer gives money to the Dutch underground banker in cash. The underground banker calls the Cambio in Suriname, who pays out the money in cash in Suriname. Since the drug business is running both ways quite well (cocaine versus ecstasy pills), clearing is not needed too often.

Money transfer offices   Money transfers via money transfer offices such as Western Union[4] and MoneyGram[5] seem to be important for money laundering, but small in size. The total amount of money transferred by the existing 30 Dutch money transfer offices is €325 million per year. According to Kleemans (2002), these relatively expensive money transfers are mainly used for smuggling illegal immigrants and women. Though they are often expensive, they are fast. The same international money transfer agents are controlled to a different extent in different countries. In the Netherlands, for example, money transfer agents have to be licensed and are supervised by the Dutch National Bank. In Suriname, the same money transfer agents do not need a license and are not supervised (see Unger and Siegel 2006). It is, therefore, very likely that these agents also behave differently in different countries.

Insurance market   One way for the launderer to use the insurance market is to arrange insurance policies on assets, either real or phantom, through a dishonest or ignorant broker. Regular claims on this insurance can then be made to return the cash to the launderer. To reduce the risk of detection, the launderer can ensure that the claims made are below the premiums paid so that the insurer makes a profit.

False contracts and documents   This is a way the launderer can avoid paying taxes on the money that has been incorporated as business income. The company enters into contracts with other entities, usually companies owned by the launderer, as a way of reducing the taxable income of that company. The second company will either operate below the taxable threshold or in a lower tax bracket so as to reduce the tax liability. In addition, these contracts may be with fictitious entities so that no tax is paid by anyone.

Fictitious sales and purchases   This method entails the use of false sales and purchase orders. These can be with legitimate organizations that will have no knowledge that these purchase orders exist. Fictitious sales documents are created to explain the extra income showing in the accounts, which has come from illegal activities.

Shell companies   Shell companies are 'businesses without substance or commercial purpose and incorporated to conceal the true beneficial ownership of business accounts and assets owned' (FATF *Report on Money Laundering Typologies*, 2002–2003). A number of shell companies are set up in countries known for strong bank secrecy laws or for lax enforcement of money laundering statutes. They can also be in the form of Special Purpose Entities (SPE's) or International Business Companies (IBC's). The dirty money is then circulated within these shell companies via two methods. The first is the loan-back system and the other is the double invoicing system. In the case of the loan-back method, the criminal sets up an offshore company and deposits the ill-gotten gains with the respective company, which subsequently returns the funds to the offender. Given that the ownership of offshore companies is very difficult to establish, it will appear as if a company is lending money to the criminal while in fact he is lending it to himself. The double invoicing system amounts to keeping two sets of books or false invoicing. Funds can be moved across borders through overcharging or undercharging imports and exports.

Trust offices[6]   Trust offices in the Netherlands provide services in the field of tax and law for foreign companies. The foreign companies do not run businesses in the Netherlands, they are only placed in the Netherlands because of tax advantages on royalties or worldwide dividends. This is completely legal. They use a trust office in the Netherlands to manage their corporation. These trust offices have been in the news recently because of some international administration scandals at several multinationals (Gorkum and Carpentier 2004). Since 2003, there has been legislation to cover the supervision of trust offices.[7] This supervision is now in the first phase, with the DNB responsible for licensing trust offices. Actual research has not yet started; this is probably the reason that no unusual business has yet been found. There were cases of trust office closures, while some of them did not seek a licence. They might have disappeared underground. More might be found once the DNB starts actual research on the licences. The total amount of money flowing through trust offices is about €8 billion per year.

The amount of trust companies was reduced drastically after they came under the supervision of the Dutch National Bank in 2003. The number of licensed trust companies in 2006 was 119, whereas there were about three times as many before the law came into force (see Statistical Bulletin DNB div. months and years).

The role of special purpose entities (vehicles)[8]   Special Purpose Entities (SPEs), also known as Special Purpose Vehicles, (SPVs) are companies settled in a country, say the Netherlands where non-Dutch resident participants are able to earn foreign income in the Netherlands and then to redistribute it to third countries and entities incorporated in third countries. From the Statistical Bulletin of the DNB (June 2003), one can see that in 2001–2002 there were, on average, €4000 billion per year flowing through these corporations. Multinational companies frequently use BFI's for internal funds transfers between subsidiary companies. For example: Esso collects the receipts from all over the world in the Netherlands and then redistributes these to its branches or to financial institutions abroad. The reason why companies such as Esso are based in the Netherlands is very often to reduce global tax exposure. In 2002, there were 12,500 registered BFI's. Eighty percent of them were represented by trust offices. But these 80 percent only account for one quarter of all BFI transactions. The very large companies are not represented through trust companies including large oil conglomerates, banks, telecommunication and automobile companies. Data released from the US Commerce Department in 2001 showed that US$107.8 billion in profits from US multinationals has been shifted to SPE/BFI subsidiaries located in 11 top offshore destinations (Sullivan, 2004, p. 590). Of these, the Netherlands held the most with US$24.6 billion in company profits, followed by Ireland holding US$19.3 billion. In his analysis of these trends Martin Sullivan (2004, p. 589) stated that:

> Recently released data from the Commerce Department indicate that the IRS cannot prevent U.S. companies from artificially shifting profits to tax haven countries like the Netherlands, Ireland, Bermuda, and Luxembourg. In 2001 subsidiaries domiciled in those four countries were assigned 30 percent of all foreign profits of US corporations, despite accounting for only 5 percent of the productive capacity and three percent of the employment of foreign subsidiaries of US corporations.

Because the amount that BFIs transfer is so huge, they are not included in the balance of payments calculations. From the geographical distribution one can see that in 2002 most transactions went to the UK (see Figure 5.2).

From the bilateral balance of payment for BFI's (De Nederlandsche Bank 2003, p. 23) one can see that Germany, the UK and the US are the countries where the BFIs have most of their credits; most debits are held in the UK and in many important offshore fiscal centres such as the Netherlands Antilles and the Cayman Islands.

The volume of these transactions is so huge that if only half a percent of the turnover was used for illegal activities such as money laundering, the amount of criminal money flowing into the Netherlands that we have estimated (€18–25 billion) could flow through these entities. Some of the experts expressed that they would not be surprised if 1 percent of BFI transactions are used for money laundering. However, a more in-depth study is necessary in order to gather more evidence. BFIs can be useful and can be abused for criminal purposes.

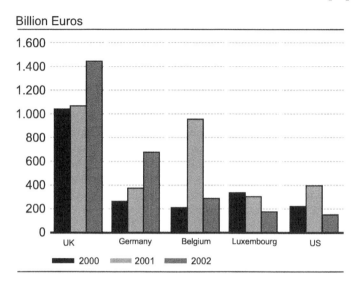

Billion Euros

Source: De Nederlandsche Bank (2003), p. 22.

Figure 5.2   Geographical distribution of gross BFI (SPE) transactions

Underground banking   In a broad definition, underground banking can be considered as any financial operation outside the conventional or regulated banking and financial sector. Due to their combination of informality, confidentiality, informal control, minimum request of information from customers, which can sometimes be, for example, illegal immigrants or legal immigrants with an unclear working status, these informal, naïve channels are extremely attractive and open to abuse. Thus, the said channels might satisfy the demand for illegal financial services and, more specifically, serve the purpose of money laundering and terrorism financing (Masciandaro, 2004[a]; see also Nawaz et al. 2002).

Due to its multicultural background, underground banking is popular in the Netherlands. In particular, the Surinamese community as well as those from Southeast Asia, South Asia and the Middle East use underground banking in order to send money back to their families. The name hawala, used for parts of underground banking, means 'transfer' in Arab. Ethnic groups often use currency exchange offices in food, telephone, and video shops as well as in other small business, which deliver local currencies to their relatives. While these systems have been traditionally used by transnational ethnic networks, due to globalization and the increased use of intermediaries these informal systems are being increasingly used by those not normally associated with a particular ethnic group. Traditionally, these systems have been used for the legal purposes of sending money to relatives in other countries. Because these systems are unregulated and unchecked, they have become increasingly attractive to those who would like to be undetected when moving money such as drug traffickers, tax evaders, money launderers and terrorist financiers. Traditionally it was thought that these informal channels could not sustain the flow of large sums of money, but there is evidence which suggests that these informal systems can indeed sustain large amounts of money (Passas, 2004). According to the DNB in 2003, €188 million left the Netherlands through formal channels each year. The Police have indications that informal channels are responsible for at least this much or a multiple of this amount. Dutch experts estimate that between 50 and 500 underground bankers are active in the Netherlands. When performing studies in Suriname, we could even identify a Dutch Hindustani underground banker ourselves (see Unger and Siegel 2006). It is important to realize that part of the money transferred through informal channels are legitimate proceeds but unknown proportions also constitute illicit funds.

Black market of foreign currency   The launderer uses the foreign currency black market both to remove the risk of transporting large amounts of currency and to avoid depositing large amounts of foreign currency in domestic banks – for instance a Mexican drug trafficker having large quantities of US dollars to deposit in a Mexican bank. These foreign exchange traders are used; they themselves are conducting an illegal enterprise and have no wish to attract attention to themselves by reporting the activities of the money launderer. Furthermore, the exchange traders charge high fees for their services. This costs the launderers money but removes some risk of having large amounts of cash on them.

5.3. THE INTEGRATION PHASE

In the third phase, money launderers want to park the laundered money safely without being detected and with profit.

Capital market investments   Capital market investments can happen in all phases of laundering. In the first phase, the launderer uses his ill-gotten cash for buying. The launderer can invest the money into financial assets so as to avoid having large amounts of cash. But he can also use capital market investments in the layering phase or for placing the money in its final spot. These assets, such as shares and bonds, are generally low risk and so the chances of losing money are small. Furthermore, the assets are highly liquid, which means they can be converted back into cash very easily. Laundered funds are co-mingled with lawful transactions.

Derivatives   These are financial assets and can be purchased by the launderer in order to invest the cash in reputable enterprises. Again, a disreputable broker is probably needed. These assets are highly liquid and so can easily be resold in order to return the cash back to the launderer. However, derivatives are much more risky than traditional financial instruments.

Real estate acquisition   The launderer can invest the illegal cash into property, which is generally a non-depreciating asset. This would normally require a real estate agent who is willing to overlook the fact that the launderer wants to pay cash for an expensive asset. This asset can then be sold fairly easily to show a legitimate source of cash. The importance of this market for Dutch money laundering will be shown in chapter 6, on sectoral effects of money laundering.

The catering industry   The catering industry is often used by launderers as it is a highly cash intensive business just like casinos, for example. The owner of a catering company can pay its employees in cash, who themselves often work illegally, and will often receive its payments in cash, which will serve as a justification for the large cash deposits. Usually, the company would have to use various fraudulent accounting practices in order to succeed in such an operation. The cash that is to be laundered is incorporated as profits. Similar exploitation of apparently legal cash intensive businesses can also be found with reference to hotels, cinemas and restaurants.

The gold market   According to the FATF, gold offers the advantage of having a so called 'high intrinsic value in a relatively compact form' and consequently, represents one of the simplest and most effective typologies. Gold can be easily purchased and bought in most jurisdictions regardless of whether it is in a rough or finished form (i.e. piece of jewellery). The advantages that gold provides:

> are highly attractive to the money launderer, that is, the high intrinsic value, conver-
> tibility, and potential anonymity in transfers. It is used, according to the FATF
> experts, both as a source of illegal funds to be laundered (through smuggling or illegal
> trade in gold) and as an actual vehicle for laundering (through the outright purchase
> of gold with illegal funds. In cases where the gold itself is the source of the illegal
> funds, some of the other typologies presented in this chapter (e.g. false invoicing) will
> be employed to make it appear that it was obtained from a legal source (FATF *Report
> on Money Laundering Typologies*, 2002–2003).

In situations where the gold is the actual vehicle for laundering it is usually related to the laundering of funds from crimes such as narcotics trafficking, organized crime activities and illegal trade in goods and merchandise (FATF *Report on Money Laundering Typologies*, 2002-2003).

The diamond market   Hiding the illicit nature of funds is easier in this case as the identity of the person making the transaction may not be publicly revealed. Furthermore, diamonds and other precious gems offer some of the same advantages as those provided by gold such as the so-called 'high intrinsic value in a compact form'. Diamonds in particular can easily be concealed and transported and will be traded with little difficulty worldwide.

> The ease with which diamonds can be hidden and transported and the very high value per gram for some stones make diamonds particularly vulnerable to illegal diversion from the legitimate channels for the exploitation and profit of criminals (FATF *Report on Money Laundering Typologies*, 2002–2003).

Buying jewels   Substantial revenues from wholesale and retail jewels sales laundered US$1.2 billion for Colombian drug kingpins in 18 months in Los Angeles in the operation La Mina, the gold mine (see Cuéllar 2003, p. 14). In the Netherlands, diamonds might be an easy way to get lightweight valuables. However, as the spending behaviour of criminals caught in the next section will show, criminals in the Netherlands do not spend their money very differently from ordinary Dutch people. But the big Columbian drug kings investing in diamonds do not get caught.

Purchase of consumer goods for export   The launderer will invest in consumer goods (such as television sets, kitchen appliances and so on) because such purchases can be easily transported across borders without arousing suspicion. These goods can then be sold abroad and produce what appear to be legitimate commercial revenues.

Acquisition of luxury goods   The launderer follows a similar logic as in the case of the purchase of consumer goods. These goods can either be kept for personal use or sold for export. One of the qualities of these products, which renders them extremely attractive, is the fact that large amounts of cash can be transformed into a less conspicuous form. Moreover, it is not unusual for purchasers of luxury goods to pay with cash and questions are unlikely to be asked as the shop is unwilling to upset the purchasers with personal questions.

Cash-intensive business   This laundering method is common in situations where the launderer uses a legitimate, cash-intensive business as a cover for laundering (such as an exchange business or a restaurant to help justify large currency deposits). It is the oldest form of laundering. The Chicago gangster Al Capone used launderettes for hiding illicit proceeds from alcohol during the American prohibition in the 1930s (see van Duyne et al. 2003 p. 73). The owner commingles the dirty money with the business's actual revenues, depositing them together into a single bank account. The deposit will not raise suspicions given the cash-intensive nature of the business and the fact that the launderer will over-report the actual revenues, thus being able to justify the dirty proceeds. The mingling of profits of crime with legitimately earned profits has been identified by Australian enforcement authorities for example, as one of the present money laundering vehicles (FATF, *Third Mutual Evaluation Report*, Australia, 2005; also Graham et al., 157, 2003).

Using currency to supplement an apparently legitimate transaction   The launderer could pay for a product worth €500,000 with a wire transfer of €300,000 and €200,000 in currency. The currency could be given to the seller under the table, who might be someone operating a currency-intensive business such as a restaurant.

Export Import Business   The Export and Import business can be used for the falsification of foreign trade prices. This is essentially a form of false invoicing and can be achieved either by overpricing imports or underpricing exports. In the first case, an importer who buys an item for an amount of US$1 million could request that the price be increased by 10 percent so that upon payment of US$1.1 million the extra U$100,000 be placed into his private bank account in the exporter's country. In the second situation (i.e. underpricing exports), an exporter will essentially sell an item to a foreign dealer for, say, 25 percent less than their negotiated value with the understanding that when the payment is made the extra 25 percent be deposited into her foreign bank account in the dealer's country. Provided the willingness of the other party, this can be an easy means to move funds across borders and to detach it from the original crime.

Acquisition and Smuggling of Arms   The acquisition of arms with ill-gotten proceeds is particularly common amongst terrorist circles (see Unger et al. 2006). Moreover, arms smuggling is also a source of illegal proceeds in itself, which are subsequently subject to laundering. Together with the proceeds of drug trafficking, organized crime, the funds derived from arms smuggling have been identified as one of the main sources of illegal proceeds for laundering especially in parts of Southern and Eastern Africa (FATF, *Report on Money Laundering Typologies*, 1996–1997).

5.4. NEW MONEY LAUNDERING RISKS

With the advent of the internet, new forms of money transfers and possibilities for launderers have occurred.

On-line banking   On-line banking makes it easier for the launderer to conduct transactions as they can avoid having to go to banks and being seen or having to complete many forms. Furthermore, it is much more difficult to trace the operators of these accounts if they never go to banks.

E-cash   E-cash, or electronic cash, is even harder to trace than real cash as the ease with which it can flow around the world makes it twice as hard for the authorities to detect. Money becomes not a real commodity, but simply a line on a piece of paper or a computer screen. The launderer then does not have to worry about depositing large amounts of cash, as the money does not physically exist. All payments and receipts are made electronically.

E-gold   One can buy gold on the internet, using addresses such as http://www. e-gold.com/examiner.html or http://goldmoney.com/. These sales and buys still need some identification, one has to register, but when used after having cleaned the money they still guarantee some anonymity.

Pre-paid phone cards   Pre-paid phone cards can be bought on the streets. One can pay with criminal cash for them and use the prepaid phone cards for shopping anonymously on the internet. The possibilities and variety of products for sale increases steadily. The Dutch Banking Association calculated that payments over the Internet valued €2 billion (5–7 million transactions) in 2004. Payments via mobile phones amounted to about €1 billion in the Netherlands (Netherlands Bankers' Association 2006).

Proprietary systems   Proprietary systems refer to a specific set of payment and funds transfer rights owned and patented, with intellectual property protections, to a financial services provider located anywhere in the world. Proprietary systems enable customers to access electronic banking or funds transfer routing systems located offshore and hence avoid local reporting requirements such as those specified in the FTR Act. This does not mean that customers are engaging in money laundering, but it does mean that customers can make undetectable financial transactions that may increase the risk of money laundering. These proprietary systems may include international funds transfers between offshore accounts/entities, cheque writing, trading facilities, letters of credit and securities trading. They also involve alternative payment systems with the conversion of funds into a virtual currency with e-credits, Pay PAL and e-gold. Funds can then be disbursed offshore without triggering the reporting requirements of the FTR Act (Hackett 2003, p. 3).

The FTR Act does not readily capture activities and transactions that proprietary systems can facilitate. Users of proprietary systems can directly access the financial service provider's global routing payment instructions for settlement. Under section 17B of the FTR Act it is uncertain whether or not customers and financial service providers (who may not come under the definition of cash dealers if located offshore) are under any reporting obligations. Any attempt to calculate volumes of money laundering nationally and/or globally should consider the risks posed by these new proprietary systems to enter into transactions that are largely invisible.

The use of electronic offshore access and payment methods is related to the growth of proprietary systems that potentially escape reporting requirements and detection strategies. This involves accessing overseas accounts, trusts and companies. Money is permanently kept offshore and shifted between offshore jurisdictions that have a high degree of bank secrecy. These overseas accounts are then accessed at ATMs using offshore debit/credit cards, which can also be used to make local purchases. Entities such as trusts, banks and International Business Corporations, also established offshore, then repay the credit cards and continue to deposit funds into them on a regular basis.

In 2002, the United States Internal Revenue Service (IRS) found that Master-Card alone processed 1.7 million offshore transactions for 230,000 US resident account holders with offshore debit/credit cards issued in 30 countries with strict bank secrecy laws and minimal FTR requirements (US Department of Justice 25 March 2002). In Australia, the current FTR Act will only direct AUSTRAC to collect information on credit card transactions if suspicious activities are reported by a local cash dealer or if there is a withdrawal in excess of A$10,000. Even if withdrawals exceeding A$10,000 are made and reported on an overseas card, the bank may not be able to record accurate identifying features if the card is from a bank located in an offshore jurisdiction with strict secrecy legislation and minimum FTR reporting requirements. In a submission to a parliamentary inquiry into cyber crime, AUSTRAC suggested that:

> Such an arrangement may allow the person to make use of funds, which, because they have not been directly transferred into Australia, will not be reported to AUSTRAC, and thus are invisible to AUSTRAC's partner agencies (Hackett 2003, p. 4).

There is a potential to transfer funds offshore or between different accounts using internal bank payment settlement systems and protocols in a way that will avoid detection and reporting requirements. For example, Bank A in a country with strong FTR requirements maintains Bank B as a subsidiary in an offshore jurisdiction that has bank secrecy provisions and minimal FTR requirements. A customer can open an account in Bank B either in person, by fax or with Bank

A operating as an intermediary. Bank A then allows the customer to deposit money directly into Bank B at a local branch. There is no need to make a telegraphic transfer or receive an IFTI. Bank A settles the payment with Bank B by a ledger transfer. It is unclear as to whether or not this is reportable under FTR legislation. Even if it is reportable, once funds are transferred into Bank B they become legally domiciled in a country that protects information about the use of funds by bank secrecy and weak FTR requirements. The FIU cannot gain access to information about this account even though the funds are still part of the same overall banking network. Money could be conceivably laundered using this method.

Similar concealment methods can be used with internal bank management accounts with large transactions taking place without arousing suspicion and thus escaping detection. In *The Commonwealth of Australia versus Nachum Goldberg*, a fraud case involving the laundering of A\$39,894,808,[9] the court considered the following evidence in its decision:

> 20. One of a number of remarkable features about this account and the manner in which it was operated, is that it was an internal bank management account. Moneys passing through it were relatively unlikely to attract the attention of regulatory authorities which would have little reason to suspect that they were other than normal inter-bank or intra-bank commercial transactions. Importantly from the respondent's perspective, the name of the actual holder would not be recorded on the AUSTRAC database. How he came to secure such an arrangement is unknown to the Court, but it is highly unlikely to have been unintended and is suggestive of the possession of detailed knowledge of the bank procedures, a level of co-operation from within the bank itself, and an understanding of the AUSTRAC operation and processes' (The Commonwealth of Australia versus Nachum Goldberg).

New proprietary systems, electronic access and payment methods and interbank settlement protocols are all ways in which transactions can be concealed. The extent of their use for money laundering is unclear. However, it might be appropriate to consider these new technologies when determining which variables and values to use in the measurement of money laundering. They also point to areas where FTR legislation could be amended enabling them to extend their regulatory capacities and monitor transactions that use electronic commerce and new payment technologies. In Australia, as with most other OECD economies, the FTR Act and FIU information gathering reflects the banking practices of the 1980s (Hackett, 2003). It needs to be considered whether or not money laundering is now taking advantage of the banking practices and technological advancements of the twenty-first century.

5.5. CHASING DIRTY MONEY AND CHANGES IN BEHAVIOUR

Both authorities and the money launderer seem to permanently change their behaviour when trying to hunt and escape money laundering.

One can notice changed techniques of money laundering as a reaction to regulation. Money launderers do react to changes in laws and regulations. Since unusual transactions have to be reported, offenders change money abroad, Dutch experts noted (see Unger et al. 2006, chapter 3). Also, underground banking became more popular. This reaction pattern of criminals to regulations also corresponds to findings of Boyerie et al. (2005[a]) for Switzerland, who noticed increased capital flight in the data after Switzerland had engaged in fiercer regulation (see chapter 2).

Due especially to the paradigm change in the perception and definition of money laundering, new hunting techniques have also developed. In the Netherlands, in Australia and in many other countries, privacy is a highly respected issue. Bank accounts are usually only accessible to the authorities when there is a public prosecution. When there is suspicion of terrorism, however, the police can seek access to information for an individual case. Normally this is not allowed, but if it regards terrorism it is authorized by a court order.[10] In this case, the Dutch National Bank shows the police all transfers relating to this person. This was done after September 11, when the DNB got a long list of suspected persons from the Ministry of Justice and scrutinized their transactions. In this regard, national security comes before privacy protection. The paradigm change by making terrorism part of money laundering (see chapter 2) might have far reaching consequences for chasing launderers.

An article was published in the Dutch newspaper Het Financieele Dagblad on 11 April 2005, in which President Bush stated that he wanted a precise tracing of money in order to fight terrorism. In Het Financieele Dagblad of the 28th of June 2006, one could see that the Belgian SWIFT company had to give access to its entire database which constituted all money transfers to the Americans. The US pressure regarding prosecution, following and tracing the money is strong when it comes to some European countries. In the Netherlands, there are special questions on MOT reporting forms. There is also a list of suspicious people available and transactions made by these listed individuals must be reported.

While the Australians can, in principle, follow and trace the money the way Bush would like it, the Dutch cannot at the moment. Today it is not possible for the Dutch National Bank to follow the money the Australian way by, in principle, being able to trace each transaction, where it comes from and where it goes. Previously it would have been, in principle, possible in the Netherlands also to trace every transaction, where it comes from, where it goes, from whom the transaction was made and to whom. But because of the present registration system this is now no longer possible. The number of reporting units went down from 40,000 to 2,000 in 2003 because of reforms aimed at changing the Dutch balance of payment statistics into a survey system and reducing reporting costs (see DNB *Statistical Bulletin* March 2003). There is no reporting requirements for banks anymore regarding their cash position or their incoming and outflowing transfers. The only reporting requirement is for suspicious transactions (see Unger and Siegel 2006).

Finally, one also has to ask the question what the limits of chasing dirty money should be. In principle, it is possible to trace every movement of every citizen, especially with new technologies, then we would be in Orwell's 1984 world.

NOTES

1. In Dutch: Raad voor de casinospelen, later transformed into raad voor kansspelen.
2. In Dutch: Raad van Commissarissen.
3. See article about money exchange offices by Dirk van der Wal in DNB Report 2005.
4. In the Netherlands there are three banks connected with Western Union: Postbank, Cash Express and Goffin Bank (Kleemans, 2002, p. 110).
5. In the Netherlands there are three banks connected with MoneyGram: Grens Wissel Kantoor (GWK), Thomas Cook and American Express (Kleemans, 2002, p. 110).
6. In Dutch: trustkantoren which function differently from US trust companies.
7. In Dutch: Wet op Toezicht Trustkantoren (Wtt), since 17 December 2003.
8. In Dutch: bijzondere financiële instellingen (BFI's).
9. A$39,894,808 = €23,542,173.
10. In Dutch: gerechtelijk bevel.

6. Short Term Effects of Money Laundering[1]

In Unger et al. (2006) we did a systematic literature research on 'money launder-ing' and on the Dutch word for it, 'witwassen', in order to find out which effects of money laundering have been identified so far. We searched the publications from the international organizations IMF, OECD and FATF. In addition, we browsed through Econlit, an economic search database that includes about 750 journals and over 44,000 working papers. The Econlit search produced 56 hits. We also searched the Dutch Central Catalogue, NCC. This database includes, in total, around 14 million books and 500,000 magazines. This search turned up another 55 hits. Furthermore, we browsed through the *Journal of Money Laun-dering Control* and the *Journal of Financial Crime*. The period covered by our searches was 1990–2004. For more details on these searches see Unger et al. (2006, chapter 4).

Altogether, we found 25 different effects of money laundering mentioned in literature. Most of these studies are merely speculations about what might happen. Some of the publications refer to estimates without ever mentioning the source. One good example of this is the work of Bartlett (2002). He lists all sorts of effects of money laundering, using sentences such as 'it is clear from avail-able evidence' that money laundering has such and such effects, without ever giving a hint of where this evidence should be found. Furthermore, as is the case with the papers on the amounts of money laundering, one source refers to the other – without much of a solid empirical back up. Only five articles within our search tried to empirically measure, in a serious manner, some of the effects of money laundering. These are the works of the IMF by Tanzi (1997) and by Quirk (1996 and 1997), who measured the effects of money laundering on the demand for money and on growth, as well as the works of AUSTRAC, by Walker (1995), who calculated macroeconomic effects on output and employ-ment by means of multipliers; and the work of Masciandaro (1999) who devel-oped a model for measuring the effect of money laundering on crime.

The following table gives an overview of the literature on the potential effects of money laundering and the underlying crime. Among the 25 different effects of money laundering, we identified one direct effect of crime, which is the loss to the victims and gain to the perpetrators of crime. The rest are indirect effects of crime and money laundering. These effects can be of economic, social or political nature. Money laundering can affect the real sector, that is, the production and consumption sphere, business activities, relative prices, saving, output, employment and growth. It can also affect the financial sector – its liquidity, reputation, integrity and stability. Or it can affect the public sector through unpaid taxes and a threat to privatisation efforts. The monetary sector can be affected by means of higher capital inflows or volatile interest rates and exchange rates.

There are also social effects such as increased crime, corruption, bribing, and contamination of legal activities through illegal activities. The political effects are the undermining of political institutions. One effect, terrorism, is dealt with in more depth, since there is an ambiguous relationship between money laundering and terrorist financing.

The 25 effects of money laundering that are summarized in the table below do not all occur immediately or in the short term but can also pose long-term dangers to the economy, society and politics. This chapter concentrates on the short-term effects of money laundering, while the next chapter deals with the long-term effects of it.

Table 6.1   The effects of money laundering described in the literature

Short-term Effects	Authors [2]	Indirect			Real Sector	Financial Sector	Public & Monetary Sector
		Economic	Social	Political			
1. Losses to the victims and gains to the perpetrator	Boorman & Ingves (2001) p. 9; Camdessus (1998) ip. 2; Mackrell (1997) ip. 3; Walker (1995) ip. 30				x		
2. Distortion of consumption and savings	Barlett (2002) p. 19; Mackrell (1997) ip. 2; Walker (1995) ip. 30ff	x				x	
3. Distortion of investment	Aninat & Hardy & Johnston (2002) ip. 1; Bartlett (2002) p. 19; Camdessus (1998) ip. 2; Mackrell (1997) ip. 3; McDonell (1998) p. 10f; McDowell (2001) ip. 1ff; Quirk (1997) ip. 4; Tanzi (1997) p. 95f; Walker (1995) ip. 30	x				x	

Short-term Effects	Authors [2]	Indirect			Real Sec-tor	Finan-cial Sector	Public & Mone-tary Sector
		Eco-nomic	Social	Poli-tical			
4. Artificial increase in prices	Keh (1996) p. 5; Alldrige (2002), p. 314	x			x		
5. Unfair competition	Mackrell (1997) ip. 3; McDowell (2001) ip. 2f; Walker (1995) ip. 33f	x			x		
6. Changes in imports and exports	Baker (1999) p. 33; Bartlett (2002) p. 18, 20; Walker (1995) ip. 33	x			x		
7. Effect on output, income and employ-ment	Bartlett (2002) p. 18; Boorman & Ingves (2001) p. 8; McDowell (2001) ip. 2, 4; Walker (1995) ip. 33	x			x		
8. Lower or higher reve-nues for the public sector	Alldridge (2002) p. 135; Boorman &Ingves (2001) p. 9; Mackrell (1997) ip. 2; McDonell (1998) p. 10; McDowell (2001) ip. 3, 4; Quirk (1997) ip. 4; Yaniv (1994 and 1999)	x					x
9. Changes in the demand for money, exchange rates and interest rates	Bartlett (2002) p. 18; Boorman & Ingves (2001) p. 9; Camdessus (1998) ip. 2; FATF (2002) ip. 3; McDonell (1998) p. 10; McDowell (2001) ip. 2f; Quirk (1997) ip. 3; Tanzi (1997) p. 97	x					x
10. Increase in the volatility of interest and exchange rates	Tanzi (1996) p. 8; McDonell (1998) p. 10; Camdessus (1998) p. 2; FATF (2002) ip. 3; Boorman & Ingves (2001) p. 9	x					x
11. Greater availability of credit	Tanzi (1996) p. 6	x				x	
12. Higher capital inflows	Keh (1996) p. 4; Tanzi (1996) p. 6	x				x	x
13. Distortion of the econo-mic statistics	Alldridge (2002) p. 306; McDonell (1998) p. 10; Quirk (1997) ip. 4; Tanzi (1997) p. 96			x			x

Long-term Effects	Authors	Indirect			Real Sector	Financial Sector	Public & Monetary Sector
		Economic	Social	Political			
1. Threatens privatisation	McDowell (2001) ip. 4; Keh (1996) , p. 11	x		x			x
2. Changes in foreign direct investment	Boorman & Ingves (2001) p. 9; FATF (2002) ip. 3; Walker (1995) ip. 34	x				x	x
3. Risk for the financial sector, solvability, liquidity	Alldridge (2002) p. 310; Aninat & Hardy & Johnston (2002) ip. 1; Boorman & Ingves (2001) p. 9, 11; Camdessus (1998) ip. 2; FATF (2002) ip. 3; McDonell (1998) p. 10; McDowell (2001) ip. 1, 3; Tanzi (1997) p. 98	x	x			x	
4. Profits for the financial sector	Alldridge (2002) p. 310	x				x	
5. Reputation of the financial sector	Aninat & Hardy & Johnston (2002) ip. 1; Bartlett (2002) p. 19; Boorman & Ingves (2001) p. 9, 11; Camdessus (1998) ip. 1; FATF (2002) ip. 3; Levi (2002) p. 184; McDonell (1998) p. 9; McDowell (2001) ip. 2, 3, 4; Quirk (1997) ip. 4; Tanzi (1997) p. 92, 98; Walker (1995) ip. 34		x			x	x
6. Illegal business contaminates legal business	Alldridge (2002) p. 315; Camdessus (1998) ip. 1f; FATF (2002) ip. 3; Levi (2002) p. 184; McDonell (1998) p. 11; Quirk (1997) ip. 4	x		x	x	x	
7. Corruption and bribe	Alldridge (2002) p. 308; Bartlett (2002) p. 18f; Camdessus (1998) ip. 1; FATF (2002) ip. 3; Keh (1996) p. 11; McDowell (2001) ip. 1, 4; Tanzi (1997) p. 92, 99; Quirk (1997) p. 19; Walker (1995) ip. 33f		x			x	x

Long-term Effects	Authors	Indirect			Real Sector	Financial Sector	Public & Monetary Sector
		Eco-nomic	Social	Poli-tical			
8. Negative or positive effect on growth rates	Aninat & Hardy & Johnston (2002) ip. 1; Bartlett (2002) p. 18ff; Camdessus (1998) ip. 2; McDonell (1998) p. 10; McDowell (2001) ip. 4; Quirk (1997) ip. 4; Tanzi (1997) p. 92, 96	x			x		
9. Undermines political insti-tutions	Camdessus (1998) ip. 1; FATF (2002) ip. 3; Mackrell (1997) ip. 3; McDonell (1998) p. 9; McDowell (2001) ip. 1, 3f; Tanzi (1997) p. 92, 99			x			x
10. Under-mines foreign policy goals	Baker (1999) p. 38f			x			x
11. Increases crime	Bartlett (2002) p. 18ff; FATF (2002) ip. 3; Levi (2002) p. 183; Mackrell (1997) ip. 3; Masciandaro (2004) p. 137; McDonell (1998) p. 9; McDowell (2001) ip. 1, 4; Quirk (1997) p. 19	x	x		x		x
12. Increases terrorism	Masciandaro (2004) p. 131	x	x				x

6.1. LOSSES TO THE VICTIM AND GAINS TO THE PERPETRATOR OF A CRIME

Money laundering is associated with the commission of a predicate offence (i.e. fraud, theft, drugs, tax evasion). This means that resources are illegally and unfairly transferred from the control of the victim to the offender. The illegal nature of the proceeds of crime renders the laundering activity necessary in order to make the wealth appear as if it was derived by legitimate means. Thus, money laundering contributes to the process of unfair reallocation of wealth from the good to the bad by rendering detection extremely difficult and allowing crimi-nals to enjoy the fruits of their crimes undisturbed. As MacKrell (1997, p. 3) points out, 'money laundering helps make crime worthwhile. It helps give legitimacy and even respectability to some of the most unworthy in society. It gives economic power to criminals and takes it from the law abiding tax payer' (see also Camdessus 1998, Walker 1995). That is to say, as a result of money laundering, crime pays off. This direct effect of money laundering, the losses to the victims of crime and the gains to the crime offenders, are also mentioned by the IMF (Camdessus 1998, p. 2) and by AUSTRAC (the Australian FATF organization, see Walker 1995).

The major criminal sources for money laundering are fraud and drugs money. There are no encompassing estimates on fraud and losses from fraud, but there are some comprehensive studies on drugs and some estimates on a few sub-forms of fraud for some countries (Critical remarks on estimating drugs and fraud have been made in chapter 3 and 4).

Losses from Drugs   Few comprehensive studies have been undertaken to measure the costs of drugs and drug abuse for society. The UNDP (1996) gives a survey on international studies regarding cost benefit analyses of drugs.

The costs in Australia related to illicit drug abuse were estimated to be equivalent to 0.4 percent of GDP. Thirty-two 32 percent of the costs were estimated to be due to reduced productivity, 26 percent to substance abuse related mortality, 18 percent to costs of the justice system (court, prisons), 13 percent to resources used in addictive consumption, and 9 percent to additional costs for police and customs (UNDP 1996). Collins and Lapsley (1996) estimated A$1.6 billion of tangible and intangible costs resulting from illicit drug abuse in Australia for 1992. This amounts to about 0.4 percent of GDP. According to their findings an even higher share, 45 percent, resulted from loss of productivity, 27 percent was spent on law enforcement and 25 percent was spent on health care. (see Figure 6.1).

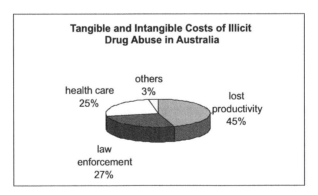

Source: Own graph based on data from Collins and Lapsley (1996).

Figure 6.1   Tangible and intangible costs of illicit drug abuse in Australia

The costs of drug abuse in the UK were also estimated to be 0.4 percent of GDP in 1988. A more recent study regarding Germany, done in 1995, came up with costs amounting to 0.4 percent of GDP as well. Based on these findings, the calculated costs per abuser of cocaine, heroin and synthetic drugs are approximately €30,000 per annum (UNDP 1996, p. 33).

In Canada, the costs of illicit drug abuse were estimated at US$ 1.1 billion in 1992, equivalent to 0.2 percent of GDP, which is only half of what has been estimated for other countries. These costs include law enforcement (29 percent), health care (6 percent), and productivity losses as a result of illness and premature death (60 percent). Further costs not included in this study are costs for society due to drug-related criminal activities, such as theft, damages etc.

Both from the Australian and the Canadian studies one can see that productivity losses due to illness and premature death are the highest costs resulting from drug abuse. Contrary to these findings, a US study sees the costs for the justice systems and property losses as a larger cost component than productivity losses. A study carried out in the State of California showed the following cost components of drug abuse: 35 percent for criminal justice system costs; 26 percent for stolen property losses; 17 percent for healthcare and losses in productivity of the victims of drug-related crime; 14 percent for costs of healthcare for the drug abuser and 8 percent for welfare and disability payments (UNDP 1996, p. 33).

Worldwide, the UN finds that drug abuse imposes high costs on countries.

* 'Identifiable costs of drug abuse, including drug-related crime costs, law enforcement costs and health costs, range from 0.5 to 1.3 percent of gross domestic product in most consumer countries' (UN 1998[a]).
* 'Due to increased global consumption of illicit drugs, substance abuse-related mortality has more than tripled over the last decade. Recent figures suggest drug injection is responsible for between 100,000 and 200,000 deaths per year' (UN 1998[a]).
* 'Drug abusers earn about 60 percent less than non-drug abusers for the same age and gender. Health expenditures are double as much as for non-drug abusers. The drug related mortality rate is between 0.3 percent–0.5 percent of hard core abusers. About 22 percent of the world's HIV/AIDS population are drug injectors' (UNDP 1996, p. 33).

Besides the economic costs such as reduced productivity, higher expenditures for health, police, judges and prison, for insurances, damages from burglary and theft, there are also social costs due to a lower level of education, environmental damages in third world countries that destroy forests for drug cultivation, corruption and other dangers to civil society.

There is a strong probability that drug addicts tend to be deeply involved in criminal activities, with daily users of drugs showing a significantly higher rate of criminality than non-drug users. The National Crime Victimization Survey of the United States revealed that 30 percent of the victims of violent crime in 1992 perceived their attacker to have been under the influence of drugs or alcohol. A UK study revealed that 50 percent of all theft and burglary was drug related (see UNDP p. 33).

Unfortunately, no encompassing study of the Netherlands is mentioned. However, if one applies the findings of international studies to the Netherlands, and assumes that drug abuse costs about 0.4 percent of GDP, then the economic costs from drug abuse in Holland would amount to €2 billion.

In a survey, 51 percent of Dutch companies reported to have been the victim of some sort of crime in the preceding three years. This does not necessarily mean that it relates to money laundering, but if – as we show later – money laundering stimulates more crime – the costs for the private and the public sector, as well as for society, need some consideration.

The direct losses for companies and institutions in the Netherlands resulting from crime amounted to €1.3 billion in 2001 (Van der Heide and Eggen, 2003, p. 60). Evidently, not all of it relates to money laundering. If one believes the UK study quoted above, almost 50 percent of burglary and theft are drug related. In an earlier chapter, we found that fraud and the drug trade are crimes that necessitate the largest part of money laundering.

In order to prevent these kinds of crime, companies have to spend about € 620 million a year on alarm installations, internal control against fraud, etc. If one adds these prevention costs to the total damage, then it amounts to about € 2 billion a year. Still to be added are the insurance fees Dutch companies are paying for protection against crime.

If one takes into account the costs for society, for insurance, for the government, the health expenditures to treat drug addicts, the legal system, the judges, the lawyers, the costs of prison, the social consequences such as dismantling the family or corruption, the costs of crime related to money laundering are certainly higher than the ones estimated. From the numbers above one can also conclude that additional crime is costly both for companies and society.

Economic benefits of drug abuse and trafficking are mainly the profits of the suppliers and traffickers of illicit drugs. For example, one gram of 100 percent pure cocaine retailed for US$4.30 in Colombia is ultimately sold for between US$59 and US$297 in the United States. The gross profit margin, or value added, is hence between 93 percent and 98.5 percent of the retail value. Worldwide estimates of the 'benefits' from illicit drugs to the US economy amounted to 6 percent of GDP. But about 90 percent of this money went to the drug traffickers and only about 10 percent went to processing and farmers (UNODC 2004).

Reuter and Greenfield (2001) present an even more drastic example from the UNDP (1994). According to their study, the farm gate price of opium originating in Pakistan was about US$90 per kilogram. This implies that the farm-gate value of a kilogram of heroin is about US$900. The wholesale price of heroin in Pakistan was US$2,870 per kilogram; the wholesale price in the US was US$80,000 per kilogram; and the retail price in the US was US$290,000 for a kilogram at 40 percent purity, equivalent to US$725,000 for a pure kilogram. This would amount to a gross profit margin or value added of 99.6 percent–99.8 percent of the retail value and a mark-up of 80,555 percent from farm gate value. In particular, the shipment from Pakistan to the US makes the price 30 times higher, a mark-up that dwarfs those of traditional agricultural products, which have a mark-up of 10 percent–12 percent (see Reuter and Greenfield 2001).

The economic benefit to the industrialized countries of the production and processing of drugs is, therefore, of much less importance than the amount of money circulating as a result of it (UNODC 2004, p. 2). However, from these calculations one can also see that money laundering of drug profits by drug traffickers will be huge.

Table 6.2   Estimates on the costs and benefits of drugs

Type of Crime	Country and Year	Amount of Estimate	Source of Estimate
Costs of illicit drug abuse	Australia 1996 UK 1988 Germany 1995	0.4% of GDP	UNDCP 1996 survey
Costs of illicit drug abuse	Australia 1992	1.6 million A$ = 0.4% of GDP of which 45% due to productivity loss	Collins and Lapsley 1996
Costs of drug abuse	Canada 1992	0.2% of GDP	UNDCP 1996
costs of drug abuse	global	0.5%–1.1% of GDP	UN 1998[a]
Direct losses for companies and institutions from crime	The Netherlands 2001	€1.3 billion	Van der Heide and Eggen, WODC 2003
Economic Benefits from Cocaine	US no year	6% of GDP gross profit margin 93–98% of retail value in Colombia	UNODC 2004
Economic Benefits from Heroin	US 1994	Farm price in Pakistan US$900, sales price in US$725,000	Reuter and Greenfield 2001 UNDCP 1994

Table 6.2. summarizes the findings on the costs and benefits of drugs. As one can see, the benefits estimated at 6 percent of GDP exceed the costs of 0.4 percent of GDP. Dry economically speaking this means that crime still pays. There are costs and benefits, which are not included in the calculations, though. For example, the disutility of being caught and imprisoned might make crime less attractive as it appears in the cost benefit analysis above. The profit margins for drugs are much higher than those of regular export and import products. This implies that the costs and benefits of the drug business are not evenly distributed among countries. The producers of opium, heroine and cocaine are placed in countries like Myanmar, Pakistan and Colombia. The consumers and final retailers are in the US and in Europe. It is here where the big gains and costs from drug addiction occur. Laundering money in the US and Europe makes the drug business pay even more.

Losses from Fraud   Estimating the losses of fraud is complicated by the fact that the definitions of fraud vary widely and that one sometimes does not know which types of fraud the data include.

The Australian Institute of Criminology estimated the overall cost of fraud in Australia at more than A$5 billion per year, which is almost a third of the A$19 billion 'total cost of crime' (Caslon, no year). One major concern in many countries at the moment is identity fraud. Estimates of the cost of identity-related offences in Australia vary from around A$1.1 billion to A$6 billion in 2002–03. Identity fraud refers to stolen passports, credit cards or any way in which one person uses another person's identity.

At the lower end, there is SIRCA (2003). SIRCA's research, which is the first of its kind in Australia, estimates the cost of identity fraud in 2001–02 to be A$1.1 billion, with an estimation error of A$130 million. It also identifies patterns in identity fraud behaviour and develops an explanatory model on the efficiency of current prevention and detection strategies (SIRCA Report 2003).

Wealth offences include falsifying, theft, obscuring, fraud and fencing. It is not clear whether or not the number of wealth offences has increased or declined in the Netherlands. The number of wealth crime incidents has declined since late 1990, according to the victims survey report (Van der Heide and Egge, WODC 2003, p. 47). However, if one counts the wealth crimes registered at the court one finds an increasing amount. In 2001, 919,000 wealth offences were registered.

For the UK, the losses from identity fraud were estimated in February 2006 at £1.72 billion by the Identity-Theft Organization, which equals about €2.5 billion. http://www.identity-theft.org.uk/ID%20fraud%20table.pdf.

According to research conducted by the Association of Certified Fraud Examiners (ACFE), US organizations lose an estimated 5 percent of annual revenues to fraud. Based on the U.S. Gross Domestic Product in 2006 – U$13.037

trillion – this percentage indicates a staggering estimate of losses around US$652 billion among organizations, despite an increased emphasis on anti-fraud controls and recent legislation to combat fraud. The results are based on a survey of 1,134 Certified Fraud Examiners (CFEs) in the US (Association of Certified Fraud Examiners, ACFE 2006).

The US Federal Trade Commission, for example, claimed that identity-related offences cost US consumers and businesses around US$53 billion in 2002 (Caslon, no year). Credit card fraud was the most common form of reported ID theft (28 percent), followed by phone or utilities fraud (19 percent), bank fraud (18 percent), and employment fraud (13 percent) (Leyden 2005). Also, Gartner (2002) found that credit card fraud was the highest. More than 5 percent of online consumers suffered from credit card fraud.

The sixth annual survey of eCommerce fraud released by CyberSource Corporation (Nasdaq: CYBS) shows that US merchants expect to lose an estimated US$2.6 billion to online fraud in 2004, US$700 million more than in 2003. The new estimate beats the prior fraud loss record of US$2.1 billion established in 2002. The Sixth Annual CyberSource Fraud Survey was sponsored by CyberSource Corporation and undertaken by Mindwave Research. The survey was fielded September 17 through October 1, 2004 and yielded 348 qualified and complete responses (vs. 333 the year before). The sample was drawn from a database of companies involved in electronic commerce activities. Incentive to respondents was a summary of the research findings.

Gartner (2002) found a somewhat more moderate number for online sales losses. He noted that more than US$700 million in online sales were lost to fraud in 2001, representing 1.14 percent of total annual online sales of US$61.8 billion.

The highest costs associated with the management of fraud are, typically, loss of potential income and revenue. A key source of revenue loss occurs when legitimate orders are rejected for fear of fraud. According to the survey done by Gartner, rejection rates during 2004 were nearly 6 percent, up from 4.6 percent the year before. So for every confirmed fraudulent order, merchants are refusing to accept another 4 to 5 orders on suspicion of fraud (Gartner, 2002).

Social Fraud and Insurance Fraud are also very important ways of creating criminal income. Furthermore, insurance fraud can also be used directly for laundering. If the launderer can get a receipt of insurance payments (even if these were not actually made) he has created legal income.

In the US, US$1 out of every US$7 spent on Medicare is lost to fraud and abuse. In 1998 alone, Medicare lost nearly US$12 billion to fraudulent or unnecessary claims. False claim schemes are the most common type of health insurance fraud. The goal in these schemes is to obtain undeserved payment for a claim or series of claims (Barrett, 2005).

Another estimate states that fraud and abuse cost Medicare and Medicaid in the US about US$ 33 billion each year (Roman 1995, Alper 1997).

A serious concern for many countries is tax fraud. In the Netherlands, the largest concern is money laundering in connection with tax evasion. For more than 25 years, rough estimations have been made regarding the amount of fiscal fraud. There are estimates of 15 percent of the GDP (€70 billion), but these seem to be too high. The CBS produced an estimate of approximately €20 billion (de Kam, 2004).

Tax fraud and financial fraud discovered in 2003 are reported to amount to about €275 million (FIOD-ECD 2003) by the fiscal police in the Netherlands. In the Netherlands, social fraud is reported to be €84.6 million by the social police (SIOD 2004, see also chapter 3 and Unger et al. 2006). However, the rate of detection is unknown. In chapter 3, we estimated Dutch fraud at 3.6–7.2 billion Euros by assuming that 5 percent–10 percent of the perpetrators get caught. These data are much lower than the ones quoted in de Kam (2004).

Within the European Union, the Commission has no detailed figures on the level of tax fraud. However, in economic literature estimates of tax fraud of 2 to 2.5 percent of GDP are mentioned. This would represent about €200 to €250 billion at EU level.

In 2006 value added tax (VAT) fraud became a big issue in the EU. On the VAT fraud, estimates of up to 10 percent of losses in VAT receipts are often quoted, the EU Commission says (EU 2006). Germany recently estimated the overall losses in VAT receipts at €17 billion per year. In the UK, the so-called 'VAT-gap', meaning the difference between the theoretical VAT receipts and the actual VAT receipts, is estimated at 13,5 percent of the VAT receipts. The revenue losses due to carousel fraud are estimated at between €1,5 billion and €3 billion a year. This represents about 1.5 percent to 2.5 percent of the total UK VAT receipts, a much lower number than the one stated for the whole EU (see EU 2006).

Regarding the excise fraud, Member States estimated in 1998 that for alcohol alone, fraud amounted up to €1.5 billion yearly. This was approximately 8 percent of the total excise duties receipts on alcoholic beverages. On the excise fraud related to tobacco, national EU customs authorities seized, in 2004, more than 41 million packets of counterfeit cigarettes. Nowadays the market share of illegal cigarettes is equivalent to approximately 9 percent of the total excise duty receipts on tobacco products.

An acute problem within the EU at the moment is the so-called Carousel Fraud. Company (B) acquires goods in another Member State without having to pay VAT to his supplier (A). Subsequently, it makes a domestic supply for which it charges VAT to the customer (C). However, the company (B) does not pay the VAT to the Treasury and disappears. The customer (C) claims a refund of the VAT paid to the company (B). Consequently, the financial loss is for the

Treasury, which has to refund VAT to the customer (C), which it never collected from the supplier (B).

Subsequently, Company C may declare an exempt intra-community supply to Company (A) and, in its turn, (A) may make an exempt intra-community supply to (B) and the fraud pattern resumes, thus explaining the term 'Carousel fraud' (EU 2006).

The benefits of fraud are mainly the income received. One can conclude that the costs of crime are substantial. The costs of drugs amount to about 0.4 percent of GDP. Fraud is still so widely and vaguely defined that it is difficult to draw conclusions from the estimates. Some include only fraud against business, some refer to vertical fraud (citizens cheating the government) and some to horizontal fraud (customers cheating business, business cheating business). Some refer only to fiscal fraud, others to social fraud. Some show the numbers of fraud detected, others try to estimate the underlying population. The fraud numbers are summarized below in Table 6.3. One can see that the numbers vary widely.

But in any case, crime is the prerequisite for money laundering. Without crime there would not be money laundering. To make crime pay, therefore, enhances the profitability of crime.

Table 6.3   Estimates on the costs and benefits of fraud

Type of Crime	Country and Year	Amount of Estimate	Source of Estimate
Fraud	Australia 2002	A$5 billion	Australian Institute of Criminology,
Identity Fraud		A$1.1 –$6 billion	SIRCA 2003,
Total Cost of Crime		A$19 billion	Caslon no year
Wealth Crime	Netherlands 2001 no total fraud estimate available	919.000 offences registered at the courts	WODC 2003
Fiscal Fraud and Social Fraud	The Netherlands 2004	€7–€15 billion	Unger et al. (2006)
Losses from Identity Fraud	UK 2006	€2,5 billion	Identity Theft Organization
Losses of Organizations from Fraud	US 2004	5% of GDP US$652 billion	Association of Certified Fraud Examiners (ACFE)
Costs for Consumers and Business from identity-related Offences	US 2002	US$53	The US Federal Trade Commission in Caslon, no year

Type of Crime	Country and Year	Amount of Estimate	Source of Estimate
Credit Card Fraud	US 2002	Most important type of identity fraud. More than 5% of consumers suffer from credit card fraud	Leyden 2005 Gartner 2002
Estimated loss from online fraud by merchants	US 2004	US$2.6 billion	The sixth annual survey of eCommerce fraud released by CyberSource Corporation (Nasdaq: CYBS)
Losses from online fraud	US 2002	US$700 million	Gartner 2002
Social fraud and abuse	US 1998 and 1994	15% of Medicare expenses. Cost Medicare and Medicaid US$33 billion	Barrett 2005 Roman 1995 Alper 1997
Social fraud and abuse discovered	The Netherlands 2003	€84.5 million	SIOD (2004)
Tax fraud and Financial Fraud Discovered	The Netherlands 2003	€698 million	FIOD-ECD 2003
Fiscal fraud, tax evasion	The Netherlands 2003	€20–€70 billion or 6%–15% of GDP	CBS, de Kam 2004
Value Added Tax Fraud	EU wide	10%–15% of VAT tax revenues	EU Memo 2006
Tax Fraud	EU wide	2%–2.5% of GDP €200–250 billion	EU Memo 2006

6.2. DISTORTION OF CONSUMPTION AND SAVINGS

Once the money is transferred from the victim to the offender, the latter will use the money in a different way than the former. The spending patterns of criminals might be different from those of ordinary citizens. Furthermore, the money laundering activity itself involves the purchase of assets such as real estate, jewellery, art and other luxury products, since these assets give launderers the possibility to conceal large amounts of illicit money without arousing suspicion (Bartlett 2002, p. 19). These spending choices may differ from those of the victims who may have intended to use the money for their everyday expenses, old age, 'rainy days' (Walker 1995, p. 30). This triggers a multiplier effect through the economy from a) the reduced and different spending of the victims and b) the increased and different spending of the criminals. The net effect is, according to Walker (1995) who tries to measure this effect, the collateral damage to the national economy. Thus, as Walker (1995, p. 31f) points out

> those industries supplying goods and services to the superannuates will suffer a reduction for demand for their services, and this will ripple through their suppliers and their supplier and so on. At the same time, the industries supplying goods and services to the launderer will experience an increase in demand, which will ripple through their suppliers and so on.

The effect of these two sets of ripples is a net loss to the economy as a result of money laundering operations.

In order to measure the multiplier effects from reduced consumption by the victims and from increased spending by the criminals empirically, Walker used input-output tables (see under output and employment effects).

Do criminals behave differently from normal people? From criminal case studies we can learn something about the behaviour of criminals and money launderers. Meloen et al. (2003) did a research on crime money, the amount, the characteristics and the spending of it in the Netherlands.

In the Netherlands, and probably in most countries, a small group of criminals makes a lot of money, while most criminals make small amounts of money. This can be seen from the following table, where 83 percent of suspects accounted for only 11.7 percent of criminal proceeds (the proceeds estimated by the judge, i.e. the WVV, the 'wederrechtelijk verkregen voordeel'), whereas 2.1 percent of suspects accounted for 57.9 percent of proceeds.

Table 6.4   Total amount of crime money and number of suspects by size 1993 till 1999

	Number of suspects		Total crime money WVV[3] (guilders)	
	N	%	N	%
1 till 100.000 guilders	6236	83.1	118,710,841	11.7
100.000 till 1 million guilders	1107	14.8	308,057,368	30.4
1 million guilders and more	159	2.1	587,160,369	57.9
Total	7502	100	1,013,928,578	100

Source: Unger et al. (2006) own calculations from Table 3.4 in Meloen et al. (2003) p. 66.

Note: 1 Euro = 2.2 Dutch guilders.

Meloen et al. (2003) analysed 52 cases of criminals ('ontnemingszaken') with unlawful advantages, where the judge estimated the proceeds (WVV) of more than 1 million guilders (400,000 Euros) per case. They divided the spending behaviour of criminals into four categories: (1) hoarding the crime money (this is mostly temporary) (2) consumptive lifestyle, spending the money on luxuries like jewels, art, expensive vehicles, boats or a plane (3) conventional investment, temporarily put it on a bank account or spend it on stocks, bonds or options or convert into loans or other securities (4) making irregular business investments or reinvesting in a business, legal or illegal, to influence it or use it for own purposes.

Table 6.5   The spending behaviour in 52 big criminal cases in millions of guilders

Hoarding	19
Consumptive lifestyle	15
Conventional investments	127
Irregular business investments	51
Total	222

Source: Unger et al. (2006) own calculations from Meloen et al. (2003).

This micro study can explain what happens with 222 million of guilders or 100 million Euros of criminal money. Using this study, one can estimate the amount of money being laundered. In the case of hoarding, there will be no money laundering involved, because it is not given an apparent legal source. In the case of consumptive lifestyle, there is also no actual 'money laundering' in the context of most research, because no banking sector is involved. In the case of conventional investments there must be money laundering involved, because in order to buy bonds or investment items one usually must prove the origins of the money used. This also holds true in the case of irregular business investments, since even establishing an illegal business requires at least some clean money.

From the micro study one can compute the amount of crime money involved with money laundering. In these 52 'million cases' the amount of money laundered is $(127 + 51) / 222 = 0.80$, which equals 80 percent. The way of spending as described above in the 52 cases shows similarities to some national statistics. The spending behaviour of big Dutch criminals seems to follow a pattern that is similar to national statistics with regard to consumption and investment shares. The spending behaviour of poorer criminals also displays the same pattern as that of honest poorer Dutchmen, as Table 6.6 reveals.

Households with a low income will spend more of their income on consumption than households with a higher income. A household with a higher income will invest more of its income since there is a limit to the amount of cars, luxury goods, jewels airplanes etc. that one person can consume with enjoyment. This logic of behaviour can also be seen with criminals.

Table 6.6 also tells us something about the laundering of money in relation to the amounts of crime money. Money laundering is more important for the rich criminals than for the poor. The rich criminals hoard and consume less than the poor ones, but they invest 59.3 percent of the crime money, double as much as the poor (29.5 percent).

Table 6.6   The behaviour of criminals in the 52 'million cases'

Spending Pattern CEBES	WVV-segments Rapsody (the amount of crime money)					
	1 till 100.000		100.000 till 1 million		1 million and more	
	guilders	%	guilders	%	guilders	%
Hoarding						
1 Cash Money NL	**3,565,220**	**36.2%**	**9,659,836**	**41.9%**	**11,487,907**	**24.0%**
2 Cash Money Foreign	541,583	5.5%	878,011	3.8%	2,820,971	5.9%
Consumption						
3 Consumptive Lifestyle	8,095	0.1%	1,300	0.0%	9,370	0.0%
4 Consumption Goods	311,335	3.2%	1,999,370	8.7%	694,477	1.5%
5 Jewellery, Musical Instruments, Art	667,787	6.8%	948,484	4.1%	1,012,104	2.1%
6 Vehicles	**1,672,090**	**17.0%**	**2,874,646**	**12.5%**	3,179,762	6.7%
7 Planes, Boats	172,850	1.8%	829,598	3.6%	227,435	0.5%
Investment						
8 Bank Accounts	**1,334,454**	**13.6%**	902,294	3.9%	632,213	1.3%
9 Immovable Property NL	718,850	7.3%	**4,527,500**	**19.6%**	**13,476,500**	**28.2%**
10 Securities			69,157	0.3%		
11 Fixed Interest Assets	854,516	8.7%	375,963	1.6%	**14,246,988**	**29.8%**
Total	9,846,753	100.0%	23,066,158	100.0%	47,787,727	100.0%
Total Hoarding	4,106,803	41.7%	10,537,847	45.7%	**14,308,878**	**29.9%**
Total Consumption	2,832,112	28.8%	6,653,398	28.8%	**5,123,148**	**10.7%**
Total Investment	2,907,821	29.5%	5,874,913	25.5%	**28,355,702**	**59.3%**
Total	9,846,753	100.0%	23,066,158	100.0%	47,787,727	100.0%
Total Number of Cases	2,399		2,786		1,666	

Source: Own calculations from Table 5.5 in Meloen et al. (2003, p. 116).

Among the 52 cases that are researched in Meloen et al. (2003) (see Table 6.7), there are 26 cases with drugs involved and 22 cases with fraud involved, which means that there are four cases of other types of crime. The question 'Does the spending behaviour of criminals differ depending on the types of crime they commit?' can therefore only be answered for the cases of drugs and fraud. But since these two categories are the most important when it comes to the amount of money as well as money laundering, it seems worthwhile to investigate them.

The most remarkable difference in spending behaviour is in the frequency of money being hoarded. For drug money, in 20 out of 26 cases, i.e. in 77 percent of cases, some of the money is hoarded in order to reinvest it in new drug sales. This happens much less often in fraud cases.

Table 6.7   Spending behaviour of drug dealers and fraud committers

Type of spending	Form of Spending	26 drug cases		22 fraud cases		4 other cases	All 52 cases	
		Num-ber	%	Num-ber	%	Num-ber	Num-ber	%
Hoarding	Cash Money NL	20	**77%**	5	**23%**	3	28	**54%**
	Cash Money Foreign	13	**50%**	2	**9%**	1	16	**31%**
Consump-tion	Luxurious Lifestyle	8	**31%**	7	**32%**	0	15	**29%**
	Consumption Goods	11	**42%**	5	**23%**	0	16	**31%**
	Jewellery, Music instruments, Art	10	**38%**	7	**32%**	2	19	**37%**
	Vehicles	21	**81%**	17	**77%**	3	41	**79%**
	Planes, Boats	11	**42%**	6	**27%**	0	17	**33%**
Conven-tional Investment	Bank Accounts NL	17	**65%**	13	**59%**	1	31	**60%**
	Bank Accounts Foreign	16	**62%**	9	**41%**	1	26	**50%**
	Immovable Property NL	8	**31%**	9	**41%**	0	17	**33%**
	Immovable Property Foreign	8	**31%**	9	**41%**	1	18	**35%**
	Securities	9	**35%**	12	**55%**	2	23	**44%**
	Fixed Interest Assets	18	**69%**	15	**68%**	2	35	**67%**
Irregular Business Investment	Business Activities NL	20	**77%**	15	**68%**	1	36	**69%**
	Business Activities Foreign	12	**46%**	8	**36%**	1	21	**40%**
	Reinvestment	8	**31%**	5	**23%**	2	15	**29%**

Percentages have to be read horizontally. For drug cases 100% equals 26 cases; for fraud cases 100% equals 22 cases; For the total of 52 cases 100% equals 52 cases; For 'other cases' no percentages have been attributed since there are too few cases.

Source: Unger et al. (2006) own calculations from Table 14.2 in Meloen et al. (2003) p. 246.

Table 6.8 Asset ownership of Dutch households from survey data in 1998

Assets	As a percentage of total financial assets
Checking and saving accounts	35.1
Bonds	2.2
Stocks	23.8
Mutual funds	13.3
Defined-contribution plans	7.9
Cash value of life insurance	10.4
Employer-sponsored saving plans	2.9
Other financial assets.	4.5
Total financial assets (average amount in guilders)	81,563

	As a percentage of total assets
Total financial assets.	27.6
Total non-financial assets	72.4
Real estate	63.8
House	58.8
Other real estate	4.9
Business equity	3.7
Stock of durable goods	4.9
Total assets (average amount)	295,000

Source: Alessie, Hochguertel, van Soest (2002) p. 358, Table 9.4

There can only be a distortion of consumption and savings if criminals behave differently from normal people with regard to consumption and savings. If one compares the case studies on criminal spending behaviour from Meloen et al. (2003) shown above, with Household Spending Behaviour according to the Tilburg study done by Alessie, Hochguertel and van Soest (2002, Chapter 9) one can see that criminals basically behave like normal people.

With regard to assets, Dutch households show the following picture in 1998. On average they possess 295,000 guilders, i.e. €134,000. They hold about €37,000 in financial assets (27.6 percent of their total assets) and about €97,000 (72.4 percent of their total assets) in non-financial assets. The largest part of financial assets is held in checking and savings accounts (35 percent of their total financial assets) and in stocks and mutual funds (23.8 percent and 13.3 percent). The largest part of non-financial assets is in real estate. About 5 percent, i.e. €6,700 are held as a stock of durable goods (Alessie, Hochguertel and van Soest 2002, p 358). When distinguished by net worth quartiles, one can see that the richer households are, the more likely they are to hold a smaller amount of cash and a larger amount of stocks, business equities, and other real estate (other than houses). The share of durable goods gets smaller in the port-folio.

The table on asset ownership (Table 6.9) shows the percentage of Dutch households that hold specific assets, according to a survey amongst them. It reveals that 95.4 percent of households have checking and saving accounts. Bank accounts are also attractive for money launderers. Sixty percent of the cases of laundering studied by Meloen et al. (2003) made use of bank accounts.

Table 6.9   Asset rates of Dutch households from survey data in 1998

Assets	By % of households
Total financial assets	95.4
Checking and savings accounts	93.2
Bonds	3.5
Stocks	15.4
Mutual Funds	21.6
Defined-contribution plans	17.5
Cash value of life insurance	23
Employer-sponsored savings plans	35.8
Other financial assets	14
Total non financial assets	79.2
Real estate	51.6
House	50.8
Other real estate	4.5
Business equity	5.1
Stock of durable goods	72.7
Total assets	97.1

Source: CentER Savings Survey, sampling years 1993–1998, in Guiso, Haliassos, and Jappelli (2002) *Household Portfolios*, p. 356.

With regard to real estate, more than 50 percent of Dutch households own real estate. About 30 percent–40 percent of criminal cases laundered by putting money into immovable property. The data on criminals and on Dutch house-holds are not directly comparable. First, the Dutch household data do not include consumption patterns. Second, most of the criminal spending statistics stem from 52 cases of rich criminals, whereas the other data are for the average Dutch household.

A more precise study has to be done to reach solid conclusions. In particular, the consumption patterns of honest Dutchmen also have to be included. But, at first glance, the patterns seem to not be extremely diverse. Distortions of consumption and savings from money laundering is, given the relatively similar spending and saving pattern of Dutch households and of money launderers, not expected to be large in the Netherlands. From the Dutch findings, one can conclude that criminals behave like normal people. There are a few rich ones and many poor ones and those who are rich have a higher propensity to save.

6.3 DISTORTION OF INVESTMENT AND SECTOR EFFECTS

The negative impact of money laundering on investment stems mainly from the fact that in their investment choices, money launderers are primarily guided by the desire to escape control and detection rather than by investment return maximizing considerations. However, these investment choices can be detrimental to the economy because they lead to a redirection of funds to assets that generate very little economic activity or employment (Bartlett 2002, p. 19).

Money launderers tend to opt for investments that afford them the largest degree of concealment even if this entails lower rates of return. This diverges income from good investments to risky and low-quality investments. Fullerton and Karayannis provide evidence that this is prevalent in the United States, where funds from tax evasion are directed to risky investments in the small business sector (Fullerton and Karayannis (1993) paraphrased in Quirk 1996).

Money laundering causes a misallocation of resources due to distortions in relative assets and commodity prices arising from money laundering activities (McDonell 1998 and McDowell 2001). Money launderers are not looking for the highest rate of return on the money they launder, but for the investment that most easily allows the recycling of the illegally obtained money. Money may move from countries with good economic policies and higher rates of return to countries with poorer economic policies and lower rates of return. This implies that world capital is invested less optimally than would occur in the absence of money laundering (Tanzi 1997).

Money laundering redirects income from high savers to low savers or from sound investments to risky, low-quality investments. There is evidence that funds from tax evasion in the US are channelled into riskier but higher yielding investments in the small business sector. Similarly, crimes against persons, such as theft and kidnapping, seem likely to be directed at wealthier individuals and thus to be biased against savings (Quirk 1997, p. 19).

In which sectors do criminals invest? Criminals reinvest their criminal proceeds in companies and real estate with the purpose of making further profits, legal or illegal. Most of these investments are in sectors that are familiar to the criminal, such as bars, restaurants, prostitution, cars and transport (Kleemans et al. 2002, p. 124–136). Criminals tend to invest in the country of their origin or the country where they perform their criminal activities. Dutchmen have a tendency to invest in the Netherlands, Turks in Turkey.

It also looks like as if each country has its own special attraction for money launderers. In Italy, Masciandaro (1999) found out that the bond market was particularly popular for criminal investors since it allowed one to disguise their true identity for quite some time.

In the Netherlands, the real estate sector is particularly attractive for launderers. It is the largest sector for money laundering and is the most vulnerable to it. Real estate is important for money laundering because it is a non-transparent market, where the values of the objects are often difficult to estimate and where big value increases can happen. In the last few years, the real estate sector got a lot of attention due to the killing of real estate agent Willem Endstra. He was shot right out in the open on the street in Amsterdam in May 2004. He was suspected of fencing and of being connected to the Mafia. The boss of the criminal organization under suspicion is Willem Holleeder, previously convicted for kidnapping beer-brewing magnate Heineken. Several people who wanted to testify against Holleeder got killed on an open street. Before his death, Endstra revealed the criminal circle and the money laundering techniques in the real estate sector to the police. The protocols, which lasted 15 hours, were published without editing in the Dutch language in the so-called 'Endstra tapes' (Middelburg and Vugt, 2006).

The real estate sector is very attractive for criminals and the Dutch real estate sector seems to be even more so. The Dutch real estate sector has relatively high investments. A comparison of the European Central Bank of investments with the housing sector within the EU shows that the Dutch are among the top four investors (after Ireland, Spain and Germany) (see ECB 2003). Furthermore, prices increased more than with other assets. In the Netherlands, prices increased while they started to stagnate in other countries (ECB 2003, CBS 2005[a]). There is speculation on land so that price movements in the real estate sector are less conspicuous (Nelen, 2004).

Meloen et al. (2003) showed that 29 out of the 52 cases analysed invested in immovable property. Nineteen of them were in housing, ranging from apartments to villas. Second, investments in coffee shops, shops, brothels and hotels took place. Sometimes these are only financial investments, sometimes the goal is to earn on business. Also, investments in big construction projects are popular. The WODC (Kleemans et al. 2002, p. 132) also finds, from analysing 80 cases, that investing in real estate is an efficient method of placing large amounts of money. The price increase in real estate is profitable and the annual profits in the real estate business create a legal basis for income.

Nelen (2004) points out that investment in real estate has the following features, which make it attractive for criminal money:

- it is a safe investment
- the objective value is difficult to assess
- speculation is a tradition in this market
- it allows the distinguishing between legal and economic ownership
- it allows realization of 'white' returns
- it can be used to perform criminal activities

Abuse of legal persons can happen because:
- they can buy sleeping enterprise licenses
- there is no central registration of foreign corporations
- it is unknown what Dutchmen do with foreign legal persons abroad
- the European Court necessitates that foreign legal persons cannot be refused

Eichholtz (2004) points out that the real estate sector has the biggest value and exceeds the size of the bond market. Therefore, it attracts big wealth, both from legal and from illegal sources. Compared to the bond market, the real estate sector is less transparent and about three times as large. In 2005, the total value of the real estate sector in the Netherlands (this includes housing and business objects) was €1771 billion, as compared to an average total value of nominal bonds to €521 billion. The difference became even bigger when compared to the year before (Unger et al. 2006, CBS, 2005).[4,5]

It looks as if each country has its own specialties when it comes to how to reintegrate money. Investment distortion effects of money laundering on specific sectors such as the bond market, the real estate sector, and the gem sector are very likely.

6.4. ARTIFICIAL INCREASE IN PRICES

Launderers have an incentive to invest their illegal proceeds in an attempt to disguise their illegal origin. Consequently, they are willing to pay for particular assets more than their actual worth as well as to purchase otherwise unappealing property or enterprises simply because it gives them the possibility to increase their share of a particular market and gain stronger foothold in a particular economy (Keh 1996[b], p. 5). This will lead to an artificial increase in prices. For example, in Colombia it appears that in the 1980s the Medellin group bought large tracts of land, which pushed prices up from US$500 to US$2,000 per hectare (Keh 1996[b], p. 5). Similarly, investments in the capital market could work the same way leading to an artificial increase in share prices.

When launderers use real estate for laundering purposes, the housing prices can increase. Usually, the different parties at the market are the project developers, whose profit can range between €10 and €275 per square metre depending on the location and use in the Netherlands. The individual investors can earn from small enterprises that they run themselves, or from trading with objects and from renting houses. The return is stable but not spectacular, maximum 10 percent–15 percent. Institutional investors are insurance companies and pension funds that hold long-term portfolios. There is strict control and a low risk profile. Profits are less than 10 percent (Eichholtz 2004, Nelen 2004). The danger that the real estate market is used for money laundering lies in the fact that buyers can pay far too high a price in order to disguise criminal money. This means that artificial price increases and unfair competition are connected with it.

6.5. UNFAIR COMPETITION

Gresham's law that 'bad money drives out good money' seems to apply to money laundering as well. Holding on to illicitly obtained cash is incriminating for the offenders. Consequently, they will attempt to convert it into assets (i.e. real estate, business), which are less conspicuous and can give the appearance of legitimate wealth. To achieve this aim, money launderers engage in extensive purchases and due to their large availability of funds, they will be able to outbid potential honest buyers (Walker 1995, p. 33). Furthermore, since their interest in the respective asset does not stem from its actual value but rather from the benefits that accrue to them in terms of concealment, they are willing to pay far more than the true value of the asset. This will artificially drive purchase prices up and make them unaffordable to honest buyers (Walker 1995, p. 33).

Moreover, if launderers acquire and operate a business and use additional criminal funds to subsidize it, this provides them with a competitive advantage over legitimate ventures to the point where they will drive them out of business (Keh 1996, p. 5). This assertion can be substantiated by the study conducted by Arlacchi (1986) on the anti-competitive business behaviour of the mafia. It appears that 'the considerable capital sums acquired in the course of the mafia's illegal activity did in fact tend to be transfused into its legal entrepreneurial operations. (...) The mafia had access to a reserve of its own finance capital that far exceeded the firm's own present dimensions – and far exceeded what was available to non-mafia firms, which often found themselves squeezed out by lack of credit and therefore subordinated to finance capital' (Arlacchi 1986, p. 102–103).

6.6. CHANGES IN IMPORTS AND EXPORTS

Money laundering activities can also bring about a distortion of a country's imports and exports. As mentioned above, money launderers tend to engage in (often imported) luxury consumption. As a consequence, there will be balance of payments problems. Such imports do not generate domestic economic activity or employment and can depress domestic prices, thus reducing the profitability of domestic enterprises. Particularly, this appears to be the case in developing countries (Bartlett 2002, p. 20).

Furthermore, money laundering affects imports and exports in terms of prices. One of the most common tactics used for laundering money and generating illegal flight capital is to overprice imports and to underprice exports (Baker 1999, p. 33). For example, an importer of particular foreign machinery could make an agreement with the seller that the purchase price be increased by a considerable margin (e.g. 30 percent). The purchaser can pay the seller the whole sum in cash on the understanding that the addition in price (i.e. the 30 percent) be placed on his account in the foreign country. Clearly, if these activities are conducted recurrently and on a large scale this can artificially affect import and export prices.

As shown in an earlier chapter of this book, Zdanovic calculated capital flight from Russia and Switzerland to the US by means of transfer pricing. His findings confirm the view of Baker (1999) on the importance of overpricing of imports and underpricing of exports.

The Dutch expertise in logistics and its excellent location make the Netherlands a perfect place to use the existing business structure for criminal purposes. Money laundering activities intermingle with legal export and import businesses. In order to estimate this effect, a more in-depth analysis of customs and tax authorities reports would have to be performed.

In order to measure the macroeconomic consequences of, say, 18 billion additional Euros of money laundering in the Netherlands, as has been estimated in Unger et al. (2006) on imports, one needs a macroeconomic model. For example, in a Keynesian macroeconomic model, the additional money supply could lower interest rates, stimulate investment and output and as a consequence, increase imports. But in countries within the Eurozone, of which the Netherlands is a part, there is no longer a model which measures the effect of changes in the money supply or demand (see e.g. the Morkmon model of the Dutch Central Bank or the Jade model of the Dutch Central Planning Bureau CPB). This has to do with the fact that the Netherlands has no longer control over the money demand. However, this also means that the macroeconomic effects of monetary aggregates cannot be evaluated any longer. Both the Morkmon and the Jade model only allow for effects of changes in the world interest rate. It is therefore not possible anymore to measure the macro economic effects of money laundering on imports and exports.

6.7. EFFECT ON OUTPUT, INCOME AND EMPLOYMENT

Money laundering also reduces output and employment by diverting resources, as mentioned above, from sectors with high additional productivity (i.e. clothing, footwear) to sterile sectors (i.e. dwelling properties, jewellery, art). The multipliers for the latter are the lowest in terms of output, income and employment, thus resulting in a net loss to the total economy regardless of where the money would have otherwise been spent. Walker (1995, p. 32) tries to measure these effects by means of an input output model and estimates that if A$1 million of laundered money is invested in dwelling properties rather than in more productive sectors of the economy this would result, on average, in a net loss to the Australian economy of A$1.126 million of output, A$609,000 of lost income and 25 lost job (Walker 1995, p. 33). Once these figures are multiplied by the actual amount of money laundered, the effects become stark indeed.

Walker uses input output data, from which he calculated multipliers per sector (see Table 6.10 for Australia). Read the first line the following way: 1 million of additional expenditures for agriculture spills over through the whole economy (farmers have to buy more fertilizers, stimulating the chemical industry, etc....), increases output by 2.178 millions and (net) income by 0.38. Some part of this goes into imports (0.094) so that the domestic employment effect is 28 jobs.

He then calculates different scenarios, depending on the consumption pattern of victims and criminals. Suppose A$1 million is transferred from relatively poor victims, who reduce their consumption of clothing and footwear, and is laundered through real estate purchases. The loss of A$1 million regarding the demand for clothing and footwear will lead to a total loss of 2.877 million in output, 692,000 in lost wages and salaries and 34 jobs. Almost half of it would be from the clothing and footwear industry, the other half from the rest of the economy. On the other hand, the 1 million increase in demand for real estate will increase output by 2.611 million, 786,000 extra wages and 29 new jobs. The net effect is a loss of 266,000 in output, a gain of 94,000 in wages and a decrease of five jobs.

Not knowing exactly how criminals spend their money, Walker states that if A$1 million of laundered money is invested in dwellings, this has the following effects:
- A net loss of output from A$578,000 to A$1,675,000.
- A net loss of income from A$199,000 to A$1,019,000.
- Net imports will fall by A$46,000 to A$250,000.
- Net employment will fall by 7 to 42 jobs.

Walker's (1995) idea behind the multiplier model was that criminals and victims have different spending behaviour. In particular, he assumed that criminals spend and invest the money less productively. If our findings about Dutch criminals and Dutch households are right, then such a difference in spending behaviour is less likely.

Similar input output tables could be used for all countries in order to measure the effects of money laundering on output, income and employment. However, this model is designed for a closed and not for a small and open economy, like the Netherlands. Walker (1995) himself does not see a problem there. He claims that laundered money flowing into the Netherlands should be treated the same way as laundered money produced within the Netherlands. They would have the same output effect, whereas laundered money that leaves the Netherlands would produce its effects in the country where it is received. Even if one accepted this, one would still have to know in detail what the victim and the offender do with the money.

Walker discusses the effects of money laundering for Australia by using a model that assumes one big closed economy. But money laundering mainly refers to transferring illegal and laundered money all over the world. The big problem of the Dutch is not the illegal money generated and laundered in the Netherlands, but the money coming from illegal activities abroad, which flows partly through the Netherlands, and is partly invested in the Netherlands.

Furthermore, the input-output multipliers do not replace a model for economic effects. They only concentrate on the amounts of demand in other sectors that are generated by an original stimulus of demand in one sector. These amounts are 'technically' determined through the technical relations of the production function, which shows how much output can be maximally produced if one increases the input by one, but effects of changed behaviour are missing.

In order to measure macro-economic output and employment effects one would need to know about the effects of large amounts of extra money flowing into the Netherlands through laundering. However, as already mentioned under Changes in Imports, such a model is no longer available for countries within the Eurozone.

Most likely, the Dutch profit from money laundering. The large amount of money flowing through the country stimulates financial services, employs lawyers and financial experts. These are among the highest paid and, hence, highest productive jobs. If the money is reintegrated into the Dutch real estate or diamond sector, this again creates jobs. However, a lot of the money laundering just flows through the Netherlands, referring hence to the layering phase of money laundering which creates less real effects than at the reintegration phase.

Table 6.10   Input output multipliers, by sector of industry for Australia

Industry	Output	Income	Imports	Employment
A$1 million increase in demand for industry in Column 1 produces the indicated total changes in output, income, imports and jobs:	A$million	A$million	A$million	# jobs
01 Agriculture	2.178	0.38	0.094	28
02 Forestry, fishing, hunting	2.485	0.646	0.128	26
03 Mining	2.136	0.428	0.114	15
04 Meat and milk products	3.008	0.511	0.097	29
05 Food products nec	2.926	0.588	0.137	27
06 Beverages, tobacco prod.	2.629	0.495	0.132	22
07 Textiles	2.778	0.582	0.239	26
08 Clothing and footwear	2.749	0.692	0.282	34
09 Wood, wood products nec	2.877	0.704	0.202	34
10 Paper, printing etc	2.595	0.646	0.226	27
11 Chemicals	2.597	0.512	0.243	21
12 Petroleum and coal products	2.438	0.339	0.239	12
13 Non-metallic mineral prod.	2.63	0.564	0.145	22
14 Basic metals and products	2.642	0.463	0.154	16
15 Fabricated metal products	2.911	0.639	0.189	27
16 Transport equipment	2.554	0.552	0.265	22
17 Machinery etc nec	2.649	0.631	0.252	26
18 Miscell. manufacturing	2.641	0.601	0.239	26
19 Electricity, gas and water	2.386	0.459	0.78	17
20 Construction	2.694	0.632	0.158	27
21 Wholesale and retail	2.656	0.772	0.105	35
22 Repairs	2.549	0.759	0.165	33
23 Transport, communication	2.463	0.638	0.128	27
24 Finance, property, etc	2.611	0.786	0.094	30
25 Ownership of dwelling	1.558	0.14	0.032	5
26 Public admin., Defence	3.233	0.951	0.194	36
27 Community services	2.983	1.159	0.124	42
28 Recreational etc services	2.762	0.747	0.131	36

Source of data: Australian Bureau of Statistics, 1994, Australian National Accounts, Input-Output Multipliers 1989–90 (Cat. #5237.0).

6.8. LOWER REVENUES FOR THE PUBLIC SECTOR

Money laundering can have a detrimental effect on government revenues by decreasing government income from tax. Money laundered also represents income that evades taxes (Quirk 1996, p. 19 and Alldridge 2002, p. 315). Misreporting or underreporting income is one of the most common methods of conducting money laundering. Consequently, money laundering negatively affects tax collection efforts.

At the same time, an increase in predicate offences and money laundering demands public enforcement expenditure, which draws further on public revenues (McDonell 1998, p. 10). This will indirectly impact honest taxpayers by bringing about an increase in tax rates.

Yaniv (1999) developed a model demonstrating how money launderers respond to tax policies. The incentive to launder increases with lower tax rates and laxant money laundering regimes, according to him.

A point not mentioned in the literature is that money laundering can also increase the revenue of the public sector. Criminals want their money to be 'legal'. A way of doing this is to pay taxes on income. Non-existent high turnovers from restaurants with no clients are sometimes voluntarily declared to the tax authorities. This way, the illegal money is turned into taxed legal money.

It can occur that the public sector also profits from money laundering, if criminals deliberately pay taxes in order to make their income from criminal activities appear legal.

The Netherlands is one of the most popular countries for multinationals because of low taxes. As shown in chapter 3, the Dutch are classified by the American tax authorities IRS as one of the biggest tax havens in Europe.

Internal Revenue Service cannot prevent companies from artificially shifting their profits to tax haven countries like the Netherlands, Ireland, Bermuda and Luxembourg. Subsidiaries in these four countries were assigned 30 percent of the profit from US corporations (Sullivan 2004, p. 589).

Also, other organizations such as the OECD (2000[a]) on Harmful Tax Practices or the Primarolo Rapport by the European Union classify the Netherlands as an intense tax competitor.

The Dutch government announced in 2004 that it would cut the country's corporate tax rate to 31.5 percent in 2006 from 34.5 percent, with a further cut to 30 percent slated to take place by 2007. The Netherlands has 100 tax treaties in place (Belgium has 66, Denmark has 78 and the UK has 110). The greater a country's network of double taxation treaties, the greater its leverage to reduce withholding taxes on incoming dividends. An elaborate network of double taxation treaties is, thus, a key factor in the ability of a territory to develop as an attractive holding company jurisdiction (see Unger et al. 2006).

When a Dutch holding company comes within the 'participation exemption rules', all income received by the holding company from the subsidiary, whether by way of dividends or otherwise, is tax free. The criteria that have to be fulfilled in order to qualify for the participation exemption rule are e.g. the 5 percent rule: the Dutch holding company must hold at least 5 percent of the subsidiary's shares. This share is much lower than in many other countries and makes the Netherlands very attractive for holding companies and other investors (see http://www. lowtax.net/lowtax/html/offon/netherlands/nethold.html).

Though tax rates might be low, and many holding companies are tax free, the large volume of transactions will, nevertheless, create extra tax income, if only from employing additional Dutchmen in the financial sector.

The suspicion is that a lot of money laundering takes place through these big entities. The public sector does not loose income because the Netherlands is a transit country for money laundering and doesnot suffer from the negative effects of it. According to de Kam (2004) the Netherlands received €500 million in taxes as a result of being a tax haven.

6.9. CHANGES IN THE DEMAND FOR MONEY, EXCHANGE RATES AND INTEREST RATES

Money laundering also affects the money demand. The IMF found that a 10 percent increase in crime results in a 6 percent reduction in overall money demand (Quirk 1997, p. 3). A 10 percent increase in crime, will, furthermore, discourage the demand for this country's currency equally by 10 percent. Money laundering can, therefore, have a negative impact on the demand for money, on the exchange rate and on interest rates.

Quirk (1997) gets these results by running the following regression: $Mi = Mi$ (y, ep, id, Li). The demand for money Mi depends positively on income (y), negatively on the expected inflation (ep), the deposit interest rate (id) and on money laundering (Li). Proxies for ML are crime, fraud and drug offences. Separate proxy variables can be included for money laundering associated with crime (L1), with tax evasion (L2) and with unemployment and labour participation (L3).

In another study done by Tanzi (1997), the IMF estimated that US$5 billion per year was being taken out of the US in cash through the illegal drugs trade in 1984. This creates a potential instability for the world financial system because of the possibility that these dollars could be unloaded in exchange for foreign currency. In order to estimate these US$5 billion, Tanzi calculated the difference between the money printed and the money circulating in the US.

To calculate the money circulating within the countries of the Eurozone is more difficult, for cash in particular. Though Central Banks still publish the money supply per country (see e.g. De Nederlandsche Bank DNB, Statistisch Bulletin March 2005 which shows M3 including cash money to be about €500 billion in January 2005), it is impossible to distinguish the money demand per country. By definition, the Euro does not have to be exchanged at country boarders within the Eurozone. Therefore, one does not know how much of each country's money supply is circulating in which Eurozone country. The Tanzi model can, therefore, not be applied for estimating the effect of money launder- ing on a single EU country.

The effects of money laundering on the money demand are practically impossible to measure for the Dutch economy anymore, since monetary aggre- gates and their effects cannot be isolated for one of the Eurozone countries any longer. Furthermore, Dutch econometric models only reveal the effects of world or Euro interest rates but not of an increase in the money supply.

Chinn and Frankel (2005) give an overview of the present debate on the relationship between the world interest rate and the national interest rates. There is an ongoing debate in economics whether interest rates are almost entirely determined on global markets, due to high capital mobility and the integration of capital markets or whether national factors are still important. The first group is represented by Barro and Sala-i-Martin (1990), the second by Breedon and Williams (1999), to give an example. Many of these studies relate to the ques- tion of whether or not national public debt affects national interest rates. Chinn and Frankel (2005) do find a relation between the expectations regarding public debt and national interest rates (p. 23). Government bond markets are, therefore, not fully integrated.

Expectations might also play an important role with regard to criminal money. €18 billion of criminal money will not affect interest rates by much, per se, in the Euro area. However, if financial investors suddenly get suspicious with regard to the source of this money, this could have a strong effect on expecta- tions. The expectations regarding Dutch money – the perception of it – might change and then have a similar effect on national interest rates as had expecta- tions regarding public debt.

The recently published GEM-model by the IMF (Bayoumi 2004) takes into account international spill-overs. They find that within two years, real effects of the US interest rate on national economies will vanish.[6]

Traditionally, money laundering would bring about an increase in money demand but this trend has lately been inversed due to changes in money launder- ing methods from cash and the banking system to non-monetary instruments and bartering, according to Quirk (1997, p. 3). Needless to say, these shifts in money demand and capital flows from one country to another are unanticipated and not related to economic factors and to this extent they bring instability to the world economy. In other words, they:

could have internationally destabilizing effects because of the integrated nature of global financial markets. The destabilizing effects could arise because these capital movements would not be seen to reflect differences in economic fundamentals across countries. Thus, they send confusing signals to the world community' (Tanzi 1996, p. 8).

6.10. INCREASE IN THE VOLATILITY OF INTEREST RATES AND EXCHANGE RATES

Money laundering leads to volatility in exchange rates and interest rates due to unanticipated inflows and outflows of capital (Tanzi 1996, p. 8, McDonell 1998, p. 10, Camdessus 1998, p. 2, Financial Action Task Force 2002[a], p. 3 and Boorman and Ingves 2001, p. 9). As Tanzi points out, a large inflow of laundered money can result in the depreciation of the exchange rate and/or an expansion of the country's monetary base (Tanzi 1996, p. 8). An increase in exchange rates is associated with a reduction in exports and a heavier reliance on imports whereas an expansion of the monetary base would bring about an increase in prices (Tanzi 1996, p. 8). Additionally, as mentioned above, interest rates are also affected because launderers invest funds where their schemes are less likely to be detected rather than where lending rates are lower or rates of return are higher. Moreover, due to the unpredictable character of such choices impacting economic fundamentals, the soundness of economic policy is also affected (McDowell 2001).

6.11. GREATER AVAILABILITY OF CREDIT

If there is an infusion of criminal funds, this could lead to a greater availability of credit, even for legitimate businesses. As a result of money being laundered through banks, they will have more deposits, which will entail a greater availability of funds they could potentially loan. If this effect is large enough, it could conceivably make interest rates go down. This argument holds true for closed economies and for big countries that can still set prices and interest rates at the world market.

In a small open economy however, this argument does not hold, since interest rates are determined at the global market and with indefinite capital mobility, funds available are almost unlimited.

6.12. HIGHER CAPITAL IN- AND OUTFLOWS

Money launderers can channel funds towards financial institutions or countries in which the money can be most easily placed without too many questions asked. This can lead to capital flight from countries with sound economic policies and higher rates of return to countries with less efficient policies and lower rates of return (Tanzi, 1996, p. 6). Thus, as Tanzi points out, 'because of money laundering, the world capital tends to be invested less optimally that would be the case in the absence of money laundering activities'.

Money laundering could have a reverse impact on economic policies recommended by the IMF, aiming at fighting inflation by means of a reduction of the money supply. In such circumstances, a strong influx of illegally obtained hard currency in the economy can conceivably be beneficial for employment by serving to increase the country's foreign reserves, decreasing its foreign debt as well as alleviating some of the difficulties associated with policies aimed at reducing expenditure (Keh 1996[b], p. 4). The anti-inflation policy, however, will be ineffective.

Furthermore, 'drug money could be a potentially stabilizing force, as a source of capital without the strings of conditionality attached' (Keh 1996, p. 4). However, one should not be too quick in proclaiming the benefits derived from money laundering. There are *always* a multitude of costs attached. The problem inherent in a heavy infusion of illegal hard currency is that it escapes government control. As a result, 'spending behaviour becomes influenced not only by the official money supply but by the infusion of informal credits as well. In turn, the demand for money in the official banking system reflects only a part of domestic economic activity. Interest rates become less useful as a barometer of money demand.' (Keh 1996[b], p. 4).

6.13. DISTORTING ECONOMIC STATISTICS

Furthermore, money-laundering activities could bring about errors in macro-economic statistics, which can subsequently give rise to errors in policy making (Tanzi, 1997, p. 10). This happens primarily for two reasons. First, money launderers base their investment choices not on the usual economics considerations, but are instead primarily motivated by other factors such as avoiding detection, low penalties, etc. (Alldridge 2002, p. 306). Thus, capital movements associated with money laundering are often counter-intuitive from an economic point of view. As a result, policy makers could get confused and make erroneous policy judgments on the basis of these unusual capital movements. As Tanzi explains, 'policy makers of a country, that, in the face of high inflation, overvalued exchange rate, and a large fiscal deficit experienced capital inflow might be less inclined to change their current policies' (Tanzi 1997, p. 96).

Second, money laundering can skew economic data due to the difficulty of measuring the exact scope and implications of this phenomenon (Quirk, 1997, p. 4). When money laundering takes place on a significant scale, it is essential for the policymaker to take it into account. Failure to do so or, alternatively, an under- or overestimation of the exact scope of this activity can lead, once again, to mistaken policy decisions.

Some estimates exist regarding how much official statistics get distorted through the shadow economy (Schneider and Klingmair 2004). These include, for example, the overestimation of unemployment rates due to the fact that the unemployed receive unemployment benefits but nevertheless do illegal jobs. Or the works of Zdanovicz (1999), who shows how balance of payment statistics get deterred by the use of wrong export and import prices. For the distortion of statistics through money laundering, however, no such estimates exist.

The Dutch seem to attract quite a lot of foreign direct investment. In particular, the role of special purpose entities as described under techniques of money laundering has to be stressed here. According to the OECD (2000[a] and [b]) transactions that are done purely for reasons of tax evasion and other money laundering purposes can lead to inflated FDI statistics.

Among the numerous short-term effects listed in the literature, sectoral effects and effects of money laundering on export and imports seem particularly important. Laundering implies unfair competition, since the launderer does not have to realize the same profits as regular business.

NOTES

1. Wouter de Kruijf and Joras Ferwerda, to whom I am very grateful, did the literature research.
2. The term ip denotes that this is not an official page number used. It refers to the page number in case the document as found on the Internet (without page numbers) is printed out.
3. WVV is the proceeds estimated by the judge.
4. Centraal Bureau voor de Statistiek (2005[a]). *'Waarde onroerende zaken'*. Statline Database: www.cbs.nl. This is a provisional number. Taxations of real estate for real estate taxes (onroerend zaak belasting) were used as value per real estate object.
5. Centraal Bureau voor de Statistiek (2005[b]). *'Nominale waarde obligaties op Euronext Amsterdam'*. Statline Database: www.cbs.nl. Nominal value of all outstanding bonds of Dutch companies and the Dutch public sector quoted at Euronext Amsterdam.
6. I owe this point and the literature references on interest rate effects to Frank van Erp.

7. Long Term Effects of Money Laundering

Money laundering can have short term effects, which usually happen within one or two years, and it can have long term effects which usually take more than four years. Some of the effects listed below even might take more than ten years before they are likely to occur. In the literature one can find twelve long term effects of money laundering.

7.1. THREATENS PRIVATIZATION

Money laundering can have extensive detrimental effects to privatisation efforts. First, as discussed in Chapter 6 in the context of unfair competition, money launderers can outbid honest purchasers for formerly state-owned enterprises (McDowell 2001).

This will result in a large-scale criminal presence in the economy. Criminals are driven by other considerations than conventional business entrepreneurs and react to different stimuli. For example, 'the criminal proprietor will occasionally shift output and pricing patterns according to non-economic factors: like feeling a police crackdown or changing investment locations because of the passage of constraining legislation' (Keh 1996[b], p. 11). As a result, significant sectors of the economy could become insulated from market-oriented stimuli, which can further prolong the readjustment process of the newly privatised economy. Additionally, it will also bring about a speculative and anti-competitive approach to conducting business in these sectors' (Unger et al. 2006).

Furthermore, as a result of structural change, these economies become highly susceptible to informal and illegal lending arrangements conducted by money launderers. Such developments have been extensively documented in reforming economies, Russia being a notable example (Keh 1996, p. 15–19, Boyrie et al. 2005). As part of the process of economic reform and liberalization, governments liberalized prices. This brought about an increase in consumer and producer prices. Faced with a continued rise in producer prices and an associated decrease in consumer expenditure, firms lacked the ability to finance production or, alternatively, were swamped in accumulated inventories of unsold output and increasing debt. As a result, firms displayed a stringent need to resort to credit (Unger et al. 2006).

However, the need for more credit in reforming economies is difficult to fulfil. Banks have serious difficulties in meeting credit needs. Their portfolios are burdened by the extensive volume of debt of weak state enterprises and thus will tend to cut back on lending as well as increase lending rates (Keh 1996[b], p. 7). Unable to obtain much-needed credit from the formal lending system, firms struggling with liquidity problems will seek credit in the informal system. Criminals and money launderers do not face similar lending problems as domestic banks. Criminal lenders have a great availability of funds and are not burdened by high transaction costs (i.e. repayment delays) (Keh 1996[b], p. 7). Consequently, they have a competitive advantage over domestic banks. They can afford to provide slightly lower lending rates as well as more attractive deposit rates and, thus, even drive legitimate lending institutions out of the market. To summarize, informal lending arrangements provided by money launderers and other criminals can prolong the adjustment process of privatising economies. They impact the banking system and its reforming process in particular. With criminal lending alternatives in the economy, commercial banks remain a marginal source of credit (Keh 1996[b], p. 17).

The argument that criminals strategically buy up state enterprises when they become privatized does not seem to hold true for Australia and the Netherlands any more, since a large part of the Australian and Dutch economy is already privatised. In other countries, where trains, steel, construction, telecommunication, electricity and gas, postal services etc. are still state owned, this point might be of greater relevance.

7.2. CHANGES IN FOREIGN DIRECT INVESTMENT

The damaged integrity of the financial sector as a result of its association with money laundering and the entrenched presence of organized crime can have a negative impact on foreign direct investment. Once a country's commercial and financial systems are perceived as being under the influence of criminal elements, this may compromise the country's reputation and undermine foreign investor's trust. Thus, appearing on the black lists published by the FATF and OECD can have serious detrimental effects on foreign direct investment (Boorman and Ingves 2001, p. 9). At the same time however, if perceived as a lax regulatory environment and a tax haven, the respective country will increasingly attract capital of an illegal nature and can draw significant benefits from it, especially if the money is directly invested in the economy rather than simply being transited through the country (Boorman and Ingves 2001, p. 9 and Walker 1995, p. 34). Rawlings and Unger (2005) refer to the 'Seychelles-effect' in this respect; the Seychelles competed for criminal money by deliberately inviting criminal capital (see also under 7.5. reputation of the financial sector).

7.3. RISKS FOR THE FINANCIAL SECTOR, SOLVABILITY, LIQUIDITY

The effect of laundering on the financial sector is of additional concern. When conducted in large amounts, it impacts banking solvability or liquidity in particular, which leads to the compromising of bank soundness (McDowell 2001 and Alldridge 2002, p. 309). Launderers' economic behaviour and choices are less predictable than those of conventional investors. Consequently, financial institutions or groups of such institutions could make wrong policy choices concerning the proportion of assets that they need to keep liquid, and as a result, become unable to satisfy unexpected solvability requirements and/or even collapse (Alldridge 2002, p. 310). Given the integrated and interrelated nature of the financial system this could further create the risk of systemic crises and monetary instability (McDonell 1997, p. 10).

7.4. PROFITS FOR THE FINANCIAL SECTOR

The opposite argument could also hold true in certain circumstances. Banks, and investment funds might actually regard launderers as desirable customers. As long as they are ensured secrecy, launderers will not be very picky about the rates of return provided. In other words:

> they will not care whether or not the highest interest rates are available. They will be happy to receive a lower or even a negative rate. The bank need not make any risky investment with their money and it can conform easily to any liquidity requirements (Alldridge 2002, p. 310, Unger et al. 2006).

7.5. REPUTATION OF THE FINANCIAL SECTOR

A great majority of authors are concerned with the effects of money laundering on the reputation of the financial sector. Organized crime can infiltrate financial institutions (FATF 2002a). Money laundering impairs the development of the financial sector for two reasons: First, it erodes financial institutions themselves, as there is a direct correlation between money laundering and fraudulent activities undertaken by employees. Second, customer trust is fundamental to the growth of sound financial institutions (Bartlett 2002, Unger et al. 2006).

Once a financial institution becomes involved in money laundering operations and this is detected, it will lose credibility and customer confidence (Bartlett 2002). Due to the perceived risk of fraud and corruption associated with money laundering, economic agents will try to avoid such institutions and conduct their business elsewhere. This negative effect is not restricted solely to the particular institutions implicated. In smaller countries, the involvement in money-laundering operations of several of its financial institutions can result in the loss of reputation for the entire financial system (McDonell 1997, p. 9). Furthermore, money-laundering operations do not actually have to happen. Even the potential for such an involvement is sometimes sufficient to damage financial credibility. As an illustrative example, Rawlings and Unger (2005) cite the Seychelles, which in 1996 passed legislation affording immunity from prosecution to anyone placing at least US$10 million in certain investments. One of the incentives provided was complete immunity from prosecution in criminal proceedings and the protection of assets from forfeiture even if investments were earned as a result of crimes committed outside the Seychelles. An investor could deal in drugs or commit violent offences anywhere else in the world and then safely invest the proceeds in the Seychelles free from forfeiture or prosecution. All that the individual had to do was invest a minimum of US$10 million and the Seychelles government would grant immunity from prosecution. The effect was that Foreign Direct Investment was reduced rather than increased, because legal investors lost confidence in the country.

The aforementioned law was viewed upon by the international community as encouraging money laundering and brought about a warning to banks to deter the engagement of financial transactions with the Seychelles (McDonell 1997, p. 10). The Seychelles finally gave in to the FATF requirements and got off the blacklist (Rawlings and Unger 2005).

The international reputation of the Netherlands is that it is one of the most efficient financial centres and a tax haven (see Chapter 6 under Revenues of the Public Sector). Dangers to the reputation can occur when a country deliberately declares that it wants to attract criminal money, as the Seychelles did. To compete with lower taxes, as the Dutch do with regard to the corporation tax, still seems a different issue than to deliberately declare to compete for criminal money. A Seychelles effect is, therefore, not to be expected for the Netherlands. Though being confronted with harmful tax practices of its offshore centres and being criticized for lax anti money laundering policy by the FATF (2005), Australia also does not deliberately compete for criminal money.

7.6. ILLEGAL BUSINESS CONTAMINATES LEGAL BUSINESS

Illegal transactions can contaminate legal ones. According to Quirk (1997, p. 4), certain perfectly legal transactions involving foreign participants are reported to have become less appealing as a result of alleged association with money laundering. Quirk does not provide any evidence in support of his assertion, which was subsequently taken up as a given in the literature (FATF 2002a, p. 3 and Camdessus 1998). His contention seems, however, logical, given that association with money laundering or even just the possibility of such an association leads to erosion of other economic agents' confidence. On the other hand, it is also likely that such transactions and enterprises will become more appealing in launderer circles. By gaining a reputation of willingness to cooperate with launderers, they could potentially attract illegal capital (Alldridge 2002, p. 315, Unger et al. 2006), Corruption, as shown in section 7.7, is closely connected to this.

Fijnault et al. (1998) identified the most vulnerable economic sectors of the Dutch economy for the infiltration of crime to be transport, harbours, the automobile sector, slot machines, hotels, restaurants, night clubs and industries that are controlled by organized crime in other countries: the construction industry, the waste disposal industry, the garment industry, the insurance sector, the wildlife sector and the smuggling of nuclear material.

There are some infiltrations in the transport sector (for drug transport overseas, by air and by land). Criminal groups set up their own haulage companies to import and export drugs; they use the Dutch airport Schiphol and the port of Rotterdam.

By trying to control the hotel, restaurant, nightclub and pub sector, criminal groups not only control this sector but also use its infrastructure for other illegal activities such as selling drugs, laundering money and installing illegal slot machines (Fijnault etc 1998).

Crime can also contaminate legal professions. Money laundering needs lawyers. As Nelen and Lankhorst (2003, p. 45–53) point out, for lawyers the specific interest of a client is more important than the general interest of society. They have to find a balance between this partiality and the code of conduct, which says that entanglements of interests due to financial or personal relationships should be avoided. Lawyers can assist money launderers in the following way:

- create complex legal arrangements such as trusts
- buy or sell property
- perform financial transactions
- give financial and tax advice
- provide introductions to financial institutions
- receive cash and provide the client with cash
- pay money to third parties for transactions not connected with the lawyer's underlying retainer
- passing money through their own personal or business accounts
- assist criminals in laundering from prison
  (see Nelen and Lankhorst (2003, p. 47f)).

Another profession that can get contaminated by crime is that of providers of financial services, since money laundering necessitates their cooperation, as is the case with lawyers and notary publics (see under corruption and bribe).

Fijnaut et al. (1998) conclude that *no criminal groups have gained control* over legitimate sectors of the economy. Other studies such as Kleemans et al. (2002) and Stuurgroep 'Politie 2000', Stichting Maatschappij en Politie (1991), Fijnault et al. (1998) confirm this for the Netherlands. Lately, parts of the real estate sector have become suspect of being under the control of organized crime (see under short term effects, distortion of investment sector effects).

7.7. CORRUPTION AND BRIBERY

Money laundering promotes corruption and bribery not only in financial institutions but also in whole sectors of the economy. First, it affects the financial institutions through which criminal proceeds are being processed (Financial Action Task Forde 2002, p. 3, Bartlett 2002, p. 2 and Schroeder 2001). Laundering needs not only financial institutions but also lawyers and notary publics who cooperate (see Kleemans et al. 2000). These institutions and professions become vulnerable to corruption by launderers seeking to further infiltrate and gain a foothold in a particular market. Thus, 'the (respective) institution could be drawn into active complicity with criminals and become part of the criminal network itself' (Financial Action Task Forde 2002, p. 3). This starts a veritable snowball effect and, if successful, launderers will expand and corrupt professionals (i.e. lawyers, bankers, accountants) (Alldridge 2002, p. 308) and public officials responsible for financial market regulation.

> Money laundering activities can corrupt parts of the financial system and undermine governance of banks. Once bank managers have become corrupted by the sizable sums of money involved in laundering, non-market behaviour can be introduced into operating areas other than those directly related to money laundering, which creates risks for the safety and soundness of banks (Alldridge 2002, p. 308).

Therefore, the corrupting effect is not restricted to the financial sector. Once launderers have infiltrated a particular economy, they will further invest or bribe public officials in order to gain control of large sectors of the economy (Alldridge 2002, p. 308). Once established, they will drive out legitimate business competitors and introduce a parasitic, anti-competitive approach to business (Keh 1996[b], p. 11). Also 'the balances accumulated after laundering could be used to corner markets or even smaller economies to the extent that they remain controlled by large-scale organized crime interests' (Quirk 1997, p. 19). The growing economic and political influence of organized crime will affect not only the economy but also the society at large by eroding the social fabric and preying on collective ethical standards (FATF 2002a, p. 3).

Transparency International (2005) published a Corruption Perception Index, in which Australia and the Netherlands rank very low with regard to corruption. The Netherlands turned out to be amongst the six countries perceived the least corrupt within the European Union. Worldwide it takes rank 11 among the 102 countries rated. Two years earlier it even had rank 7 (Transparency International 2003). Australia has surpassed the Netherlands in 2005 and holds rank 9 in 2005 (11 in 2003) out of 102 countries rated. The rank numbers below refer to the ranking of the 102 countries investigated by Transparency International.

Table 7.1   *Corruption perception index for the European Union countries and selected other countries in 2005*

Country	Ranking	Country	Ranking	Country	Ranking
Iceland	1	Canada	14	Cyprus	37
Finland, New Zealand	2–3	Hong Kong	15	Hungary Italy	40–41
Denmark	4	Germany	16	Lithuania	44
Singapore	5	US	17	Czech Republic Slovakia Greece	47–50
Sweden	6	France	18	Latvia	51–55
Switzerland	7	Belgium Ireland	19–20	Poland	70–77
Norway	8	Spain	23		
Australia	9	Malta	25		
Austria	10	Portugal	26		
Netherlands United Kingdom	11–12	Estonia	27		
Luxembourg	13	Slovenia	31		

Source: Transparency International (2005).

Several police corruption reports showed that there is very little bribery in the Netherlands. Only 25 out of 1600 cases investigated by the Bureaux of Internal Affairs in 1999–2000 had some connection with bribery. Bribery at Schiphol is necessary for drug dealers, whereas ports need less of it (Kleemans et al. 2002, p. 323f). Several other studies, such as Nelen and Lankhorst (2003) (for an overview see Kleemans et al. 2002), also conclude that there is little corruption and bribery in the Netherlands.

7.8. NEGATIVE OR POSITIVE EFFECT ON GROWTH RATES

Money laundering has a significant negative impact on growth rates. Since in the context of this activity funds are redirected from sound to risky ventures, from productive to sterile investments and crime and corruption are facilitated, economic growth can suffer (Bartlett 2002, p. 1). When a particular venture or industry is no longer appealing to launderers, they simply tend to abandon it, causing the potential collapse of these sectors and serious damage to the respective economies (McDowell 2001). Moreover, through its damaging effect on financial institutions, which is crucial for economic growth, as well as through its distorting effect on the allocation of resources, laundering further dampens economic growth (Tanzi, 1997, p. 96). These assertions appear to be corroborated by the empirical study conducted by Quirk in 18 industrial countries for the period 1983–90, which found that reductions in annual growth rates were associated with increases in money laundering activities (Quirk 1997, p. 6).

However, money laundering can also have positive effects on growth. For example, if a country is a transfer country for criminal money flows, additional value added is created for financial services without the countries having to bear the costs of crime. Money is simply flowing through.

If money is transferred from the country with criminal activities to the laundering country, then the latter does not bear the negative effects of predicate crimes associated with money laundering. It benefits from crime abroad; it is a free rider on criminal activities. This is the case, in particular, for countries with less strict anti-money laundering regulations than neighbouring countries because less strict regulation can have a positive effect on the capacity to attract illegal capital. The reverse is true as well. The more strict the anti-money laundering regulations, the more the country will suffer from a negative externality effect, the inability to attract illegal capital (Bagella, Becchetti and Lo Cicero 2003).

For the purpose of the money-laundering project of Unger et al. (2006), Ferwerda and Bosma (2005) did an empirical research regarding the effect of money laundering on economic growth.

The only empirical research in this field so far was done by Quirk (1996) and was taken as a starting point. He based his estimations on the work of Barro (1991). The latter estimated whether initial GDP and human capital played a role in economic growth by using cross-section data from 98 countries for the period ranging from 1960–1985. For human capital, Barro (1991) used school enrolment rates at the secondary and primary level as proxies. Barro (1991) ran several regressions alternating these variables, adding or leaving out some new ones such as fertility rate, life expectancy, government expenditures, political instability, economic systems and market distortion. He showed that initial growth and human capital play an important role for growth in 98 countries, for the period extending from 1960–1985.

Quirk (1996) extended the model and replaced human capital with a proxy for money laundering, the level of crime. In his model, growth depends on private domestic capital, government consumption, education measured as student enrolment at the tertiary level, and on crime. Quirk (1996) found that the most significant difference in the regressions he ran emerged when he excluded government consumption. Instead of being positive and significant, the sign became negative. According to Quirk (1996), this implied that money laundering was closely and positively related to the level of government consumption. The more the government consumed, e.g. the higher the number of civil servants, the more money was laundered. Knowing this, Quirk (1996) estimated the effect of money laundering on economic growth by the following equation:

$$DGDP = C + \beta1(PI) + \beta2(TER) + \beta3(CRIM) + \varepsilon$$
$$DGDP = -1.94 + 1.06(PI) + 0.068(TER) + -0.015(CRIM) + \varepsilon$$

DGDP = Growth of GDP, 1983–1990
PI = Private gross domestic capital formation in constant prices
TER = Student enrolment at the tertiary level (in millions)
CRIM = Total number of offences contained in national statistics

From this equation, Quirk (1996) concluded:

> The elasticity at the means in the equation is an estimated 0.1 percentage point reduction in industrial country annual GDP growth rates for each 10 percent rise in money laundering associated with crime (Quirk, 1996, p. 20).

The problem with Quirk's results is that they are outdated and because of his elasticity approach cannot be applied to other countries. Money laundering has increased substantially since the 1980s. Furthermore, some improvements can still be made such as relating crime to the size of the population or per 1000 of population, in order to account for the country size.

Because money laundering worldwide is heavily concentrated in Europe and North America, the dataset used by Ferwerda and Bosma (2005) was restricted to Europe (EU-15)[1] and North America (US and Canada). The countries in these areas display the same economic structure and forms of development and have the best international comparable crime statistics. Taking these countries into account results in a similar number of countries as in the Quirk study (1996).[2] Several proxy variables have been selected for money laundering, and a pooled regression has been done. The pooled data set contains the 17 countries mentioned above and within a six-year period, from 1995 till 2000. This gives a total of 102 observations.

The growth of GDP was taken as an indicator for economic growth. The disadvantage of using GDP growth is that demographic trends show up in the variable. To solve this, TFP (total factor productivity)-growth can be used as a dependent variable.[3] The reason why they opted for GDP growth instead of TFP is that the latter also has its problems. Money laundering could, indeed, decrease the total factor productivity (TFP), but money laundering could also have an effect on e.g. the capital accumulation in a country. Because it is not exactly clear which part of the economy is affected by money laundering, Ferwerda and Bosma (2005) opted for GDP growth as the dependent variable. Another advantage of using GDP growth is that it facilitates the comparison with Quirk (1996).

Quirk (1996) used 5 control variables; GDP per capita, investment, government consumption and two human capital variables.[4] He ran several regressions, all with different control variables. The regression that he used to estimate the effect of money laundering on economic growth as described above, is a regression with two control variables; investment and third level education for the human capital variable. Ferwerda and Bosma (2005) used these two control variables plus the other control variables used by Quirk (1996), in case these would be significant. In order to avoid causality problems, the control variable used in the regressions was lagged by one year. This was done in order to account for the fact that investment and human capital accumulation in year t have only an effect on economic growth in the year after, t+1.

Quirk (1996) presented the result of his regression as elasticity for industrialized countries. It is not possible to transfer the conclusion of the countries in the regression to other countries, since this elasticity depends on the absolute size of the crime variable. Firstly, this variable is not scaled to the size of the country and secondly, the elasticity is not constant when the absolute number changes.[5]

The most important improvement done by Ferwerda and Bosma (2005) in Unger et al. (2006) was the inclusion of a greater variety of proxy variables for money laundering.

The following variables were used as a proxy for money laundering:
- The number of crimes (from crime statistics)
- Money laundering based on the percentages given by Walker (1999[a])
- Money laundering calculated with the attractiveness index of Walker (1999[a])
- Money laundering calculated with the attractiveness index of Unger et al. (2006)

Quirk (1996) used the crime statistics of Interpol, the International Crime Statistics. This source is not available for research purposes anymore. Therefore, they used the European Sourcebook of Crime and Criminal Justice Statistics

(WODC, 2003), and the data from the United Nations Office on Drugs and Crime (UNODC).[6,7]

In the datasets of UNODC and WODC, the number of times each crime was reported is only partly published. This means that for some countries the information on the number of times a specific crime is recorded was not available. This problem was solved in two ways:

- First, by filling in the missing data. For this they took the mean of the countries available. In Table 7.2 these percentages are marked with an *. This way of completing the data will be called 'original'.
- Second, by assuming that the relative amount of each crime (as a percentage of total recorded crimes) is constant over countries and over years. The share of each crime does not seem to change significantly over time. Between 1995 and 2000 for the EU-15 and North America the shares were quite stable.

Table 7.2   Types of crime reported, in percentages (in 1995)

Country	Drugs	Total fraud	Theft	Robbery	Burglary
Austria	2.4	2.6*	43.9	0.4	14.6*
Belgium	4.1	0.9	46.5	1.8	14.6*
Canada	2.3	2.6*	31.5	1.1	14.3
Denmark	0.1	2.0	52.3	0.4	19.8
Finland	1.8	3.9	20.4	0.4	19.3
France	2.2	2.6*	62.5	2.0	14.6*
Germany	2.4	2.6*	57.7	1.0	14.6*
Greece	0.9	2.6*	24.1	0.4	12.7
Ireland	3.8	2.8	50.7	2.6	30.3
Italy	1.7	2.6*	59.0	1.3	14.6*
The Netherlands	0.3	2.0	58.6	1.3	9.9
Norway	5.9	3.4	45.6	0.2	1.0
Portugal	2.0	2.4	22.0	4.4	15.5
Spain	1.3	2.6*	40.3	9.0	15.6
Sweden	2.5	4.3	29.3	0.5	12.4
United Kingdom	0.4	2.6*	72.4	1.3	14.6*
United States	5.7	1.7	30.7	2.2	9.9
Mean	**2.3**	**2.6**	**44.0**	**1.8**	**14.6**

* These percentages are filled in by using the corresponding mean of that crime.

Source: Ferwerda and Bosma (2005) in Unger et al. (2006)

But the shares *do* differ across countries. It is hard to tell what the reason for these differences is. Partly this can be due to the fact that countries differ in the way they define crime typologies and in the way they collect and present their statistics (WODC, 2003, p.19). The differences can also be partly due to the fact that the chance of being caught differs between countries.

If these factors explain the differences in relative amounts across countries, one can assume the percentages to be the same across countries. The mean of the known percentages of each crime in 1995 will count as the relative amount of each crime. These percentages are shown at the bottom of Table 7.2. This way of completing and harmonizing the dataset is called 'average'.

When these 'original' and 'average' percentages are multiplied with the relevant types of crime one gets the generated money for laundering.

The regressions show that the two control variables Quirk (1996) left out, GDP per capita and government consumption, are not significant. Therefore, they will also be excluded from our model. The control variables that are included by Quirk (1996), investment and human capital, also turned out to be significant.

This means that the regression that is finally estimated is the following:

$$GDPGR_t = C_t + \beta1(POPGR)t\text{-}1 + \beta2(I/y)_t\text{-}1 + \beta3(ML \text{ variables}) + \varepsilon_t$$
(regression 1-6 in Appendix 1)

C = Constant Term
GDPGR = Growth of GDP
POPGR = Population Growth
I/y = Investment Share of Income
ML = Money Laundering

If one takes a look at the separate effect of each control variable, one finds that the relation between population growth and economic growth is always positive with a beta between 280 and 350, indicating that one percent of population growth would increase the growth of GDP by 0.28–0.35 percent. This is an effect that has to be expected here, because if the population rises, the amount of human capital goes up. This then will lead to a higher steady state, which again will lead to higher economic growth.

The negative coefficient -0.2 of of the investment share is harder to interpret. This would mean that if the investment share of GDP increases, and thus the (government) consumption share of GDP decreases, the economic growth will decline. The negative effect of the investment share may be due to measurement problems, the short time period of only six years (business cycle effects) and the estimation method used. The high constant C may be a sort of trade off for the negative investment effect. If one uses a pooled OLS model, without taking country dummies into account, the growth rate will be estimated not as a result of a yearly change of the investment shares but in actuality as a result of a change in investment shares (since the computer treats all pooled observations equally, and is not told that one is dealing with one specific point in time or country).

The model presented here can in later steps definitely be refined and much richer results can be exploited from it by introducing country dummies and doing fixed effect pooled regressions. For this, one has to increase the time span in order to get more observations. This would allow one to say something about differences between countries and differences in one country over time.

The diverse proxies for money laundering with some control variables were included in a regression with real GDP growth as the dependent variable. The results of these regressions are that money laundering dampens economic growth. If money laundering increases from its initial level with US$1 billion, the economic growth will decrease by 0.03 to 0.06 percent points in the 17 countries explored. This confirms the results of the literature on the effects of money laundering, and the only empirical estimation regarding the effect of money laundering on economic growth available, by Quirk (1996).

When crime was included in the regressions as a proxy for money laundering (regression 7 in Appendix 1), this led to the result that if crime increases from its initial level by 1 percent, the economic growth will decrease by 0.12 percentage points. This is comparable with the 0.1 percentage points Quirk (1996) found in his regression.

The most interesting point is that one can theoretically[8] separate the effect of money laundering on economic growth from the effect of crime on economic growth (regression 8–13). All these regression results show that money laundering has a positive effect on growth. Money laundering increases growth rates between 0.06 percent and 0.14 percent, depending on the proxy for money laundering chosen (see Appendix 1, regression number 8–13). Three of the estimated money laundering coefficients are significant at the 5 percent level. However, while money laundering increases growth, this effect is counteracted by crime, which dampens growth. The coefficients of crime have a negative sign in all regressions. An increase in crime by one percent reduces growth by 0.26–0.48 percent. When one compares the results of regression 7 (crime alone) with the following ones, one can see that the crime coefficient increases when money laundering is introduced in the regressions 8–13 in Appendix 1. However, since money laundering and crime are not independent of one another, the interpretation of separate effects must be done carefully. Regressions 8–11 include money-laundering proxies that are calculated from the proceeds of crime; therefore they are definitely dependent on crime. In order to find a somehow independent indicator for money laundering, Ferwerda and Bosma (2005) took the attractiveness indicator (see Chapter 4) as a proxy in regression

12 and 13. As the significant results in regression 12 show, money laundering has a very small but positive effect of 0.06 percent points on growth, but crime dampens growth by 0.45 percent points. The overall effect of on the one hand a positive effect of money laundering on growth and on the other hand a negative effect of crime on growth, is negative, since the crime effect outweighs the money laundering effect. Therefore, one can conclude:

> Money laundering itself does not dampen economic growth, it is the crime that is intermingled with it that does (Ferwerda and Bosma 2005 in Unger et al. 2006).

The danger of money laundering for the economy is not that it directly affects macro-economic variables such as output, employment, or growth. The danger lies in the fact that money laundering increases crime. And it is crime that has negative effects on the economy. Crime reduces growth by -0.12 to -0.48 percent.

It is, therefore, very important to study the relationship between money laundering and crime (see under 7.12). If crime increases so will money laundering and this dampens growth.

7.9. UNDERMINES POLITICAL INSTITUTIONS

If a cartel of money launderers manages to gain a hold of significant parts of the economy, they could further attempt to increase their political control as well, as a means to furthering their goals and ensuring that the authorities do not introduce stricter anti-money laundering controls. These goals can be achieved through corruption, bribery or even tampering with national elections, which would affect the very core of the democratic process. As pointed out by Tanzi:

> these criminal elements may corrupt the political process of particular economies by financing candidates who may be more likely to let these elements have their way. When the money involved is so large and the pay off to the criminal elements so important, it seems realistic to expect that attempts will be made to install more friendly administrations' (Tanzi 1997, p. 99).

In the Netherlands, mafia-like organized crime as is the case in Italy or the US is not largely present. Criminal groups have not taken over specific sectors, regions or political institutions and do not act like 'alternative governments'. Criminal groups join in with the legal and financial sector. The Dutch expertise in *logistics* and the excellent location make the Netherlands a perfect place to use the existing legal nodes and networks for organized crime. The nature of organized crime in the Netherlands can be described as *'transit crime'*. The international exposure of the Netherlands in legal trade makes it attractive for international illegal trade also. Many forms of organized crime have to do with international smuggling activities – drugs, illegal immigrants, women for prostitution, arms, stolen vehicles, cigarettes – and other transnational illegal activities such as money laundering and fraud (Kleemans et al. 2002). The large number and variety of immigrants and ethnic groups facilitate the drug trade in particular. Family ties are important for international criminal associations. The sound Dutch infrastructure combined with the social links of Colombian cocaine, Turkish heroin and Moroccan hashish make the Netherlands an important transit country for drugs in Europe (Kleemans et al. 2002, p. 308). In addition, Dutchmen produce and trade synthetic drugs. The WODC has analysed 80 cases from the WODC monitor and found that the organisation of crime does not follow the 'mafia' hierarchic pyramid structure with the 'godfather' at the peak of the organisation, but rather a network with some individuals plus facilitators such as underground bankers, money exchangers, and forgers of documents reappearing as the main 'nodes' in the network again and again.

For Australia, similar findings have been made. The presence of diverse ethnic groups makes network forms of crime more likely than mafia-like structures. Though, lately, organized crime by Asian mafia groups is feared (see e.g. the November 2004 meeting of the Australian Institute of Criminology http://www.aic.gov.au/conferences/2004/).

Violence is associated mainly with *drug trafficking* where it is used for intimidation and establishing a violent reputation. With money laundering it is mostly absent. In the Netherlands, according to the Dutch Central Criminal Intelligence Service, the number of killings lies between 20 and 30 per year (1992–1998) and 75 percent of the victims are born outside the Netherlands. Specifically, their origins lie in Turkey (21 percent), Suriname and Netherlands Antilles (11 percent), Morocco (7 percent), China (7 percent) and other countries (21 percent). It is difficult to establish a clear link between these murders and organized crime since the reason for the killings often remains unclear.

The Netherlands is also more a transit country for *smuggling illegal immigrants* than a country of destination (because of extensive registration for housing, work and taxes). Smuggling rings and clients often share the same ethnic background. Many of the prime suspects of smuggling people are involved in forging documents as well (Kleemans et al. 2002, p. 213). Forged documents are also an important way to open a bank account for money laundering purposes.

Research regarding *trafficking of women for prostitution* also shows that about 75 percent of the women arrested were born abroad. Specifically, these women come from Yugoslavia (13 percent), Nigeria (8 percent), Turkey (7 percent), Bulgaria (4 percent), Morocco (5 percent), Albania (4 percent0, Czech Republic (3 percent) and Germany (3 percent), with 25 percent of them coming from other countries. The Netherlands seems to be a special distribution point for Albanians who buy and sell victims from Eastern Europe in Holland.

Trafficking in Arms   The total number of arms smuggled into the Netherlands is estimated at 9,000–18,000 per year, of which 2,000–4,000 are firearms; the rest are small arms. The latter originate from former Eastern Bloc countries. About 15–25 importers are involved in this activity; mostly they are also involved in other types of criminal activities (Spapens and Bruinsma, 2002). The profits that are made by trafficking arms are relatively modest compared to drugs. However, it enhances one's reputation in the criminal world. From interviews with prisoners it emerged that 'middlemen' earn about *€25–75 per weapon,* whereas large-scale traders make about *€225 per weapon.* Very often arms smuggling is combined with drug smuggling. Dutch criminals and former Yugoslavians mainly do the trade in arms (Kleemans et al. 2002, p. 317).

Trafficking in Stolen Vehicles   About 30,000–35,000 cars and lorries are stolen in the Netherlands every year. Approximately 5,000–7,000 cars and 200 lorries disappear permanently. Dutch groups work in teams of 5 sharing labour (stealing, changing license plates etc.), whereas foreign groups (from Russia, Latvia, the Ukraine and former Yugoslavia) are larger. The Dutch criminal groups steal about 10–15 cars per year for local and regional sale. Usually a legal car seller is part of the group for purposes of 'recycling ' the car back into the legitimate world. If 5 people steal 15 cars per year the amount of money seems too small to be interesting for money laundering.

Eastern European Crime   The Netherlands and the Dutch Antilles are very attractive for the Russian mafia, flight capital, cigarette smuggling (as a transit country for the UK), trafficking in women for prostitution, violence, the growing drug trafficking related to Eastern Europe and the rise of organized theft such as 'hit and run' robberies' (Kleemans et al. 2002, p. 319).

Lately, killings in the real estate sector are attributed to the Yugoslavian mafia, in the Netherlands. However, there does not seem any danger of undermining political institutions.

7.10. UNDERMINES FOREIGN POLICY GOALS

Money laundering heavily impacts developing countries, thus undermining US and European aid policies, as materialized in foreign aid, World Bank financing, IMF credits aimed at reducing poverty and promoting economic development. For example, the total of US, OECD and World Bank aid to developing and former communist countries is $50 billion a year, but $100 billion comes back from these countries to Western bank accounts (Baker 1999, p. 38–39).

In 2003, the Dutch spent $3,981 million or €3,524 on Foreign Aid (net ODA) all together. The Dutch are the most important donors of gross ODA (Official Development Aid) for Suriname: in 2003, US$21.8 million was sent to Suriname, a country with a GNP per capita of about US$2000 a year. Dutch foreign aid is generous and by far the highest, compared to the US$1.4 million coming from the EU and US$1 million from the US (OECD, World Bank, www.oecd. org/dataoecd/63/53/1868905.gif and DAC www.oecd.org/dac).

More than double the foreign aid goes to the Netherlands Antilles ($56 million) and to Aruba (US$52 million) (see Table 7.3).

But how much money flows back to the Netherlands in the form of money laundering? All three countries are susceptible to a large amount of money laundering.

Table 7.3   Dutch foreign aid and criminal money flows in million €

Country	Dutch foreign aid in millions of Euro and (US$)	Net flows of money from the balance of payments	Suspicious transactions from the country to the Netherlands	Money laundering inflows esti- mated in Unger et al. (2006 Chap- ter 2)	Net effect= foreign aid minus inflows back to the Netherlands
Netherlands Antilles	44 (56)	-6,436	42.8	2.8	at the edge
Suriname	16 (21.8)	+19	5.4	10.7	at the edge
Aruba	42 (52)	-104	-	-	

Source: OECD DAC databank, DNB bilateral balance of payment data.

Explanation: As net flows from the balance of payments the statistical difference was taken. Knowing that all errors and omissions are also included in this number, it is not very reliable. However, to give an indication of size and sign it seems sufficient here.

At first glance, there is no danger that capital flight of the Netherlands Antilles and Aruba undermines Dutch foreign aid policy. In fact, the opposite is true: far more than only foreign aid money flows from the Netherlands to the Netherlands Antilles in terms of official money flows. In total, €6 billion more is going out than coming in. However, the number of executed suspicious transactions from the Netherlands Antilles to the Netherlands amounts to about the same size as the Dutch foreign aid. This would mean that money laundering counterbalances the positive effect of foreign aid. The calculations of chapter 4 show, however, much less money laundering flowing from the Antilles to the Netherlands. But as I mentioned in chapter 4, the model might underestimate special ties between these two countries. However, the MOT data could also overestimate money laundering and indicate an overreporting of banks of suspicious transactions from the Netherlands Antilles.

For Aruba, the official data indicate an outflow and not an inflow to the Netherlands. Suriname, however, might indeed suffer from the fact that the amount flowing into this poor country (€16 million) is counterbalanced by the additional money that flows back into the Netherlands of €19 million. However, both the suspicious transactions of the MOT data and the money laundering inflows to the Netherlands from Suriname do not exceed Dutch foreign aid. As a rough first estimate one can say that the undermining of foreign (aid) policy is not yet to be feared for the Netherlands. However, the positive effect of foreign aid definitely gets dampened by money flowing back to the Netherlands for laundering purposes.

7.11. MONEY LAUNDERING INCREASES CRIME

Money laundering can be regarded as a multiplier of criminal activities, giving economic power to criminals. As such, it makes crime worthwhile by permitting offenders to make use of the proceeds of their crimes (i.e. criminal proceeds are less valuable to the criminal than laundered funds) and hence can further encourage criminal behaviour (Mackrell 1997). Additionally, 'there is the contamination bred by contempt for the law, because one aspect of the law is broken, other financial infringements seem easier to make' (Quirk 1997, p. 19).

Money laundering can also facilitate crime because it provides criminal organizations with apparently legitimate funds, which they can use to subsidize, diversify and expand themselves (Levi 2002, p. 183). That is to say, 'money laundering is inextricably linked to the underlying criminal activity that generates it. Laundering enables criminal activity to continue' (FATF 2002a, p. 3).

It is important to clarify, however, that this does not hold true for tax havens and countries with lax anti-money laundering regulations that purposefully try to attract criminal funds. In such countries, there is a negative relationship between crime and money laundering; the negative effects of crime are primarily suffered abroad (Masciandaro 2004, p. 135–163). This becomes salient from a cost-benefit analysis. A policymaker will choose to pursue lax anti-money laundering regulations only if the expected national benefits outweigh the expected national costs. If money laundering were associated with a sudden increase in predicate offences, the costs of regulations that favour money laundering would become too high, and the policymaker would choose not to pursue them because they would lead to public dissatisfaction (Masciandaro 2004, p. 135–163). Hence, 'some countries which do not bear the costs associated with money laundering become predisposed to adopting lax regulations that facilitate money laundering. The other side of the coin is that both criminal and terrorist organizations and those who bear the costs stemming from money laundering will 'naturally' tend to be situated in countries other than the one where the regulations are adopted' (Masciandaro 2004, p. 137).

Masciandaro (1999) assumes that money laundering triggers financial flows, which lead to more investment in illegal activities in the country. There is, through this, a spill-over mechanism from criminal money to crime. Because of the possibility of money laundering in the financial sector, expanding illegal activities in the real sector will be the consequence.

7.11.1. The Model of Masciandaro (1999)

Masciandaro wants to analyse the effects of anti-money laundering policy. He analyses the existing interactions between the criminal economy and financial markets. He wants to provide a theoretical analysis of the mechanisms ruling the growth of the illegal activity as well as its ties with the development of a criminal economy.

1. He defines money laundering as a multiplier of criminal financial activities. This 'polluting' element increases
    a) the lower the aggregate transaction costs of doing money laundering
    b) the larger the share of reinvestment in illegal activities
    c) the more the pressure to finance reinvestment with clean money
    d) the bigger the difference between expected real returns between illegal and legal activities
    e) the larger the initial volume of illegal revenues that has to be laundered.

2. The legislator faces two (conflicting) goals. He wants to fight money laundering because of its negative economic, social and political effects; but he also does not want to burden and impose costs on the banking and financial systems with too strict anti-money laundering rules.

3. He assumes a closed economy, though no issue of money laundering would lose its significance if one introduces heterogeneous regulations in an increasingly integrated financial market.

4. He shows that money laundering can be seen as a multiplier of criminal activities that transform their illegal potential purchasing power into legal effective purchasing power.

5. Each laundering operation involves transaction costs for the criminal of CR. These transaction costs are a fixed proportion c of the amount of illegal funds that need to be laundered. Laundered money is a fixed proportion y of the initial amount of liquidity from criminal activity (ACI).

$$CR = c \ (yACI)$$

6. The laundered liquidity is what is left from the criminal money after laundering.

$$(1\text{-}c)yACI$$

7. Criminals can now decide how much of the laundered money they want to spend, save and reinvest either on legal or illegal markets. A fixed share q of laundered money is reinvested in illegal activities. This share q(r) is a function of r, the difference between the expected returns in the illegal economy ri and in the legal economy rl.

8. The new amount of money to be laundered includes also the revenue from the illegal reinvestment operations and is

$$q \ (1\text{+}ri) \ (1\text{-}c)yACI.$$

9. Critical assumption: both legal and illegal activities must be financed (at least in part) by clean money.

10. If the proportions stay constant over time, then an infinite series of money laundering can be described by a multiplier that shows by how much an original amount of liquidity from criminal activity ACI increases the total amount of illegal financial flows AFI over time.

    Total amount of money laundered AFI = (y/(1-q(1-c)(1+ri)) ACI = multiplier times original crime money ACI

11. If the supply of anti-money laundering regulation was costless, the policy maker's best decision would be to increase the costs of money laundering as much as possible so that c=1. But anti-money laundering has also costs, namely those to the banking sector and the entire economy. There is a trade-off between the effectiveness of anti-money laundering regulation, which increases the integrity of the financial sector and the efficiency of the banking sector (because of costs of regulations that make banking more

cumbersome). The politician has to find the optimal level of regulation under these constraints.

The model allows predictions about the medium term relationship between the volume of money laundering and the growth of illegal markets. The key idea of the model is that financial activities include both legal and illegal transactions. Due to the presence of money laundering, financial flows are likely to be larger. In countries with a lot of organized crime, financial flows should therefore be larger than in comparable countries with less crime.

Masciandaro (1999) does, unfortunately, not apply this model to Italy. After having explained the multiplier model, he suddenly switches to doing a cross-section analysis of the ties between bank deposits, the legal economy and illegal markets, instead of calculating the multiplier for Italy. He claims that bank deposits represent an outstanding feature of the Italian financial system.

The legal economy he measures with per capita GNP and for the illegal economy he uses per capita number of crimes. He does several correlations and regressions.

He finds a significant impact of the illegal economy and an increasing relationship between the growth of illegal activities and the involvement of banks in the money laundering business. Furthermore, he finds that the higher the diffusion of money laundering activities, the less effective anti-money laundering regulations are. Finally, there are also possibilities to measure corruption. See Bardhan (1997) and Lambsdorff (1999) for an overview.

In Unger et al. (2006) I estimated the Masciandaro model for the Netherlands. Here I compare several multipliers. From chapter 4 I conclude that the findings for the Netherlands also hold for Australia. Masciandaro (1999) assumes that money laundering triggers financial flows, which lead to more investment in illegal activities in the country. There is, therefore, a spill-over mechanism from criminal money to crime. Because of the possibility of money laundering in the financial sector, reinvestment of the money in illegal activities in the real sector will be the consequence.

As is shown in Figure 7.1 below, there is an original amount of liquidity from crime ACI. One can interpret ACI as stock and as flow. Masciandaro himself seems to have a flow in mind when he talks about the liquidity from crime. One can interpret this as the proceeds from crime. But one can also interpret ACI as the stock of criminal money. A fixed proportion y of this illegal money has to be laundered, since even criminal activities need some legal money. A part c of the criminal money gets lost in the verge of the money-laundering process. These costs c include both legal regulations (which increase c for the launderer) and costs for the individual criminal who tries to bribe somebody, has to buy a false passport, has to find somebody to bring the money over the border and loses some money while whitewashing it in the casino etc. The laundered money can be reinvested in either legal or illegal activities. A fixed share (q) of it goes back into the illegal sector and bears an interest of ri, (1-q) gets reinvested in the legal sector and has an interest rate rl. If the decision of how much money is put into the illegal sector (q) depends on the difference of the interest rate between the illegal and the legal sector ri-rl, then this interest difference must stay constant over time (otherwise the multiplier would not work the way Masciandaro designs it).

The last part of the Masciandaro graph is not convincing. Why should the return from money reinvested into illegal activities also not be split between criminal and legal activities but be entirely laundered? It seems more consistent to assume that only a share y of the return from reinvestment into illegal activities q (1-c) (1-ri)y ACI is laundered at cost c whereas the rest (1-y) q (1-c) (1-ri)y ACI is put on the illegal market.

The original multiplier of Masciandaro was:

$$\text{Total amount of money laundered AFI} = y/(1- (q(1-c)(1+r_i))) \text{ ACI}$$

Multiplier times original crime money

When the reinvested money is again split into y share for the illegal market and (1-y) for the legal, the new modified multiplier becomes:

$$\text{AFI} = y/ (1- (y\ q\ (1-c)\ (1+r_i)))\ \text{ACI}$$

Assumptions:
y = fixed proportion of crime money that needs to be laundered
c = fixed proportion of transaction costs of laundering
q = fixed share of laundered money reinvested in illegal activities (depends on difference between r_l and r_i)
r_l = return in legal economy
r_i = return in illegal economy

Note that 1> y, q, c > 0 since they are shares by definition. But the interest rate ri has basically no 'natural' restriction. However, it is limited by the model constraints. An indefinite series $x + x^2 + x^3 + \ldots x^n$ with $n \to \infty$ can be approximated with limes $n \to \infty$ $1/ (1-x)$ as long as $0 < x < 1$.

If this condition is applied to our problem, this guarantees that the multiplier is positive and that the model does not explode. For the original multiplier of Masciandaro (1999) this means that q (1-c) (1+ri) < 1. (For example, if q is 0.9 and c=0.1 then the maximal value the interest rate on criminal activities ri can have so that the model does not explode is 23 percent. With higher ri the nominator would become negative.

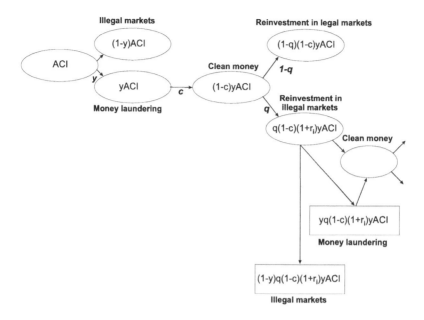

Figure 7.1   The model of Masciandaro (1999) modified

Raffaella Barone (2006) interpreted the model slightly differently. She claims that the numerator in Masciandaro's (1999) and my model should be y(1-c). So my multiplier should be:

$$AFI = y(1-c)/[1- yq(1-c)(1+r_i)]ACI$$

Masciandaro and I had looked at yACI, the criminal proceeds which are planned to put into the laundering process. We chose an input oriented approach. Barone opts for an output oriented approach. She looks at the money which has been already laundered (1-c)yACI and is then reinvested. Barone (2000) modified the model of Masciandaro (1999). She corrects the model by allowing for the (more realistic) fact that criminals will not reinvest their laundered money in the illegal sector again. They would rather keep the criminal money for paying criminal activities and use the laundered money for other needs. She does so by assuming that criminal money can also be consumed. This certainly adds to the debate, since criminals also like to spend the money on luxury goods and use it for regular life, but the multiplier then becomes more cumbersome.

The model is hence relatively robust within a range of 'normal' numbers, but once criminal returns get exorbitantly high it would not hold anymore.

Note also that the modified multiplier is smaller than Masciandaro's and it might be for reasons of realistic results that he opted for the larger one. (See below under operationalisation that for the assumptions of y=0.7, c=0.5, q=0.2 and ri=0.5 Masciandaro's multiplier is 1.11 while ours is 0.9). My multiplier can easily get smaller than 1 which would mean that money laundering leads to less and not more money laundering activities.

7.11.2. Possible operationalization of the variables

y... The fixed proportion of crime money that needs to be laundered is 70 percent (from CBS 2004) and 80 percent (from Walker 1995). The actual percentage will depend on the type of crime: a large percentage of crime money from drugs and fraud is being laundered, whereas other types of crime like theft, burglary, robbery etc. lead to proceeds of which only about 10 percent are being laundered. However, since drugs and fraud are the largest components of crime that are relevant for money laundering, we will assume y in the range of 0.70–0.80. The way in which we will present the multiplier allows us, nevertheless, to look at other possible proportions to be laundered also.

c... transaction costs of laundering. Which percentage of money is lost through the laundering process? It depends, amongst others things, on anti money laundering policy. If money is laundered through the casino, the expected return is 46 percent (except if you play red and black only, then it is definitely higher, almost 100 percent, except for the zero, but this might be too conspicuous). If you only have to declare the gains, which are then whitewashed, and forget about the losses, playing in the casino seems the best strategy. But this strategy is not good for very large amounts. You get videotaped; the casino does not hand out larger amounts in cash, reports suspicious transactions to the authorities etc. But laundering in the casino means that the expected return, c, is 46 percent. Another argument we found is that money laundering means that the criminal does want to pay taxes. There should, therefore, be at least the loss of the corporate tax of 34 percent (in the Netherlands) plus some fees for the bank or the (Dutch) income tax rate of maximum 52 percent.

Altogether, this means that it seems quite reasonable to assume c = 0.5. Half of the criminal money is lost when it is laundered, either through casino losses or through taxes. When you take the criminal money over the border and then place it into a bank account, the transaction costs c might be substantially lower and the share of money successfully laundered (1-c) might be much higher (1-c = 0.9).

q... laundered money reinvested in illegal economy. This variable is difficult to evaluate. Experts of the DNB think that there is a high incentive to make money dirty again because of the high profits in the criminal sector. There will be less of an incentive, though, to reinvest clean money into dirty business than the other way around, except for terrorism financing or if return differences are very high. But even with high returns on criminal activities, it still seems more likely that some of the illegal money will be hoarded for further illegal business purposes rather than running through the risky laundering process and then reinvesting the clean money illegally again. Following Masciandaro, however, one always needs some clean money to do illegal business. In the following we assumed that 20–50 percent of the laundered money is made dirty again, q=0.2, q=0.5.

ri... the average return of illegal business is also difficult to estimate. For drugs, the sales value of 1 kg of heroine can exceed the costs of production by 600 percent. But for cocaine the difference between wholesale and retail price or the value added is about 100 percent. For example, one gram of 100 percent pure cocaine retailed for $4.30 in Colombia is ultimately sold for between $59 and $297 in the United States. The gross profit margin, or value added, is therefore between 93 percent and 98.5 percent of the retail value (see UNDP 1996, p. 3). For other sorts of crime much lower rates of return might apply. We assume r to be between 50 percent and 100 percent.

The following graphs display the multiplier for different assumptions regarding the variables mentioned above. Read the graphs (Figure 7.2–7.5) as follows: along one line (for example changes in q, top line in the Figure 7.2) one can read how big the multiplier is if q changes, as long as the other three variables stay at their level (in the first graph y=0.7, c=0.5 and ri=0.5). If q=0.2, the multiplier is about 0.78. If – given the three other variables do not change – q increases to 0.95, the multiplier is 1.39. If q=0.75, the multiplier is 1.15 and if q=0.5 the multiplier is 0.95. Along the upwards sloping, top line the change of the multiplier can be seen for all values of q. In the same way one can look at the downwards sloping, line for c, the share of money lost with laundering. If the other three variables stay at y=0.7, ri=0.5 and q=0.2 the multiplier is 0.87 if only 5 percent of money is lost through laundering, it is 0.78 if 50 percent is lost and it is 0.70 if 95 percent of money is lost through laundering. In the same way variations in y and ri can be analysed.

The second graph, Figure 7.3, is plotted for Masciandaro's multiplier with the same basic assumptions. His multiplier is larger since the denominator is slightly smaller (it does not include the y for splitting interest receipts from laundering into legal and illegal money).

In Figure 7.4. illegal returns ri=100 percent, i.e. are double as high as in Figure 7.2. One can see that the multiplier slightly increases in that case. In the fourth graph, Figure 7.5, the interest rate r=100 percent for the Masciandaro multiplier.

The stability condition for the multiplier model is that the lower part of the fraction, the denominator, cannot get zero. If the interest rates gets high, say 600 percent, and y=0.7 and c=0.5, then the model would explode if q=0.85 or more.

This problem applies in particular to the interest rate, which is not necessarily smaller than 1, whereas all the other variables are between 0 and 1 by definition.

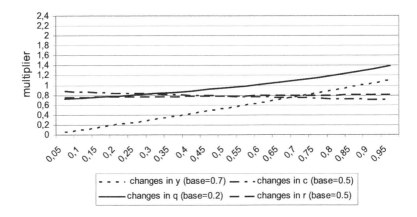

Figure 7.2   The Unger crime multiplier with an interest rate of 50 %

This means that criminal money will attract more crime because financial returns of it will partly be reinvested in additional criminal activities.

The Masciandaro (1999) model is a closed economy model. Money that is being laundered will be reinvested in the closed economy. In an open economy, as long as the reinvestment in illegal activities happens abroad, the country that accepts money laundering will not suffer. But it seems more likely that opportunities to launder will eventually also attract criminals.

Countries that have hardly any regulations against money laundering are, in principle, free riding on those countries that suffer from high crime. They accept the returns from crime as investments, but this goes either at the cost of other countries or – and this seems more likely – will backfire eventually.

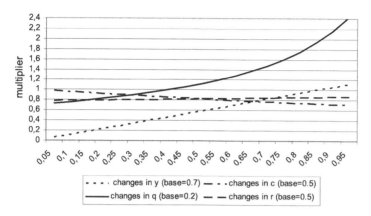

Figure 7.3 *The Masciandaro crime multiplier with an interest rate of 50 %*

My multiplier lies between 0.9 and 2 in most cases and under more likely assumptions it is about 1.06–1.1. The Masciandaro multiplier lies between 1 and 3 in most cases and under more likely assumptions it is about 1.1–1.25. This means that proceeds from crime will increase through money laundering by about 6 percent to 10 percent (Unger) or by about 10 percent to 25 percent (Masciandaro) of the original amount. Money laundering triggers an additional 6 percent–25 percent of more laundering through an increase in illegal activities.

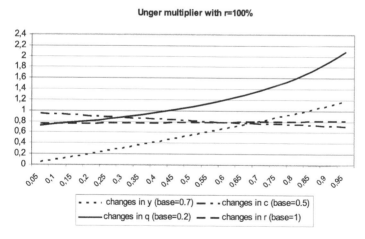

Figure 7.4 *The Unger crime multiplier with an illegal interest rate of 100 %*

Masciandaro multiplier with r=100%

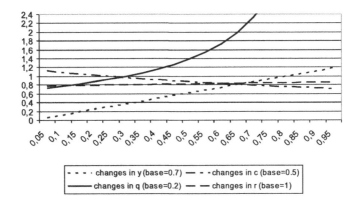

Figure 7.5   The Masciandaro multiplier with an interest rate of 100%

7.12.   INCREASES TERRORISM

According to a 1999 FBI report, there were over 14,000 international terrorist attacks between 1968 and 1999. Terrorism today has much more of an international impact because of markets' interconnectedness and of the advanced technological capabilities of terrorists (Jerry, 2002). Money laundering can contribute to an increase in terrorism in two ways. First, laundered money can be used to fund terrorist activities. A typical example is the financing of terrorism with the proceeds from the production and marketing of narcotics (Masciandaro and Filotto, 2001). Most experts agree that the sale and trade of drugs seem to be a sizable financial contributor to terrorist organizations. According to Schneider and Klingmair (2004), the origin of terrorist wealth can be broken into the following sources of financing: drug business (mainly transporting) 30–35 percent, donations or tribute payments of governments 20–30 percent, classic criminal activities (blackmail and in particular kidnapping) 10–15 percent, unknown 30–35 percent. The Taliban, for example, profited from the trafficking of opium and taxing the drug trade in areas under its control and these funds were subsequently used to support terrorist organizations like al-Qaeda. Also, profits generated from the sale of opium and heroin have been used to buy weapons and to finance the training and support of terrorists around the world (Hedges, 2001). Usually, the drug money used for financing terrorism will first be 'laundered'. This serves two purposes: concealing the illegal origin of the money as well as the illegal destination of the funds. In other words:

in those specific situations, at least on the logical level, the importance of transaction costs is at least doubled, since the need to lower the probability of incrimination concerns both the crimes that generated the financial flows and the crimes for which they are intended (Masciandaro, 2004[a], p. 131).

However, it should be made clear that very often terrorism is financed not only with illegally derived funds but also with clean money, which was never connected to a criminal activity. Supporters, friendly governments and also unsuspecting benefactors provide these clean funds. It is often the case that well-off individuals make donations to organizations that they believe to be real Islamic charities but which later on turn out to be a cover for supporting terrorism. The financing of terrorism with clean money involves a process completely different from money laundering: money dirtying (i.e. reverse money laundering). In that case, the funds are not derived from criminal activity and need to be laundered in order to 'separate' them from the original crime, but on the contrary, the money is clean and needs to be separated from its original source because it will be used for a criminal purpose (i.e. terrorism). This brings us to the second connection between money laundering and terrorism. Even if terrorism is financed with clean funds and one would be tempted to dismiss any connection between the two, such a conclusion would be erroneous. In this situation there is, just in the case of money laundering, an incentive for concealment, a need to separate financial flows from their source and destination in order to avoid the crime of terrorism being discovered (Masciandaro, 2004[a], p. 131). 'Money dirtying can also perform an illegal monetary function, responding to the demand for covertness expressed by individuals or groups proposing to commit crimes of terrorism' (Masciandaro, 2004[a], p. 131).

Thus, in their efforts to avoid detection, terrorists will exploit the same weaknesses in the international financial system as launderers and will tend to use the same channels. Banks with strict secrecy regimes, nations with sovereignty concerns, elected public officials citing freedom from government controls and financial control, intentionally or unintentionally created safe havens for the transfer and hiding of profits of organized crime and terrorism all represent avenues that are and will increasingly be used not only by launderers but also terrorists. The FATF finds that terrorists use the same money laundering methods as other criminal groups, which include cash smuggling, structure deposits and withdrawals from bank accounts, purchases of various type of monetary instruments, use of debit or credit cards, and informal financial networks. Thus, it can be said that although money laundering and terrorism are two distinct phenomena, they do share many of the same characteristics including sources, techniques, adaptability, and risks. Schneider and Klingmair (2004) identifies some of the methods of terrorist financing and its concealment as follows: *Starburst*: a deposit of dirty money made in a bank with standing instructions to wire it in small random fragments to hundreds of other bank accounts around the world (both on shore and off-shore financial centres). *Boomerang*: money sent in a long arc around the world before returning to its country of origin. On the journey, the money travels through what money launderers refer to as 'black holes' (countries that lack the means or inclination to investigate banks). *Legal money*: may come from a wealthy individual, religious charity or donation from a country. The money may use the underground banking system. *Tax optimization experts*: people who construct shell companies and other structures to hide wealth or dirty money and introduce clients to banks as new customers. Evidently, some of these strategies (i.e. starburst, boomerang and tax optimization) are methods used by launderers as well, showing a further indication of the connection between the two phenomena.

In recent years, terrorists have become very adaptable in their methods, being able to switch from traditional methods of disguising and transferring wealth to complex financial movements. There is evidence that terrorist financing networks operate globally and have the capability of infiltrating the financial systems in developed and developing countries and to exploit existing loopholes. The 'weak links' in the international financial system and its regulation, which were traditionally used by launderers, are already avenues for concealment of terrorist financing. Offshore banking centres have been considered a haven for terrorists to store large sums of money given that these centres are usually characterized by lax banking regulations and poor financial oversight (Baldwin, 2002). The situation is rendered even more worrisome, given that these banks have correspondent relationships with some of the world's biggest financial institutions. International correspondent relations exist so that banks can provide a wide range of alternate services to the their clients in areas where they do not have branches. At the same time, as a result of the creation of these self-regulating banking relationships, terrorism-intended funds can easily be transferred from offshore lax jurisdictions to some of the largest Western banks. As Johnson (2001, 131) states 'correspondent banking arrangements allow the transfer of both illegally and legally derived money from the unregulated to the regulated financial institutions (...) through the back door of the regulated institutions'. Thus, formal financial institutions become vulnerable to unknowingly facilitating money laundering and terrorist financing. It is thought that al-Qaeda moved money through poorly regulated financial centres until it was disguised sufficiently enough to move it to safer, large and reputable institutions. Nawaz et al. (2002) point out that

> investigations conducted into the financial dealings of al-Qaeda have disclosed that the terrorist network was able to use the 'correspondent network' of the Sudanese-based bank al-Shamal for cross-border transactions. These cross-border dealings have included France's Credit Lyonnais, Germany's Commerzbank, Standard Bank of South Africa and Saudi Hollandi Bank in Jeddah in which ABN AMRO of the Netherlands has a 40 percent stake. Other known al-Qaeda dealings with correspon-

dent banks have involved the movement of funds from the al-Shamal Bank through the Bank of New York to a Bank of America account in Texas.

Consequently, laxity in the fight against money laundering can lead to the further establishment of such channels (Masciandaro and Portolano 2004).

Since launderers and terrorist financers use many of the same avenues for moving and hiding money and represent similar threats to the financial system (Thony 2002), strategies put in place to fight money laundering can also be applied to fighting terrorist financing. In this context, the international response to terrorism and money laundering has been very important. In 1999, ten years after the Financial Action Task Force (FATF) developed its 40 Recommendations setting out measures national governments should take to implement effective anti-money laundering programmes, the General Assembly of the United Nations adopted the International Convention for the Suppression of the Financing of Terrorism. Initially, few countries ratified the convention, but after September 11, 2001, a large number of states committed to the convention. At the end of 2001, the FATF also expanded beyond money laundering to terrorist financing. It initially called on countries to adopt its *Special Eight Recommendations*, which were later expanded to Nine Recommendations in October 2004. Also in 2001, the UN Security Council adopted Resolution 1373 that encourages states to prevent and suppress the financing of terrorist acts, to criminalize terrorist financing and to freeze terrorist assets.

Moreover, several important regional and international bodies and organizations began supporting and contributing to international efforts against terrorist financing (i.e. FATF-style regional bodies, the Egmont group of Financial Intelligence Units, the IMF, and World Bank). This global push helped to include larger numbers of countries in the fight against terrorist financing and to develop a consistent and integrated approach against money laundering and terrorism financing (CFT). Given the transnational character of both terrorism and money laundering, such a global approach to the issue is indispensable. As observed above, strong anti-money laundering regulations undertaken in only some jurisdictions will not protect them from the combined threat of money laundering and terrorism. As long as the international financial system as a whole remains vulnerable and as long as other jurisdictions continue to adopt a lax approach to these matters, loopholes remain in the system through which both clean and dirty funds can be channelled. Once into the system, these funds can be used, among other things, for terrorist financing which will negatively affect jurisdictions regardless of them having strict financial regulations put in place. This is due to the fact that terrorist financing will then be channelled through the backdoor of regulated institutions (i.e. correspondent banks from jurisdictions with lax regulation). In light of this, the fight against money laundering and terrorist financing has to be taken up in a global, integrated fashion.

The empirical study of Blomberg, Hess and Orphanisdes (2004) uses panel data for 177 countries from 1968–2000. These data are taken from the Penn World Table, the ITERATE data set for terrorist events and data sets of external and internal conflict. By means of a cross-sectional and panel growth regression analysis and using a structural VAR model, they estimate the following equations:

$$\Delta yi = \beta o + \beta 1\ D1 + \beta 2\ D2i + \beta 3 \ln y0 + \beta 4\ I/Yi + \beta 5\ T + \beta 6\ I + \beta 7\ Ei + \varepsilon i$$

Country i's average per capita growth Δ yi depends on the log of initial GDP y0, Investment ratio I/Yi, Terrorism T, Internal Conflict I, external Conflict E plus two dummies D1 and D2 for non oil exporting countries and for Africa.

In the US, there were 20.4 terrorist events per year on average, the second highest number after Lebanon, followed by Germany in third place with 19.3 events and by France with 17.9. Terrorism mainly takes place in the US and Europe (this might have changed with regard to the situation in Iraq, Israel and so on, though).

They find a strong positive correlation between terrorism and internal conflict ($\rho=0.15$) and between terrorism and income ($\rho=0.20$). The more internal conflict a country has and the richer the country, the more terrorist attacks it has to expect.

Terrorism leads to a slight decline in per capita growth. If there were one terrorist event every year, this would lead to a 1.5 percent reduction of per capita income growth over the whole period (1968–2000). One would have to divide this by 33 to get the effect estimated for a year. The effect is, hence, quite small, much smaller than from external conflicts. But terrorism has a strong negative impact on business investment. The Investment/GDP ratio falls by 0.5 percent points, while government expenditures increase by 0.4 percent points. Investment reacts more negatively to terrorism than other spending components and government expenditures get crowded in.

For the Netherlands, a small effect has to be expected. Furthermore, as stated above, we think that the connection between money laundering and terrorism is only a very loose one.

7.13.   MAJOR FINDINGS

Most concern in the literature is given to three effects of money laundering. First, there is the economic effect of a misallocation of resources through price distortions. Criminals who want to maximize their profit have to do this under an additional budget constraint, namely that they do not lose their (illegal) business, assets or income by getting caught. This makes other investments more 'profitable' than the ones for the honest investor.

Second, there is the economic and social effect of ruining the reputation and integrity of the financial sector with all its consequences in the longer termed future such as a decline of foreign direct investment, bribe and corruption. This seems to be a major concern.

The third most mentioned effect is the political effect of an infiltration of institutions by criminal and terrorist organizations and the political undermining of state authority and democracy through criminals.

Table 7.4 summarizes the major findings and sources. Column 2 lists important sources. Most of the empirical sources refer to the Netherlands. Column 3 indicates important fields for further research. Column 4 shows major findings. Many of the findings, but not all, refer to the Netherlands.

Table 7.4   Effects of money laundering summarized

Effects mentioned in literature *Short Term Effects*	Important Sources	Remarks and suggestions for further research	Major findings
1. Losses to the victims and gains to the perpetrator – economic and social costs	WODC (2002) NIPO (2002) Stichting Maatschappij en Politie, SMP (1991) UNDCP (1996)	For households the value of damage is missing, victim reports refer to number of cases but not to the value of damages. Many international studies. A Dutch comprehensive cost-benefit analysis is not mentioned by UNDCP (1996)	Costs of drug abuse are about 0.4 percent of GDP
2. Distortion of consumption and savings	Meloen et al. (2003) show criminal spending behaviour from case studies. Alessie et al. (2002) show household spending behaviour from survey data.	A more careful look could be given to the consumption pattern, e.g. for detailed luxury goods such as diamonds.	A comparison of criminal spending behaviour from case studies with household panel data shows that the spending pattern is similar. No significant effect to be expected.

Effects mentioned in literature	Important Sources	Remarks and suggestions for further research	Major findings
Short Term Effects			
3. Distortion of investment 4. Distortion of relative prices 5. Unfair competition	Eichholtz (2004) for the real estate sector	A more in-depth study of the real estate sector and the insurance market is recommended.	Real estate sector large in value and highly non transparent. Very susceptible for money laundering.
6. Changes in imports and exports	Information missing	More information from custom and tax authorities necessary.	Very likely that criminal activities and money laundering mix with regular export and import business
7. Negative or positive effects on output, income and employment	Walker (1995)	For Australia: 1 million laundered money decreases output by 1.2 million, reduces income by 0.6 million and costs 25 jobs.	Most likely positive effect for transit countries of crime such as Australia and the Netherlands.
8. Lower revenues for the public sector	de Kam (2004)	Since the Netherlands is a transit country for crime and money laundering, positive income effects from financial sector to be expected also. Has to be studied in more depth.	In the Netherlands, the public sector loses revenues from tax evasion of approximately €20 billion. However, the public sector also gains approximately €500 million from being a tax haven.
9. Changes in the demand for money, interest rates and exchange rates	Quirk 1996 regression	Problem: In the Eurozone no more Dutch money demand identifiable	10 percent increase of crime will lead to a 6 percent reduction of money demand
10. Increase in the volatility of interest rates and exchange rates	Bayoumi (2004)	Not identifiable for one Eurozone country alone.	-

Effects mentioned in literature	Important Sources	Remarks and suggestions for further research	Major findings
Short Term Effects			
11. Greater avail-ability of credit	Does not hold for small open econo-mies	-	-
12. Higher capital in-and outflows, instability	Walker (1999[a]) plus our findings from chapter 4 Zdanowicz (1999), Boyrie (2005[a])	Transfer price method of Zdanovicz and Boyerie shows very large capital flight flows for Switzerland and Russia but it's still unclear how much is due to money laun-dering	€14–21 billion of additional capital inflows. If there is a through flow, there is no danger
13. Distortion of economic statistics	Some estimates on false statistics for shadow economy available but not for money laundering	over- and underpric-ing, see under 12. transfer pricing	-

Effects mentioned in literature	Important Sources	Remarks and suggestions for further research	Major findings
Long Term Effects			
1. Threatens privatization	No longer relevant for Australia and the Netherlands	-	-
2. Changes in foreign direct investment	According to DNB not visible in data	-	-
3 Risk for the financial sector, solvability, liquidity	-	Effect of a strategic once and for all re-moval of criminal money	Not big. The Netherlands and Australia are transit countries for crime. Prob-lem: in the long run a strategic attack

Effects mentioned in literature	Important Sources	Remarks and suggestions for further research	Major findings
Long Term Effects			
4. Profits for the financial sector	-	Still has to be studied	
5. Reputation of the financial sector	Rawlings and Unger (2005)	Seychelles effect	Not likely for Australia and the Netherlands
6. Illegal business contaminates legal business	WODC studies on organized crime	More sectors and case studies needed	Real estate sector, transport sector. restaurant sector. In total small effect
7. Corruption and bribery	WODC study, Kleemans et al. (2002)	Study on the financial sector needed	Only financial sector and customs relevant
8.Negative or positive effect on growth rates	Quirk 1996, IMF	Quirk estimated that a 10 percent increase of crime leads to 0.1 percent less growth. This would be a very large effect. We modified the model.	Money laundering itself does not dampen economic growth; it is the crime that is intermingled with it that does.
9. Undermines political and democratic institutions	WODC study on organized crime, Kleemans (2002 and 2005)	-	No evidence for Australia and The Netherlands
10. Undermines foreign policy	OECD Foreign Aid Statistics DNB Balance of Payment Statistic	Capital flowing back from developing countries might be larger than Dutch foreign aid. Differs from country to country	Not exactly proven. Might be the case for Dutch Antilles and Suriname
11. Money laundering increases crime	Masciandaro (1999) multiplier	Money laundering multiplier for different scenarios, partly solid data	Money laundering increases crime so that in the end 10 percent–25 percent more money laundering will take place

Effects mentioned in literature *Long Term Effects*	Important Sources	Remarks and suggestions for further research	Major findings
12. Increases terrorism	Blomberg et al. (2004) regression	1.5 percent less per capita growth in 30 years discourages business but stimulates government expenditures. Little effect.	Only loose connection between money laundering and terrorism. They use the same channels but for a different purpose

NOTES

1. EU-15 is Austria, Belgium, Denmark, Finland, France, Germany, Greece, Ireland, Italy, the Netherlands, Norway, Portugal, Spain, Sweden and the United Kingdom.
2. In this paper the number of countries is 17, while Quirk (1996) used a dataset of 19 countries.
3. I owe this possible solution to Ben Geurts, Ministry of Finance.
4. These human capital variables are school enrolment figures on the second and third level of education.
5. I owe this point to Ben Geurts.
6. This can be retrieved from the internet: http://www.unodc.org.
7. To check the robustness of this data we compared it with some figures available on the internet: Fact book Crime: Drug War Facts (http://www.drugwarfacts.org/crime.htm) and Disaster center: United States crime rates 1960–2000 (http://www.disastercenter.com/crime/uscrime.htm). These sources present comparable data, although this might be due to the fact that they use the same source; this is an indication that these numbers can be trusted.
8. The separation of money laundering and crime is theoretical, because there are three ways in which money laundering and crime are intermingled; the proceeds of crime are laundered, money laundering is a crime and money laundering attracts crime, as mentioned earlier.

Appendix 1

Table 7.5   The regression output of Ferwerda and Bosma (2005) in Unger et al. (2006)

#	Dependend Variable	C	Control Variables		Crime	Money Laundering Variables						Regression Statistics			n
			Pop gr (t-1)	I/Y (t-1)		Our	Our (w)	Walker	Walker (w)	Unger	Unger (w)	F-statistic	Adj. R-squared	DW	
1	GDP growth	6.46	326.08	-0.2		-0.03						7.37	0.16	1.4	102
		(3.63)	(4.36)	(-2.45)		(-2.28)									
2	GDP growth	6.67	332.41	-0.21			-0.04					8.02	0.17	1.42	102
		(3.77)	(4.53)	(-2.58)			(-2.62)								
3	GDP growth	6.56	339.89	-0.2				-0.04				8.37	0.18	1.44	102
		(3.73)	(4.63)	(-2.52)				(-2.79)							
4	GDP growth	6.63	344.02	-0.2					-0.06			8.63	0.18	1.44	102
		(3.78)	(4.69)	(-2.56)					(-2.9)						
5	GDP growth	6.52	330.1	-0.2						-0.02		8.28	0.18	1.43	102
		(3.71)	(4.57)	(-2.54)						(-2.74)					
6	GDP growth	6.7	335.45	-0.21							-0.03	8.9	0.19	1.45	102
		(3.83)	(4.7)	(-2.64)							(-3.02)				
7	GDP growth	6.99	344.33	-0.22	-0.12							9.79	0.21	1.48	102
		(4.01)	(4.87)	(-2.79)	(-3.38)										
8	GDP growth	7.91	285.08	-0.26	-0.48	0.14						10.43	0.27	1.63	102
		(4.67)	(4.06)	(-3.39)	(-4.02)	(3.12)									
9	GDP growth	7.28	311.91	-0.23	-0.41		0.11					8.87	0.24	1.55	102
		(4.25)	(4.41)	(-2.99)	(-3.06)		(2.23)								
10	GDP growth	7.32	323.96	-0.23	-0.26			0.05				7.75	0.21	1.5	102
		(4.16)	(4.47)	(-2.96)	(-2.21)			(1.22)							
11	GDP growth	7.21	327.21	-0.23	-0.24				0.06			7.56	0.21	1.49	102
		(4.1)	(4.49)	(-2.9)	(-1.91)				(0.95)						
12	GDP growth	7.9	330.05	-0.25	-0.45					0.06		8.77	0.24	1.55	102
		(4.49)	(4.74)	(-3.19)	(-2.9)					(2.16)					
13	GDP growth	7.34	340.14	-0.23	-0.34						0.06	7.77	0.21	1.5	102
		(4.17)	(4.82)	(-2.94)	(-1.92)						(1.25)				

All the coefficients are significant at a 5 % level except for those underlined
The t-values are presented under each coefficient between parantheses

The variables explained for Table 7.5

Pop gr (t-1) =   Population growth in percentages lagged by one year.

I/Y (t-1) =   Investment share of GDP lagged by one year.

Crime =   Total number of recorded crime offences in million offences

Our =   Calculation of the money laundering variable based on their calculations and the attractiveness index published by Walker (1999[a]) with the 'original' generated money calculation.

Our (av) =   Calculation of the money laundering variable based on their calculations and the attractiveness index published by Walker (1999[a]) with the 'average' generated money calculation.

Walker =   Calculation of the money laundering variable based on the percentages published by Walker (1999[b]) with the 'original' generated money calculation.

Walker (av) =   Calculation of the money laundering variable based on the percentages published by Walker (1999[b]) with the 'average' generated money calculation.

Unger =   Calculation of the money laundering variable based on their calculations and the attractiveness index in this paper with the 'original' generated money calculation.

Unger (av) =   Calculation of the money laundering variable based on their calculations and the attractiveness index in this paper with the 'original' generated money calculation.

8. Conclusions

This book is based on a study conducted by Unger et al. (2006), performed for the Dutch Ministry of Finance. The goal of this study was to present a broad overview of the amounts and effects of money laundering that have been estimated so far and to identify blind spots in research. We contributed to the money laundering research by giving an interdisciplinary overview of the state of the arts. In the study and more so in this book, Madalina Busuioc showed the legal problems associated with defining and prosecuting money laundering (see Chapter 2). In the study, we calculated the amount of money laundered for the Netherlands by making improvements to the underlying model, both theoretical and empirical, and by making it more transparent. This book improves some of the indicators. Furthermore, I explored the underlying model and possible ways of modelling money laundering in more depth here. I showed different approaches of how to measure money laundering and looked at the theoretical model lying behind existing estimation models. I discovered that the gravity approach is the model lying behind the Walker model. This means that approaches of international trade theory can also be used to theoretically underpin this model (see Chapter 3). Furthermore, with the help of my student assistant Joras Ferwerda, I compared the Netherlands with Australia with regard to the amounts of money laundered (see Chapters 4).

Together with Madalina Busuioc I identified the important techniques of money laundering and gave some examples and empirical underpinning. Money laundering can take place in three different phases. It is important for empirical estimates to identify which phase of laundering one tends to measure (see Chapter 5).

In Chapter 6 and 7 I give an encompassing and multidisciplinary overview regarding the effects of money laundering. These chapters are an extension of Unger et al. (2006) where we collected definitions, data, and research results from law, criminology, economics, and cognate social sciences. We also conducted interviews with both national and international experts in the field from organizations such as national banks, ministries, research departments, investigating authorities, and universities. In this book I also identified important points of controversy between the disciplines and areas for future research. I distinguished between the short term (see Chapter 6) and long term effects of money laundering (see Chapter 7). The most important effects of money laundering are the distortion of prices and sector effects, for example in the real estate sector, damage to the reputation of the financial sector, and increases of crime and corruption. Money laundering can have positive effects on growth (more demand for goods and services) but also negative ones, because in the long run it increases crime.

Money laundering, financial crime and terrorist financing have shattered the myth of capital neutrality. The ability of money to flow freely within and between countries has produced enormous benefits, allowing companies to engage in forms of flexible financing that led to investment in infrastructure, jobs and new technologies. These positive effects have encouraged countries to compete for highly mobile capital that moves from one country to the next in search of investment opportunities. This has also brought new risks with it. Criminals, corrupt officials, unscrupulous entrepreneurs, suspect company officers and terrorists are all able to abuse the financial system and engage in money laundering. This poses new risks to the stability, integrity and reputation of the financial system. It also has the potential to undermine social capital and corrode economic, political and social institutions and citizens' trust and confidence in them. The IMF has estimated that total global money laundering accounts for 1–2 percent of world GDP and, more recently, increased this estimate to 2–5 percent of world GDP. We have found that between €3 and €6 billion is laundered in the Netherlands alone, while €14 to 21 billion flow into the Netherlands for laundering from the top 20 countries that generate money for laundering. Australia is not one of the top 20 laundering countries. Nevertheless, US$1–3 billion is laundered and about US$12–18 billion flow into the country.

In the past 20 years, law enforcement authorities and FIUs in OECD countries have made major progress in identifying the ways money laundering works. However, much emphasis continues to be placed on relatively small money laundering operations that tend to highlight the predicate crime (such as drug dealing and fraud). There is still not enough knowledge about how large sums of money are laundered. There are glimpses of this in official reports, but the most public attention by far is directed to the most sensationalist cases. Yet, while they may be scandalous, they do not always involve vast sums of money. New measures and further investigation is needed in order to assess ways in which large sums of money are being laundered. In 1999, it was revealed that $70 billion in Russian funds were channelled through Nauru, the world's smallest republic with some 10,605 people and, at that time, 400 banks. In a scholarly analysis of this problem, de Boyrie, Pak and Zdanowicz (2005[b]) estimated the average volume of capital flight from Russia to the United States from 1995–1999 to be betweenUS$1.86 billion and US$8.92 billion. They suggested that this could be attributed to either money laundering and/or tax evasion. Such research analysis gets behind the headlines. Furthering our understanding of money laundering requires further research to aid policy formulation.

While there is good data for how relatively small sums of money are laundered, further research is needed on how large volumes of money are laundered. In laundering large sums of money, the commingling of funds between lawful and illegal fractions becomes paramount. It makes good policy to establish exactly how much money is laundered in large transactions using established commercial institutions. The Netherlands already has good reporting mechanisms in place designed to detect unusual transactions involving large fund transfers between institutions. For example, inter-institutional transfers involving amounts that exceed €4 million must be reported to MOT. We need to know if such inter-institutional transfers do indeed pose a serious money laundering risk and if so, how. Also, do conventional money laundering processes, such as smurfing play a role in large transactions? More information in this area would help in devising regulatory policy to more effectively manage this risk.

In order to find out more about large flows of capital, it is important to analyse balance of payments data in more detail and more intensely. Though there are bilateral balance of payment data available at the DNB (and for the current account at the CBS), these data are not detailed enough to draw conclusions about money laundering. We have suspicions about where the illegal money might be hiding in the official data of the balance of payments. The item in the balance of payments that is most suspect regarding money laundering is income from wealth in the current account. In the financial accounts it is shares and bonds (aandelen en kapitaalmarktpapier), other financial transactions (overig financieel verkeer), which should be split into central bank, bank, public sector, and private transactions. Large amounts of money laundering can be concealed in other items of the capital balance.

Economically speaking, laundered money is diluted like a drop of ink in the flow of finance, making it difficult to detect. This means that it is hidden in official data. One way to approach this problem is to do mirror balances (spiegelbalansen) where one looks at how far the outflow of one country to another corresponds with the inflow this country has received. Differences in booking and accounting might give hints of unusual transactions. Also, a sudden diversion of flows might give hints of unusual transactions.

Boyrie, Pak and Zdanowicz (2005[a] and 2005[b]) show how one can estimate capital flight due to abnormal pricing in international trade. They also give an overview of how to measure capital flight. In particular, what they call the 'hot money measure' follows the balance of payment identity. They take errors and omissions and private short-term capital figures from the balance of payments.

Although I also used errors and omissions for calculating money flows back from Aruba, Suriname and the Netherlands Antilles in chapter seven on long term effects and on undermining foreign policy, I have stressed the point that this number includes so much counting, reporting and other mistakes that it still needs to be improved.

One should also be aware that export under-invoicing and import overpricing are forms of money laundering that will be hidden in the current account. We do not know the precise role double invoicing, transfer pricing and illegal commissions play in money laundering for the Netherlands and Australia. More research as started by Zdanowicz et al. (1999) could be carried out to establish exactly if, how and why these methods are used in money laundering.

Money laundering in the real estate sector may well be a significant problem. However, additional data on money laundering through the real estate sector is required as this is currently under explored. Recent events in the Netherlands have only hinted at the potential scale of the problem. The FATF (2005) has hinted at this problem for Australia.

It is also very likely that each country has its specialty, its comparative advantage, for money launderers. Australia and The Netherlands seem particularly attractive for reintegrating money into the real estate sector. Furthermore, special purpose entities and trust companies seem to be a huge attraction for tax evaders and money launderers in The Netherlands. In Italy, the bond market seems particularly interesting. In Austria, the banking sector itself seems interesting.

An important step of further research should be directed towards estimating big capital flows originating from illegal activities. For the Netherlands in particular, it is important to identify the through flow niches. In our study, we assume that special purpose entities are important for the through flow of money laundered, but more research and a more in depth analysis have to be performed here.

Money laundering involves a range of techniques. Not enough is known about the risk posed by bearer instruments, correspondent banking and new forms of cybertechnology in money laundering. These areas would benefit from further investigation. Knowledge about how they contribute to money laundering could be used to develop regulatory policies designed to contain the risks posed by such techniques.

Trust companies pose a risk regarding money laundering because of their capacity to conceal the beneficial ownership of the legal persons behind the entities they manage. This has been regulated in the Netherlands as of 2003. It would make a valuable contribution to policy formulation to determine how successful these new regulations have been in combating and reducing money laundering. One of the first promising results is the fact that the number of licences for trust companies has been reduced drastically since the implementation of the new law. The Netherlands is one of the first countries in the world to introduce specific legislation that regulates the governance of trust companies and as such may contribute to providing important standards for such regulation elsewhere.

Another area particularly susceptible to money laundering is the insurance sector, which is also much less regulated than the banking sector. Further research as to the extent of money laundering and dangers faced by money laundering in this sector should be investigated.

More information is required to determine the magnitude of money laundering in specific sectors including derivatives trading and the stock market.

Bribery and corruption do not play a large role in money laundering in the Netherlands and Australia, but they might in other countries. Therefore, we need more data on the part played indirectly by third parties in laundering processes such as accountants, lawyers, bank officers and real estate agents who, through unintentional non-compliance (with reporting suspicious transactions for example) or intential support lauderers.

Furthermore, a study of the precise link between money laundering and corruption and bribery in the financial sector seems important. The magic number, that one million of laundering needs one collaborator in the financial sector, should be questioned and replaced by facts.

Terrorist financing has been slotted into money laundering because of the urgency of this problem. However, terrorist financing often uses clean money to begin with and then transforms it into criminal money through acts of political violence. It is, therefore, only loosely related to money laundering. Both groups use, however the same channels for laundering or dirtying money.

An effective system of activity monitoring should be adopted for the informal banking sector. Underground banking is an important and sizeable threat to the formal financial sector.

There are specific countries that are more dangerous for the Netherlands and Australia with regard to money laundering than others. Specific studies focusing on the links between the Netherlands (Australia) and other particular countries should be conducted to gain information about specific situations and how to better decrease money laundering activities. The corridor studies on worker's remittances that the World Bank is doing at the moment, by looking at remittances sent from one country to another and by analysing the remittance channels from both sides, seems a promising way of progressing (see Unger and Siegel 2006).

Though there is still a long way to go in order to overcome all the technical, methodological, theoretical and empirical problems related to money laundering, there are also some findings in this book which will hopefully stimulate further debate and show in which direction research should develop further.

8.1. MAJOR FINDINGS OF THE BOOK

8.1.1. Money Launders Wear 'Suits and Ties'

The archetypical image of money launderers as comprised of 'tattooed gang-sters' dealing in drugs, prostitution, people-trafficking and racketeering is largely a myth. Money laundering also involves 'white collar' crime. It includes well-dressed bankers, lawyers, notary publics, financial advisors, real estate agents, businessmen, and construction magnates; these are the actors engaged in the huge transactions needed to clean criminal money. While money launder-ing traditionally has a certain gangster-type associated 'glamour' with it in popular mythology and culture, it is also an 'unseen' crime or at least not one that is easily identified beyond the most blatant offences (again the image of the archetypical gangster sitting in a casino playing roulette with ill-gotten gains, is more a reflection of the popular imagination rather than criminological fact). In many cases it is not considered a serious crime by itself in comparison to drug offences, homicide and armed robbery. Police forces have traditionally placed more resources in combating these offences.

Since money laundering has not been considered a serious crime for police in comparison with drug offences, less emphasis has been placed on it. If combating crime is the main goal, then it makes more sense to target the infra-structure that allows money laundering and facilitates crime. This means that there should be a concerted effort to detect and prosecute money laundering, even if it involves pursuing the suited third parties who facilitate layering and integration rather than the 'tattooed gangsters' of the socio-cultural imagery who may still be making the initial placement.

8.2.2. Money Laundering Experiences a Paradigm Shift

Money laundering would not exist without law. It is the law, working its way through the fabric of the body-politic as a 'regime of truth' in Foucauldian terms, that establishes money laundering as a phenomenon, an event and a crime. In addition, it is a very recent discursive innovation indeed. Prior to the passage of the US BSA Act in 1970, money laundering did not exist as a legal concept or an objective phenomenon, except as a metaphor to explain livelihoods made on the proceeds of crime since the days of Al Capone and his Chicago gambling dens. Until the mid-1980s, money laundering as a legal phenomenon remained confined largely to the US and to the proceeds of drug dealing. Then, beginning in the mid-1980s and led largely by the US, there was an exponential expansion in the crimes associated with money laundering and a surge in the number of countries that introduced it as an offence. This followed in the wake of financial deregulation and the liberalization of foreign exchange trading. While liberal western states were keen to deregulate their economies, they soon discovered that this had unforeseen consequences. Money could be moved at the click of a mouse, giving offenders new opportunities to launder their criminal gains like never before.

In response, money laundering became an offence in its own right. A growing international consensus emerged that created the idea of money laundering and then defined it as a material practice. Countries and multilateral organisations then sought to counter the offence through AML. This exercise in constructing a new category of crime reached such a level by the late 1990s that countries with no or limited money laundering provisions had become a minority of states by the close of the twentieth century. Multilateral organizations such as the FATF could begin listing jurisdictions that had resisted or ignored the construction of the concept of money laundering as Non Compliant Countries and Territories (NCCTs). At its peak in 2000, the FATF had listed some 15 countries as Non Compliant Countries and Territories (NCCTs), which had made only minimal moves to prevent money laundering through defining, legislating and enforcing against it. Today there is only one country that still remains on this list: Myanmar (Burma). In the past thirty years money laundering has moved *vis-a-vis* a series of paradigmatic shifts from the national periphery of the world's greatest power to centre stage of global law enforcement.

8.1.3.   Money Laundering Challenges Economic Theory and Modelling

Until now, conventional economics has not been able to keep pace with these paradigmatic shifts that have created the idea and the substance of money laundering. For economics, money is neutral. It has no moral, ethical or political agency. It is a medium of exchange that accords value to the production, consumption and distribution of scarce goods and services. In classical economic thought it is impossible to distinguish lawful and criminological money. However, this is precisely what states have done. Economics cannot divorce itself from society, its laws, political institutions and cultural practices. Hence, one finding of the research presented in this volume is that money laundering has exposed the deficiencies in the view that capital is neutral.

This reinforces the observations of the Italian economist and leader in the emerging scholarship field of money laundering, Donato Masciandaro (2004, p. 4), that events such as September 11th have compelled economists to question fundamental disciplinary 'truths' about the neutrality of money. This echoes John Maynard Keynes who, at the Breton Woods talks, cautioned against deregulated capital mobility on the grounds that the wealthy could send their money abroad to avoid taxes. The same could be said about offenders who can now send their money anywhere in the world for laundering at the click of a mouse. Keynes' words of caution have been disregarded and virtually all controls on the mobility of capital (open global foreign exchange markets) have been lifted, opening up new systemic risks associated with money laundering. Economics must be able to account for the resulting distinction of 'criminal' and 'lawful' money and the unclear categories of grey in-between, symbolized by practices such as tax evasion and dealings with places like Libya and Iran (whether or not these transactions constitute money laundering varies between countries tremendously). The Walker model has been used in this volume in an attempt to address the inadequacies of conventional economics to deal with 'capital neutrality'. We have remained cognizant of the fact, however, that it is very difficult to make conclusive estimations due to the inconclusive categorizations of money laundering and variations between nation-states, despite the expansion of definitions and extension of money laundering as a legal category to almost every country in the world in the past 30 years.

8.1.4.   The Boundaries Between Clean and Dirty Money are Blurred

Nevertheless, the idea that money is neutral continues to hold a residual appeal due to the 'commingling' of funds. It can be very difficult to distinguish 'lawful' from 'criminal' money in ever more complex money laundering arrangements. Exactly when laundered money becomes 'clean' – in the placement, layering or integration phase – is unclear. When laundered funds are layered they are likely to become 'mixed-up' with legitimate money. People can also have multiple identities and subjectivities; they can be involved in both lawful enterprise and criminal activities at the same time. For example, if a businessperson owns a shop, restaurant, transport firm or warehouse and deals in lawful goods and services as producer, distributor or retailer, then that business will be turning over legitimate monies. When the same businessperson is also engaged in drug dealing, people trafficking or embezzlement, and infuses the proceeds of those crimes into the legitimate business as a way of placing and layering money, then those laundered funds become 'mixed-up' or commingled with legitimate earnings. It can be quite a challenge to distinguish between the two. Alternatively, when an offender decides to invest illegal money in collective investment schemes, mutual funds and unit trusts, and they in turn invest in third party entities, the money is commingled with investments from legal sources. Consequently, the boundaries between 'dirty' and 'clean' money become increasingly blurred. This has significant implications for measuring and estimating money laundering because laundering involves the circulation of funds and multiple transmissions between persons, entities and countries. Granted, this is only the case if money laundering is defined as an active attempt to bring illegal funds back into the legal economy. It may not always hold true that money laundering involves merely hiding ill-gotten gains. Either way, a further finding of the research presented in this volume is that money laundering facilitates the commingling of lawful and illegal funds and is much more significant in the daily operations of market economies than previously envisioned.

8.1.5.   No One Seems to Launder Anymore. And yet ...

National and international convergence on money laundering has led to all countries, except Myanmar, accepting and agreeing to implement the FATF's 40 recommendations plus nine special recommendations on terrorist financing. At the level of political rhetoric, all countries are now committed to AML. Then why is money laundering still a significant problem? Why do estimates continue to increase when there are combined national and multilateral efforts designed to counter money laundering? These questions can be addressed by another one of our major findings: *normative compliance* must be distinguished from *functional compliance* with anti money laundering (AML). While virtually all of the world's states have asserted that they are complying with AML at a normative level – compliance reflects good governance – there is a difference between these assertions and what states actually do at a functional level. A number of states have committed themselves to implementing AML at a normative level while this is at odds with what they are doing about it in practice. Several countries have refused to seriously lift bank secrecy (a key regulatory cloaking device that facilitates money laundering), but at the same time claim to be active in countering money laundering. For example, in its assessment of Liechtenstein's banking system, the US State Department noted that '[R]umours and accusations of misuse ... persist in spite of the progress the principality has made in its efforts against money laundering' (US State Department cited by Lomas 2006: Tax-News.com). How can claims that the principality has made 'progress' in its efforts against money laundering be substantiated *functionally* when the very same report observes that Liechtenstein is still refusing to abolish or amend its strict bank secrecy laws? Prince Alois of Liechtenstein claims that bank secrecy laws are unlikely to change because voters would reject such a move. He reflected: 'I don't think a draft law or international accord proposing to scrap bank secrecy would be successful in the foreseeable future. The people would reject it in a referendum' (Prince Alois cited by Lomas 2006: Tax-News.com).

8.1.6.   It is the Big Countries not the Small, Which we should Worry About: Giants Wash More

It is not just small states like Liechtenstein, Anguilla and Bermuda that pose significant risks for the laundering of funds. In fact, their total contribution to money laundering is probably relatively small. The final major finding from the research presented in this volume is that it is large, industrialized OECD economies that are the main conduits for laundering money. Small tax haven states may play a part, but their role has been overstated in the past. They could not exist without a clientele that is based in large countries. It is in those states that the crimes are committed and the proceeds earned. Moreover, many industrialized countries have ring-fenced fiscal and corporate regimes which accord one set of treatment for residents and another set of much more liberal arrangements for non-residents. Consequently, many large countries offer extremely attractive features and services for both domestic and international money launderers.

In its analysis of US shell companies, the US GAO found that corporate vehicles registered in the constituent states of America fell short of regulatory safeguards necessary to deter money laundering. In contrast, the GAO discussed the regulatory experiences of Jersey and the Isle of Man in a way that could be interpreted as the fact that they provide something of a model for good corporate regulation that would be useful in countering money laundering (GAO 2006: 41–42). These two countries are often vilified in the media as centres of 'hot money', but the US GAO (2006: 42) made a more balanced assessment of their regulatory standards and instead observed that:

> Despite strong initial resistance, the company services provider industry in these two jurisdictions is now perceived as successful because licensed companies have continued to remain profitable. In addition, one company service provider told us that the regulators have instilled a degree of professionalism in the company service provider industry. Further, law enforcement officials can obtain information about company ownership when they need it.

By contrast, the US itself remains a very attractive destination for laundered funds. Raymond Baker, a US money-laundering expert reported that:

> When it comes to large deposits from overseas, far too often American banks assume a 'don't ask, don't tell philosophy'... In fact, the Treasury Department estimates that 99.9 percent of the criminal money presented for deposit in the United States is accepted into secure amounts. It's a sad fact, but American banks, under the umbrella of conflicting American laws and policies, will accept money from overseas even if they suspect that it has been illegally obtained (Baker, cited in Napoleoni 2004: 203–204).

Similarly, in 2001 a French parliamentary report identified the City of London as a key centre for money laundering and terrorist financing. Its author, Arnaud Montebourg, who is a member of the French Parliament, writes that one has:

> ... to understand the length of time that the City of London has been used, the way it has been infiltrated, and above all the lack of reaction on the part of the British regulatory authorities ... [London is] not only a tax, banking and financial haven, but also, unfortunately, a judicial haven in many respects (Montebourg, cited in Incian, Roche and Stern, 2001: 29)

The point here is that it is not just 'small offshore' states that operate as centres and conduits for money laundering, but also major industrialised OECD economies. Indeed the widening legal, cultural and political scope of money laundering has blurred the boundaries between the 'lawful' and the 'criminal', the 'offshore' and the 'onshore', 'neutral money' and 'laundered money.' What economic estimates of the amounts and effects of money laundering have to take into account is the possibility that these paradigmatic shifts and enduring uncertainties have made the whole world an attractive place for money laundering. And the most attractive countries are the well developed industrialized countries with well established financial centres and business. Established people with white collars wash the white powdered money from drugs in established financial and business centres. It is the giants that wash more!

Bibliography

Alessie, R., S. Hochguertel and A. van Soest (2002), 'Household Portfolios in the Netherlands', in L. Guiso, M. Haliassos and T. Jappelli (eds), *Household Portfolios*, Cambridge, MA: MIT Press, pp. 340–388.

Alldridge, P. (2002), 'The Moral Limits of the Crime of Money Laundering', *Buffalo Criminal Law Review*, **5** (1) 279–319.

Alper, P.R. (1997), 'Free Doctors From Medicare's Shackles', *Wall Street Journal*, 5 November 1997.

Anderson, J.E. (1979), 'A Theoretical Foundation for the Gravity Equation', *American Economic Review*, **69**, 106–116.

Aninat, E., D. Hardy and R.B. Johnston (2002), 'Combating Money Laundering and the Financing of Terrorism', *Finance & Development, A quarterly magazine of the IMF*, **39** (3).

Arlacchi, P. (1986), *Mafia Business. The maffia ethic and the spirit of capitalism*, London: Verso.

Association of Certified Fraud Examiners (ACFE) (2006), 'ACFE's Highly-Anticipated Report to the Nation to be published in June', http://www.acfe.com/announcement-rttn-preview.asp.

Athanassiou, E. (2002), 'Terrorism, Transaction, Costs and mode of Governance, DIW Workshop on The Economic Consequences of Global Terrorism', 14–15 June, Germany.

Aufhauser, D.D. (2003), 'Terrorist financing: Foxes run to ground (Analysis)', *Journal of Money Laundering Control*, **6** (4), 301–305.

Australian Bureau of Statistics (1994) Australian National Accounts, Input/Output Multipliers 1989/90 (Cat. #5237.0).

Australian Transaction Reports and Analysis Centre (2004), *AUSTRAC Annual Report 2003–2004*, Sydney: AUSTRAC.

Bagella, M., L. Becchetti and M. Lo Cicero (2003), 'Regional Externalitieand Direct Effects of Legislation Against Money Laundering: A Test on Excess Money Balances in The Five Andean Countries', *Journal of Money Laundering Control*, **7** (4), 347–366.

Baker, R.W. (1999), 'The Biggest Loophole in the Free-Market System', *Washington Quarterly*, **22** (4), 29–46.

Baldwin Jr, F.N. (2002), 'Money laundering countermeasures with primary focus upon terrorism and the USA Patriot Act 2001 (Analysis)', *Journal of Money Laundering Control* **6** (2), 105–136.

Bardhan, P. (1997), 'Corruption and Development: A Review of Issues', *Journal of Economic Literature*, **35**, 1320–1346.

Baree, M.A. (2001), 'Money Laundering and Frauds, Changing Expectations From Accountants Profession Issues and Trends', Institute of Chartered Accountants of Bangladesh, SAFA conference at Goa, India, October/December 2001.

Barone, R. (2000), *Riciclaggio ed Usura: Un Modello Di Analisi Economica*, University of Lecce, mimeo.

Barone, R. (2003), 'Laundering and Usury: An Economic Analysis Model', University of Lecce Economics Working Paper No. 42/21 (in Italian).

Barone, R. (2006), 'Comments on Rawlings and Unger (2005)', Competing for Criminal Money, Workshop at the Bocconi University, organized by Donato Masciandaro, Milano in March 2006.

Barrett, S. (2005), 'Insurance Fraud and Abuse: A Very Serious Problem', *Quackwatch*, February 15, 2005, http://www.quackwatch.org/02Consumer Protection/insfraud.html.

Barro, R.J. (1991), 'Economic growth in a cross section of countries', *The Quarterly Journal of Economics*, **106**, 407–443.

Barro, R.J. and X. Sala-I-Martin (1990), 'World real interest rates', in O.J. Blanchard and S. Fischer (eds), *NBER Macroeconomics Annual 1990*, Cambridge, MA: MIT Press, pp. 15–59.

Bartlett, B.L. (2002), 'The negative effects of money laundering on economic development', *Platypus Magazine* (77), 18–23.

Basel Committee on Banking Supervision (2004), 'The compliance function in banks', Consultative Document, Bank for International Settlements, 31 January 2003, Basel.

Bayoumi, T. (2004), 'A new International Macroeconomic Mode', IMF Occasional Paper 239, November 2004.

Beare, M.E. (ed.) (2003), *Critical Reflections on Transnational Organized Crime, Money Laundering, and Corruption*, Toronto: University of Toronto Press.

Beck, T., A. Demitguc-Kunt and R. Levine (1999), 'A New Database on Financial Development and Structure', Policy Research Working Paper Series 2146, The World Bank.

Becker, G.S. (1968), 'Crime and Punishment: An Economic Approach', *The Journal of Political Economy*, **76** (2), 169–217.

Bergstrand, J.H. (1985), 'The Gravity Equation in International Trade: Some Microeconomic Foundations and Empirical Evidence', *Review of Economics and Statistics*, **67**, 474–81.

Bergstrand, J.H. (1989), 'The Generalized Gravity Equation, Monopolistic Competition and the Factor-Proportions Theory in International Trade', *Review of Economics and Statistics*,**71**, 143–53.

Bhattacharyya, D.K. (1990), 'An Econometric Method of Estimating the hidden economy, United Kingdom (1960–1984): Estimates and Tests', *The Economic Journal*, **100** (402), 703–717.

Biern, H.A. (2004), 'Testimony of Herbert A. Biern Senior Associate Director, Division of Banking Supervision and Regulation, The Bank Secrecy Act and the USA Patriot Act Before the Committee on International Relations, U.S. House of Representatives November 17, 2004', US Federal Reserve and the US House of Representatives, Washington DC, available at http://www.federalreserve.gov/boarddocs/testimony/2004/20041117/default.htm.

Blomberg, S.B., G.D. Hess and A. Orphanides (2004), 'The macroeconomic consequences of terrorism', *Journal of Monetary Economics*, **51** (5), 1007–1032.

Blomberg, S.B., G.D. Hess and A. Weerapana (2002), 'Terrorism From Within: An Economic Model of Terrorism', Claremont Colleges Working Papers 2002-14, Claremont Colleges.

Blomberg, S.B., D. Gregory and A. Weerapana (2004), 'Economic Conditions and Terrorism', *European Journal of Political Economy*, **20** (2), 463–478.

Blum, J.A., M. Levi, R.T. Naylor and P. Williams (1998), *Financial Havens, Banking Secrecy and Money Laundering*, United Nations Office for Drug Control and Crime Prevention.

Boon, V. van der (2006), 'Witwasstudie van Financien onder vuur', *Financieel Dagblad*, 28 February 2006.

Boorman, J. and S. Ingves (2001), 'Financial System Abuse, Financial Crime and Money Laundering', IMF Background Paper, International Monetary Fund.

Bovenkerk, F. and W.I.M. Hogewind (2002), 'Hennepteelt in Nederland: het probleem van de criminaliteit en haar bestrijding', Politiewetenschap no. 8, Utrecht: Willem Pompe Instituut voor Strafrechtswetenschappen.

Boyrie, M.E. de, S.J. Pak and J.S. Zdanowicz (2005a), 'The impact of Switzerland's money laundering law on capital flows through abnormal pricing in international trade', *Applied Financial Economics*, **15**, 217–230.

Boyrie, M.E. de, S.J. Pak and J.S. Zdanowicz (2005b) 'Estimating the magnitude of capital flight due to abnormal pricing in international trade: The Russia-USA case', Working Paper Series 2004, 1, Center for International Business Education and Research, Florida International University.

Breedon, F., B. Henry and G. Williams (1999), 'Long-term Real Interest Rates: Evidence on the Global Capital Market', *Oxford Review of Economic Policy*, **15** (2), 128–142.

Breton, A. (ed.) (2000), 'New Canadian Perspectives, Exploring the Economics of Language', Canadian Heritage http://www.pch.gc.ca/progs/lo-ol/perspectives/english/explorer/index.html.

Bruck, T. and B. Wickstrom (2004), 'The economic consequences of terror: guest editors' introduction', *European Journal of Political Economy*, **20** (2), 293–300.

Bruinsma, G.J.N. and F. Bovenkerk (1995), 'Deelonderzoek II, Branches', Bijlage IX, Deel II, onderzoeksgroep Fijnaut in Tweede Kamer der Staten-Generaal (1995), in *Enquête Opsporingsmethoden*, Vergaderjaar 1995–1996, 24072, Nr. 16. Den Haag: Sdu Uitgevers.

Bunt, H.G. van de (1995), 'Beroepsgroepen en Fraude', Bijlage X, Deel III, onderzoeksgroep Fijnaut in Tweede Kamer der Staten-Generaal (1995), in *Enquête Opsporingsmethoden*, Vergaderjaar 1995–1996, 24072, Nr. 16., Den Haag: Sdu Uitgevers.

Camdessus, M. (1998), 'Money Laundering: the importance of International Countermeasures', Plenary meeting of the FATF, Paris, 10 February 1998.

Caribbean Financial Action Task Force (2005), *Suriname Mutual Evaluation Report*, Fifth Draft September 2005.

Caslon Analytics profile identity crime, http://www.caslon.com.au/idtheftprofile. htm (July 11, 2006).

Centraal Bureau voor de Statistiek (2004), *Statistical Yearbook of the Netherlands 2004*, Voorburg/Heerlen: Statistics Netherlands.

Centraal Bureau voor de Statistiek (2005a), 'Waarde onroerende zaken', Statline Database: www.cbs.nl.

Centraal Bureau voor de Statistiek (2005b), 'Nominale waarde obligaties op Euronext Amsterdam', Statline Database: www.cbs.nl.

Centraal Plan Bureau (2003), 'JADE, A model for the Joint-Analysis of Dynamics and Equilibrium', CPB Document, No. 30, May 2003.

Centraal Plan Bureau (2003), 'SAFE, A quarterly model of the Dutch economy for short-term analysis', CPB Documents, No. 42, December 2003.

Central Intelligence Agency (2005), *The World Factbook 2005*, Washington D.C.: CIA.

Chalk, P. (1996), *West European Terrorism and Counter-Terrorism: The Evolving Dynamic*, New York: St. Martin's Press.

Chen, A.H.S. and F. Thomas (2004), 'The effects of terrorism on global capital markets', *European Journal of Political Economy*, **20** (2), 349–366.

Chinn, M. and J. Frankel (2005), 'The Euro Area and Wolrd Interest Rates', Unpublished paper.

Coalson, R. (2004), 'Analysis: Crisis of Confidence in Russia's Central Bank?', Feature Articles, Radio Free Europe, 26 July 2004.

Collins, D.J. and H.M. Lapsley (1996), *The social costs of drug abuse in Australia in 1988 and 1992*, National Drug Strategy Monograph Series No. 30, Commonwealth Department of Human Services and Health, Canberra.

Commonwealth of Australia (1988), *Financial Transaction Reports Act 1988*, Canberra: Commonwealth of Australia.

Commonwealth Law Bulletin (2001), 'International Developments', *Commonwealth Law Bulletin*, **27** (1), 468–507.

Council of Europe (1990), *Convention on Laundering, Search, Seizure and Confiscation of the Proceeds from Crime*, Strasbourg, 8 November 1990.

Cuéllar, M. (2003), 'The Tenuous Relationship between the Fight Against Money Laundering and the Disruption of Criminal Finance', *Journal of Criminal Law and Criminology*, **93** (2 & 3).

Cybersource (2006), *eCommerce Fraud Losses to Jump $700 Million in 2004*, http://www.cybersource.com/news_and_events/view.xml?page_id=1313 (11 July 2006).

Davis, K.E. (2003), 'Legislating against the financing of terrorism: Pitfalls and prospects', *Journal of Financial Crime*, **10** (3), 269–274.

Deardorff, A. (1998), 'Determinants of Bilateral Trade: Does Gravity Work in a Frictionless World?', in J. Frankel (ed), *The Regionalization of the World Economy*, Chicago: University of Chicago Press, pp. 7–28.

De Nederlandsche Bank (2003), *De Nederlandsche Bank, Statistisch Bulletin Juni 2003*, DNB, June 2003.

De Nederlandsche Bank (2004), *De Nederlandsche Bank, Statistisch Bulletin December 2004*, DNB, December 2004.

De Nederlandsche Bank (2005), *De Nederlandsche Bank, Statistisch Bulletin Maart 2005*, DNB, March 2005.

De Nederlandsche Bank, US Federal Reserve Board, State of Illinois and the New York Banking Department (2005), *In the matter of ABN AMRO N.V. Amsterdam, The Netherlands, ABN AMRO BANK N.V. New York Branch, New York, New York, ABN AMRO BANK N.V. CHICAGO BRANCH, Chicago Illinois. Order to Cease and Desist Issued Upon Consent*, FBK Dkt. No. 05-035-B-FB, US Federal Reserve, Washington DC.

Dijck, S. van and R. Koning (2003), *Holland Casino*, Onderzoekskeuzevak Economie van de Publieke Sector, Utrecht School of Economics.

Donker, M., G.H.J. Homburg and F.H.M. van Gemert (2001). *Verkeerd Gokken; een oriënterend onderzoek naar aard en omvang van illegale kansspelen in Nederland'*, College van toezicht op de kansspelen en het Nederlands Kansspel Platform, Den Haag, Amsterdam, January 2001.

Downes, S. (2004), 'Soros to maintain his opposition to Bush', *Times Online*, 4 November 2004.

Duyne, P.C. van (1996), *Organized Crime in Europe*, New York: Nova Science Publishers.

Duyne, P.C. van (1998), 'Money Laundering: Pavlov's dog and beyond', *Howard Journal of Criminal Justice*, **37** (4), 359–374.

Duyne, P.C. van (2006), 'Witwasonderzoek, luchtspiegelingen en de menselijke maat', *Justitiële verkenningen*, **32** (2).

Duyne, P.C. van and R. Janssen (2006), 'De stelling van Petrus van Duyne: maak criminelen niet groter dan ze zijn', *NRC Handelsblad*, 11 February 2006 (interview by R. Janssen).

Duyne, P.C. van, K. von Lampe and J.L. Newell (eds) (2003), *Criminal Finances and Organizing Crime in Europe*, Nijmegen: Wolf Legal Publishers.

Duyne, P.C. van, K. von Lampe and N. Passas (eds) (2002), *Upperworld and Underworld in cross border crime*, Nijmegen: Wolf Legal Publishers.

Duyne, P.C. van, J. Matjaz, K. von Lampe and J.L. Newell (eds) (2004), *Threat and Phantom of Organized Crime, Corruption and Terrorism*, Nijmegen: Wolf Legal Publishers.

Duyne, P.C. van and H.A. de Miranda (1999), 'The emperor's cloths of disclosure, hot money and suspect disclosure', *Crime, Law and Social Change*, **31** (3), 245–271.

Duyne, P.C. van, J.M. Reijntjes and C.D. Schaap (1993), *Misdaadgeld, 1993*, Arnhem: Gouda Quint.

The Economist (1997), 'Money Laundering: That Infernal Washing Machine', *The Economist*, 26 July 1997.

Eggen, A.Th.J. and W. van der Heide (eds), *Criminaliteit en rechtshandhaving 2004: ontwikkelingen en samenhangen*, Den Haag, WODC/CBS, 2005.

Eichholtz, P. (2004), 'De Vastgoedwereld: Spelers, Activiteiten en Geldstromen', Presentation held at the seminar *Zicht op misdaad en onroerend goed*, 15 December, 2004, Centre for Information and Research on Organised Crime, Amsterdam, Vrije Universiteit.

Eldor, R. and M. Rafi (2004), 'Financial markets and terrorism', *European Journal of Political Economy*, **20** (2), 367–386.

Enders, W. and T. Sandler (1993), 'The Effectiveness of Anti-Terrorism Policies: Vector Autoregression Intervention Analysis', *American Political Science Review*, **87** (4), 839–844.

Enste, D.H. and F. Schneider (2000), *Schattenwirtschaft und Schwarzarbeit: Umfang, Ursachen, Wirkungen und wirtschaftspolitische Empfehlungen*, Forum Wirtschaft und Soziales (FWS), R. Oldenbourg Verlag, München-Wien.

European Central Bank (2003), *Structural Factors in the EU Housing Market*, European Central Bank, 2003.

European Central Bank (2004), *Monthly Bulletins Jan–Dec 2004*, Frankfurt am Main: European Central Bank.

European Committee on Internal Market and Consumer Protection (2004), 'Proposal for a directive of the European Parliament and of the Council on the prevention of the use of the financial system for the purpose of money laundering including terrorist financing', (Presented by the Commission), Brussels, COM/2004.

European Council (1998), *98/699/JHA: Joint Action of 3 December 1998 adopted by the Council on the basis of Article K.3 of the Treaty on European Union, on money laundering, the identification, tracing, freezing, seizing and confiscation of instrumentalities and the proceeds from crime.*

European Council (1991), *Council Directive 91/308/EEC of 10 June 1991 on prevention of the use of the financial system for the purpose of money laundering.*

European Council (2001), *2001/500/JHA: Council Framework Decision of 26 June 2001 on money laundering, the identification, tracing, freezing, seizing and confiscation of instrumentalities and the proceeds of crime.*

European Council (2005), *Convention on Laundering, Search, Seizure and Confiscation of the Proceeds from Crime and on the Financing of Terrorism*, Explanatory Report, 16 May 2005, Warsaw http://www.coe.int/t/dcr/summit/conventions_en.asp.

European Council and Parliament (2001), *Directive 2001/97/EC of the European Parliament and of the Council of 4 December 2001 amending Council Directive 91/308/EEC on prevention of the use of the financial system for the purpose of money laundering.*

European Council and Parliament (2005), *Directive 2005/60/EC of the European Parliament and of the Council of 26 October 2005 on the prevention of the use of the financial system for the purpose of money laundering and terrorist financing.*

European Journal of Political Economy (2004), Economic research on terror (preface)', *European Journal of Political Economy*, **20** (2), 291–292.

European Union (2006), *EU coherent strategy against fiscal fraud*, MEMO/06/221, Brussels, 31 May 2006.

Faber, W. and A.A.A. van Nunen (2002), *Het ei van Columbo? Evaluatie van het project financieel recherchere*, Oss: Faber Organisatievernieuwing.

Faber, W. and A.A.A. van Nunen (2004), *Uit onverdachte bron*, Meppel: Boom Juridische uitgevers.

Federal Bureau of Investigation (1999), *Countering Terrorism Threat Assessment and Warning Unit, Terrorism and the United States*, United States.

Feenstra, R.C. (2002), 'Border Effects and the Gravity Equation: Consistent Methods for Estimation', *Scottish Journal of Political Economy*, **49**, 491–506.

Ferguson, R.W.J. (2003), 'Financial Bailout of September 11: Rapid Response', *Challenge: The Magazine of Economic Affairs*, **45**.

Ferwerda, H., N. Arts, E. de Bie and J. van Leiden, (2005), *Georganiseerde Autodiefstal, Kenmerken, achtergronden van een illegale branche in beeld gebracht*, WODC, Ministerie van Justitie.

Ferwerda, J. and Z.S. Bosma (2005), 'The effect of money laundering on economic growth', Paper for Onderzoekskeuzevak Economie van de Publieke Sector, Utrecht School of Economics.

Ferwerda, J. (2006), 'Notes on the Amounts and the Effects of Money Laundering by Unger et al. (2006)', Paper written at the Utrecht School of Economics, July 2006, mimeo.

Fijnaut, C.J.C.F., F. Bovenkerk, G.J.N. Bruinsma and H.G. van de Bunt (1995),
'Eindrapport Georganiseerde criminaliteit in Nederland'. Bijlage VII, Eindrapport onderzoeksgroep Fijnaut in Tweede Kamer der Staten-Generaal,
vergaderjaar 1995–1996, 24072, Nr. 16, *Enquête Opsporingsmethoden*, Den
Haag: Sdu Uitgevers.

Fijnaut, C.J.C.F., G. Bruinsma and H. van de Bunt (1998), *Organized Crime in
the Netherlands*, Den Haag: Kluwer Law International.

Fijnaut, C.J.C.F. and L. Paoli (eds) (2004), *Organised Crime in Europe, Concepts, Patterns and Control Policies in the European Union and Beyond*,
Studies of Organized Crime, Vol. 4, New York: Springer.

Financial Action Task Force (1997–2003), *Financial Action Task Force, Annual
Reports 1997–2003*.

Financial Action Task Force (2000), *Financial Action Task Force, 1999–2000,
Money Laundering Typologies*, Paris, 2000.

Financial Action Task Force (2001), *FATF Cracks Down on Terrorist Financing*, Washington, 31 October 2001.

Financial Action Task Force (2002a), *Basic Facts about Money Laundering*,
FATF website (www1.oecd.org/fatf).

Financial Action Task Force (2002b), *Report on Money Laundering Typologies
2001–2002*, Paris.

Financial Action Task Force (2003), *Financial Action Task Force, The forty
recommendations*, 20 June 2003.

Financial Action Task Force (2005), *Third Mutual Evaluation Report on anti-
money laundering and combating the financing of terrorism*, Australia, 14
October 2005.

Financial Action Task Force and Organization for Economic Co-operation and
Development (1999), *Money Laundering*, Policy Brief, July 1999.

Financieel Dagblad (2006) Chef Air france genoemd in witwaszaak, Franse
Justitie verhoort ceo Spinetta, July 13, p. 13.

FIOD-ECD, Fiscale Inlichtingen- en Opsporingsdienst en de Economische
Controledienst, Fiscal Intelligence and Investigation Office and the Economic
Control Office (the Netherlands), diverse annual reports.

FitzGerald, V. (2004), 'Global financial information, compliance incentives and
terrorist funding', *European Journal of Political Economy*, **20**, 387–410.

Frey, B.S. and H. Weck (1983), 'Estimating the Shadow Economy: a 'Naïve'
approach', *Oxford Economic Papers, New Series*, **35** (1), 23–44.

Frey, B.S. and F. Schneider (2000), 'Informal and Underground Economy', in
O. Ashenfelter, *International Encyclopedia of Social and Behavioral Science*,
Bd. 12 Economics, Amsterdam: Elsevier Science Publishing Company.

Frey, B.S. and L. Simon (2002), 'Terrorism: Deterrence May Backfire', DIW Workshop on The Economics Consequences of Global Terrorism, Berlin, 14-15 June.

Frey, B.S. and L. Simon (2004), 'Decentralizations as a disincentive for terror', *European Journal of Political Economy*, **20**, 509–515.

Fullerton, D. and M. Karayannis (1993), 'Tax Evastion and the Allocation of Capital', NBER Working Paper No. 4581, National Bureau of Economic Research, Cambridge.

GAO, United States Government Accountability Office (2006) Minimal Ownership is Collected and Available, GAO-07-196T, November 14.

Gartner (2002), *Survey of US Consumer Fraud*, Stamford, USA: Gartner.

Gauws, A.R. (2005), 'The determinants of South African expo', PhD university of Pretoria, South Africa, February 2005, http://upetd.up.ac.za/thesis/available/etd-04182005-141139/unrestricted/06chapter6.pdf.

Gilmore, W.C. (1994), *Dirty Money: The Evolution of Money Laundering Countermeasures*, Strasbourg: Council of Europe Press.

Golberg, N. (2001), *Supreme Court of Victoria, Court of Appeal (VSCA), 107 (27 July 2001)*, The Hon. Winneke, Batt and Vincent, JJ. Paragraphs 1–62.

Goldsmith P. (2004), 'Financial crime, terror and subversion – The control of risk in a destabilised world economy', *Journal of Financial Crime*, **11**(4), 312–315.

Gorkum, W.M.E. van and J.R. de Carpentier (2004), *Toezicht op Trustkantoren*, Bank Juridische Reeks 50, NIBE-SVV.

Graaf, F. and M. Jurgens (2003), 'The Netherlands', in T. Graham (ed.), *Butterworths International Guide to Money Laundering Law and Practice*, Second Edition, Butterworths.

Grabosky, P. and J. Braithwaite, (1993), *Business Regulation and Australia's Future*, Canberra: Australian Institute of Criminology.

Graham, T. (2003), *Butterworths International Guide to Money Laundering Law and Practice* (Second Edition), Edinburgh: Butterworths LexisNexis.

Graycar, A. and P. Grabosky (eds) (1996), 'Money Laundering in the 21st Century: Risks and Countermeasures', Australian Institute of Criminology, Research and Public Policy Series, Seminar held on 7 February 1996, Canberra, Australia.

Guiso, L., M. Haliassos and T. Juppelli (2002), *Household Portfolios*, Cambridge: The MIT Press.

Gupta, S., C. Benedict, R. Bhattacharya and S. Chakravarti (2004), 'Fiscal consequences of armed conflict and terrorism in low- and middle-income countries', *European Journal of Political Economy*, **20**, 403–421.

Gupta, S., H. Davoodi and R. Alonso-Terme (1998), 'Does Corruption Affect Income Inequality and Poverty', International Monetary Fund Working Paper, No. 98/76, May 1998.

Hackett, A. (2003), *AUSTRAC Submission No. 2, Inquiry into Cybercrime*, Parliamentary Joint Committee on Australian Crime Commission, Sydney: AUSTRAC.

Haller, D. and C. Shore (2005), *Corruption: Anthropological Perspectives*, London: Pluto.

Head, K. (2003), 'Gravity for Beginners' Version prepared for UBC Econ 590a students, 5 February 2003, Faculty of Commerce, University of British Columbia, Vancouver, Canada.

Hedges, M. (2001), 'Afghan Opium Benefits Taliban/Al-Gaeda Protects Heroin Smuglers, Collects Drug Tax', *Houston Chronicle* (online), Houston.

Helleiner, E. (2000), 'The Politics of Global Financial Reregulation: Lessons from the fight against Money Laundering', CEPA, Working Paper Series III.

Helliwell, J.F. (1998), *How Much Do National Borders Matter?*, Washington: Brookings Institution.

Helliwell, J.F. (2000), 'Language and Trade, Gravity Modelling of Trade Flows and the Role of Language', The Department of Canadian Heritage, http://www.pch.gc.ca/progs/lo-ol/perspectives/english/explorer/page_01.html

Helpman, E. (1984), 'A Simple Theory of International Trade with Multinational Corporations', *Journal of Political Economy*, **92** (3), 451–471.

Heide, W. van der and A.Th.J. Eggen (2003), *Criminaliteit en rechtshandhaving 2001*, WODC: 211 Onderzoek en Beleid. Centraal Bureau voor de Statistiek, Meppel: BOOM Juridische Uitgevers, Den Haag: WODC.

Holland Casino (2003), *Jaarverslag Holland Casino 2002*, Holland Casino.

Hunter, B. and S. Lawrence (2003), 'Australia', in T. Graham (ed.), *Butterworths International Guide to Money Laundering Law and Practice*, Second Edition, Butterworths.

Identity-Theft Organization (2006), 'Updated estimates of the cost of indentity fraud to the UK economy', Table, 2 February 2006, http://www.identity-theft.org.uk/ID%20fraud%20table.pdf.

Incian, E., M. Roche and B. Stern (2001), London 'is lax on money laundering: French MPs accuse Britain of dragging feet over tracking down terrorists' funds, *Guardian Weekly*, October 18-42, 29.

International Monetary Fund (2001), *World Economic Outlook – The Global Economy After September 11*, World Economic and Financial Surveys, Washington, December 2001.

International Monetary Fund (2004), *The IMF and the Fight against Money Laundering and the Financing of Terrorism, A Fact Sheet*, September 2004.

International Monetary Fund and the World Bank (2001), 'Enhancing Contributions To Combating Money Laundering', Policy Paper, International Monetary Fund and World Bank.

Interpol (2004), *Funds derived from criminal activities*, Lyon: Interpol.

International Organization of Securities Commission, Technical Committee (1992), *Report on Money Laundering*, IOSCO Report No. 25, October 1992.

Jain, S.M. and W. Sharun (2004), 'The economics of high-visibility terrorism', *European Journal of Political Economy*, **20**, 479–494.

Jayasuriya, D. (2002) 'Money laundering and terrorism financing: The role of capital market regulators', *Journal of Financial Crime* **10** (1), 30–36.

Jerry, R.H. (2002), 'Insurance, Terrorism, and 9/11: reflections on Three Threshold Questions', *Connecticut Insurance Law Journal*, **9**, 113.

Johnson, J. (2001) In Pursuit of Dirty Money: Identifying Weaknesses in the Global Financial System, Journal of Money Laundering Control, 5:2, p. 122–132.

Johnston, R.B. and O.M. Nedelescu (2005), 'The impact of terrorism on financial markets', IMF Working Paper (WP 05/60), 22.

Jordan, D.C. (1999), *Drug Politics: Dirty Money and Democraties*, Norman: University of Oklahoma Press.

Jurith, E. (2003), 'Acts of Terror, Illicit Drugs and Money Laundering', *Journal of Financial Crime*, **11** (2), 158–162.

Kam, F. de (2004), 'Belastingparadijs Nederland, Judasloon voor de schatkist', *NRC Handelsblad*, 6 March 2004.

Kaspersen, H.W.K. (2005), 'De Wet op kansspelen en handhaving in Cyber space', Presentation held at the seminar *Gokken en georganiseerde criminaliteit*, 6 April 2005, Centre for Information and Research on Organized Crime, Amsterdam, Vrije Universiteit.

Keh, D.I. (1996a), 'Economic Reform and Criminal Finance', *Transnational Organized Crime*, **2** (1), 66–80.

Keh, D.I. (1996b), *Drug Money in a Changing World: Economic Reform and Criminal Finance*, UNODC, 1996–4.

Kendall, R.E. (2004), 'Financial crime, terror and subversion', *Journal of Financial Crime*, **11** (4), 363–365.

Kleemans, E.R., M.E.I. Brienen and H.G. van de Bunt (eds) (2002), *Georganiseerde criminaliteit in Nederland, tweede rapportage op basis van de WODC – monitor*, Ministerie van Justitie, Wetenschappelijk Onderzoek- en Documentatiecentrum.

Klerks, P.P.H.M. (2000), *Groot in de hasj, theorie en de praktijk van de georganiseerde criminaliteit*, Politie Studies 26, Alphen ad Rijn: Samson, Antwerpen: Kluwer rechtswetenschappen.

Knaap, T. (2006), *Distances between countries*, http://knaap.com/data/location 06.xls

Lackó, M. (2000) 'Hidden Economy – An Unknown Quantity? Comparative Analysis of Hidden Economies in Transition Countries in 1989–1995', *Economics of Transition*, **8** (1), 117–149.

Lambsdorff, J.G. (1999), 'Corruption in Empirical Research', A review, presented at the 9th International Anti-Corruption Conference, Durban, South Africa, 10–15 December, 1999.

Lensvelt-Mulders, G.J.L.M., P.G.M. van der Heijden and O. Laudy (2006), 'A validation of a computer-assisted randomized response survey to estimate the prevalence of fraud in social security', *Journal of the Royal Statistical Society: Series A*, **169** (2), 305–318.

Leong, A.V.M. (2004), 'Definitional analysis: The war on terror and organised crime', *Journal of Money Laundering Control*, **8** (1), 19–36.

Leun, J.P. van der, G. Engbersen and P. van der Heijden (1998), *Illegaliteit en criminaliteit: schattingen, aanhoudingen en uitzettingen*, Rotterdam EUR/ FSW (rapport).

Levi, M. (2002), 'Money Laundering and its Regulation', *Annals of the American Academy of Political and Social Science*, **582** (1), 181–194.

Lewis, S. and D. Macfarlane (2003), '$5bn lost to foreign tax rorts', *The Australian*, 6 January 2003.

Leyden, J. (2005), 'US hit for $548m in fraud losses', *The Register*, 2 February 2005.

Linnemann, H. (1966), *An Econometric Study of International Trade Flows*, Amsterdam: North-Holland.

Lomas U. (2006) Liechtenstein Will Resist Moves To End Bank Secrecy, Says Prince, Tax-News.com, Brussels, March 21, 2006.

Mackrell, N. (1997), 'Economic Consequences of Money Laundering', in A. Graycar and P. Grabosky (eds), 'Money Laundering in the 21st Century: Risks and Countermeasures', Australian Institute of Criminology, Research and Public Policy Series, Seminar held on 7 February 1996, Canberra, Australia.

Masciandaro, D. (1995), 'Money laundering, banks and regulators, an economic analysis', Working paper No. 73, Innocenzo Gasparini Institute for Economic Research, January 1995.

Masciandaro, D. (1998), 'Money Laundering Regulation: The Micro Economics', *Journal of Money Laundering Control*, **2** (2).

Masciandaro, D. (1999), 'Money Laundering: The Economics of Regulation', *European Journal of Law and Economics*, **7**, 225–240.

Masciandaro, D. (2004a), *Global Financial Crime: Terrorism, Money Laundering, and OffShore Centres*, Global Finance Series, Ashgate: ISPA.

Masciandaro, D. (2004b), *Combating Black Money: Money Laundering and Terrorism Finance, International Cooperation and the G8 Role*, University of Lecce Economics Working Paper No. 56/26, June 2004.

Masciandro, D. and U. Filotto (2001), 'Money Laundering Regulation and Bank Compliance Costs. What Do Your Customers Know? Economics and Italian Experience', *Journal of Money Laundering Control*, **5** (2), 133–145.

Masciandaro, D. and A. Portlano (2002), *Terrorism and Organised crime, Financial Regulation and non Cooperative countries: inside the Black (List) Box*, University of Lecce Economics Working Paper No. 32/14, November 2002.

McCallum, J.C.P. (1995), 'National Borders Matter: Canada–U.S. Regional Trade Patterns', *American Economic Review*, **85**, 615–623.

McDonell, R. (1997), 'An Overview of the Global Money Laundering Problem, International Anti-Money Laundering Standards and the World of the Financial Action Task Force', Delivered at the International Conference on Global Drugs Law, New Delhi, 28 February 1997.

McDonell, R. (1998), 'Money Laundering Methodologies and International and Regional Counter-Measures', Presented at: Gambling, Technology and Society: Regulatory Challenges for the 21st Century, Rex Hotel, Sydney, 7–8 May 1998.

McDowell J. (2001). 'The Consequences of Money Laundering and Financial Crime, Economic Perspectives', *Economic Perspectives, an Electronic Journal of the U.S. Department of State*, **6** (2).

Meldpunt Ongebruikelijke Transacties (2004), *Jaarverslag 2003, vooruitblik 2004*, MOT, Ministerie van Justitie. Breda: Koninklijke Drukkerij Broese & Peereboom.

Meloen, J., R. Landman, H. de Miranda, J.van Eekelen and S. van Soest (2003), *Buit en Besteding, Een empirisch onderzoek naar de omvang, de kenmerken en de besteding van misdaadgeld*, Den Haag: Reed Business Information.

Middelburg, B. and P. Vugts (2006) *De Endstra-Tapes*, Amsterdam: Nieuw Amsterdam.

Mills, J.W. and I. Robert (2004), 'Responding to terrorism and achieving stability in the global financial system: Rational policy or crisis reaction?', *Journal of Financial Crime*, **11**(4), 380–396.

Ministry of Justice, Ministry of Finance (2004), *Meer aandacht voor vervolging en opsporing van witwassen*, Letter to parliament, 11 May 2004, www.minjus.nl.

Morais, H.V. (2002), 'The War Against Money Laundering, Terrorism, and the Financing of Terrorism', *Lawasia Journal*, 1–32.

Morris-Cotterill, N. (2001), *Think Again: Money Laundering*, Money Laundery Special, 17 July 2002, Sanders Research Associates.

Napoleoni, L. (2003), *Modern Jihad: Tracing the Dollars Behind the Terror Networks*, London: Penguin Books.

Napoleoni, L. (2004), *Terror Inc: Tracing the Money Behind Global Terrorism*, London: Penguin Books.

North Atlantic Treaty Organization Parliamentary Assembly (1998), *Transnational Organized Crime – an Escalating Threat to the Global Market*, November 1998.

Nawaz, S., R. McKinnon and R. Webb (2002), 'Informal and Formal Money. Transfer Networks: Financial Service or Financial Crime?', *Journal of Money Laundering Control*, **5** (4), 330–337.

Naylor, R.T. (1999), *Follow-the-Money methods in Crime Control Policy*, Nathanson Centre for the Study of Organized Crime and Corruption, Toronto: University of Toronto Press.

Nederlands Wetboek van Strafrecht (2004), *XXXA: Witwassen*, Artikel 420bis, 420quarter and 420ter 18 Oktober 2004.

Nelen, H. and F. Lankhorst (2003), 'Legal professions', in H.G. van de Bunt and C.R.A van der Schroot (2003), *Prevention of Organized Crime*, WODC: 215. Meppel: BOOM Juridische Uitgevers, pp. 45–53.

Nelen, H. (2004), 'Criminaliteit en onroerend goed', Presentation held at the seminar *Zicht op misdaad en onroerend goed*, 15 December 2004, Centre for Information and Research on Organised Crime, Amsterdam, Vrije Universiteit.

Netherlands Bankers' Association (2006), *Dutch Issuers of Electronic Money (NVIEG)*, Round Table Meeting Brussels, 8 March 2006.

NIPO Consult (2002), *Monitor Bedrijven en Instellingen 2002*, NIPO Consult Amsterdam, July 2002.

Nitsch, V. and S. Dieter (2004), 'Terrorism and international trade: an empirical investigation', *European Journal of Political Economy*, **20**, 423–433.

Nordstrom, C. (2004), *Shadows of War: Violence, Power, and International Profiteering in the Twenty-First Century*, California Series in Public Anthropology, Berkley: University of California Press.

Norgren, C. (2004), 'The control of risks associated with crime, terror and subversion. (Analysis)', *Journal of Money Laundering Control*, **7** (3), 201-206.

NRC Handelsblad (2006), 'Sectie Binnenland, korte berichten, subject: 2 million cash found on roof in Amsterdam', *NRC Handelsblad*, 20 March 2006.

Organization for Economic Co-operation and Development (2000a), *2000 Report: Towards Global Tax Co-operation: Progress in Identifying and Eliminating Harmful Tax Practices*, Paris: OECD Publications.

Organization for Economic Co-operation and Development (2000b), *Improving Access to Bank Information for Tax Purposes*, Paris: OECD Publications.

Organization for Economic Co-operation and Development (2002), *Measuring the Non-Observed Economy – A Handbook*, Paris: OECD Publications.

Paauw, K. (2005), 'Witwassen in een Nederlands casino', Presentation held at the seminar *Gokken en georganiseerde criminaliteit*, 6 April 2005, Centre for Information and Research on Organized Crime, Amsterdam, Vrije Universiteit.

Pak, S., M. Boyrie and J. Zdanowicz (2004), 'Estimating the Magnitude of capital flight due to abnormal pricing in international trade: the Russia–USA case', CIBER Working Paper.

Parliamentary committee Van Traa (1996), *Inzake Opsporing*, Den Haag: Sdu Uitgevers.

Passas, N. (2004), 'Informal Value Transfer Systems and their Mechanics', presentation at a 2004 APEC conference in Tokyo.

Ping, H. (2004), *Fight Against Money Laundering. A Comparative Perspective*, Rotterdam: Erasmus University.

Pollard, N. (2005), 'UN Report puts Worlds Illicit Drug trade at Estimated $ 321 billion', *Reuters, Boston Globe*, 30 June 2005.

Proximal Consulting (2006), 'Proximal white paper 8, an overview of the global level of fraud and financial crime', Proximal Consulting, The Money Laundering & Business Crime Mitigation Firm, 11 July.

President's Commission on Organized Crime (1984), *The Cash Connection: Organized Crime, Financial Institutions, and Money Laundering*, Interim Report to the President and Attorney General, Reagan Administration Report, United States.

Projectbureau Politiemonitor (2003), *Codeboek Politiemonitor Bevolking 2003*, Projectnummer 77300. Den Haag: B&A Groep Beleidsonderzoek & -Advies BV, Hilversum: Intromart BV.

Quirk, P.J. (1996), *Macroeconomic Implications of Money Laundering*, IMF Working Paper, International Monetary Fund, No. 96/66.

Quirk, P.J. (1997), 'Money Laundering: Muddying the Macroeconomy', *Finance & Development*, **34** (1), 7–9.

Rajwade, A.V. (2005), 'The story behind Refco's collapse', in *rediff.com*, 7 November 2005, available at http://www.rediff.com/money/2005/nov/07 spec3.htm

Rawlings, G. (2004), 'Laws, Liquidity and Eurobonds. The making of the Vanuatu Tax Haven', *The Journal of Pacific History – Pacific Currents*, **39** (3), 325–341.

Rawlings, G. and B. Unger (2005), 'Competing for Criminal Money', Paper prepared for the Society for the Advancement of Socio-economics, Budapest 30 June–2 July 2005.

Reuter, P. and V. Greenfield (2001), 'Measuring Global Drug Markets: How good are the numbers and why should we care about them?', *World Economics*, **2** (4).

Rider, B.A.K. (2002), 'Laundering terrorists! (Editorial)', *Journal of Money Laundering Control*, **5** (4), 255–256.

Ringguth, J. (2002), 'Money Laundering – The Criminal Dimension', Paper presented at the 'Stop Money Laundering' Conference, 26 February 2002, London.

Risen, J. (2002), 'Money Transfers by Hijackers Did Not Set Off Alarms for Banking Regulators', *New York Times*, 17 July 2002.

Roman, N.E. (1995), 'Medicare Scam Veterans Tell Panel How Easy It Was to Cheat', *Washington Times*, 3 November 1995.

Ruiz, M. (2003), 'Argentina', in T. Graham (ed.) (2003), *Butterworths International Guide to Money Laundering Law and Practice*, Second Edition, Butterworths.

Sandler, T. and W. Enders (2002), *What do we know about the substitution effect in transnational terrorism?*, School of Business at the University of Alabama, April 2002.

Sandler, T. and W. Enders (2004), *Transnational terrorism: An economic analysis*, Center for Risk and Economic Analysis of Terrorism Events University of Southern California, Los Angeles California.

Sandler, T. and W. Enders (2004), 'An Economic Perspective on Transnational Terrorism', *European Journal of Political Economy*, **20** (2), 301–316.

Savona, E.U. (1997), *Responding to Money Laundering, International Perspectives*, London: Harwood Academic Publishers.

Savona, E.U. (1999), *European Money Trails*, Amsterdam: Harwood Academic Publishers.

Schaap, C.D. (1998), *Fighting Money Laundering: With Comments of the Legislation of the Netherlands Antilles and Aruba*, London & Boston: Kluwer Law International.

Schaap, C.D. (1999), 'Heling getoetst', PhD thesis Sanders Instituut, Erasmus University Rotterdam, Arnhem: Gouda Quint.

Schaap, C. (2005), 'Witwassen in een Arubaans Casino; mythen en feiten', Presentation held at the seminar *Gokken en georganiseerde criminaliteit*, 6 April 2005, Centre for Information and Research on Organized Crime, Amsterdam, Vrije Universiteit.

Scharpf, F.W. and V.A. Schmidt (2000) *Welfare and Work in the open Economy, Volume II Diverse Responses to Common Challengers*, New York: Oxford University Press.

Schmid, A.P. (1983), *Political Terrorism: A Research Guide to Concepts, Theories, Databases and Literature*, Amsterdam: New Brunswick.

Schneider, F. (2002). 'Money Supply for Terrorism, The hidden financial flows of Islamic terrorist organizations: Some preliminary results from an economic perspective'. Paper prepared for the workshop '*The Economic Consequences of Global Terrorism*', organized by DIW Berlin, June 14–15 2002.

Schneider, F. (2006), 'Shadow Economies of 145 countries all over the world: what do we really know?', Revised version May 2006, http://www.econ.jku. at/Schneider/ShadEconomyWorld145_2006.pdf.

Schneider, F. and D.H. Enste (2000), 'Shadow Economies: Size, Causes, and Consequences', *Journal of Economic Literature*, **38**, 77–114.

Schneider, F. and D.H. Enste (2002), *The Shadow Economy, An International Survey*, Cambridge: University Press.

Schneider, F. and R. Klingmair (2004), 'Shadow Economies around the World: What Do We Know?', Institute for the Study of Labour (IZA) Bonn, Discussion Paper No. 1043, March 2004.

Schroeder, W.R. (2001), 'Money Laundering, A Global Threat and the International Community's Response', *FBI Law Enforcement Bulletin*, **70** (5), 1–9.

Schudelaro, T. (2003), *Electronic Payment Systems and Money Laundering, Risks and Countermeasures in the Post-Internet Hype Era*, Nijmegen: Wolf Legal Publishers.

Seagrave, S. (1995), *Lords of the Rim: The Invisible Empire of the Overseas Chinese*, New York: Putnam's Sons.

Securities Industry Research Centre (2003), *Identity Fraud: An evaluation of its nature, cost and extent*, SIRCA Securities Industry Research Centre of Asia-Pacific.

Shapiro, G. (2006), 'Austrian bank hit by Refco scandal', in *Law and tax news. com*, 2 May 2006, Available at http://www.lawandtax-news.com/asp/story. asp?storyname=23481.

Siegmann, A. (2006), 'Cadastre prices of real estate objects in the city of Amsterdam', Unpublished graph, University of Amsterdam, UvA.

Silberbauer, K. and R. Krilyszyn (2003), 'Austria', in T. Graham (ed) (2003), *Butterworths International Guide to Money Laundering Law and Practice*, Second Edition, Butterworths.

SIOD, Sociale Inlichtingen- en Opsporingsdienst, Social Intelligence and Investigation Office (the Netherlands), diverse annual reports.

Smekens, M. and M Verbruggen (2004), *De Illegale Economie in Nederland*, Centraal Bureau voor de Statistiek, 20 September 2004.

Smit, P.R., F.T. van Tulder, R.F. Meijer and P.P.J. Groen (2003), *Het ophelderingspercentage nader beschouwd*, WODC: 213 (onderzoek en beleid), ministerie van Justitie, Meppel: BOOM Juridische Uitgevers.

Smith, R.G. (1997), *Measuring the Extent of Fraud in Australia.*, Australian Institute of Criminology, Trends & Issues, November 1997.

Spapens, A.C. and M.Y. Bruinsma (2002), *Smokkel van handvuurwapens vanuit voormalige Oostbloklanden naar Nederland*, Instituut voor sociaal-wetenschappelijk beleidsonderzoek en advies, Tilburg.

Stessens, G. (2002), *Money Laudering: A New International Enforcement Model*, Cambridge: University Press.

Stuurgroep 'Politie 2000', Stichting Maatschappij en Politie (1991), *Veiligheid en politie: een beheersbare zaak*, Deel 7 uit de SMP-publikaties, Arnhem: Gouda Quint, Antwerpen: Kluwer Rechtswetenschappen.

Sullivan, M.A. (2004), 'US Multinationals Move More Profits to Tax Havens', *Tax Notes International*, **27** (4), 589–593.

Takáts, E. (2006), 'A Theory of "Crying Wolf": The Economics of Money Laundering Enforcement', Paper presented at a workshop organized by Donato Masciandaro at Bocconi University, Milano, March 2006.

Tanzi, V. (1996), 'Money Laundering and the International Financial System', IMF Working Paper, International Monetary Fund, No. 96/55.

Tanzi, V. (1997), 'Macroeconomic Implications of Money Laundering', in E.U. Savona, *Responding to Money Laundering, International Perspectives*, Amsterdam: Harwood Academic Publishers, pp. 91–104

Tedds, L.M. and D.E.A. Giles (2000), 'Modeling the Underground Economies in Canada & New Zealand: A Comparative Analy', Working Paper, University of Victoria.

Tegelaar, J. (2005), 'De fiscale en bestuurlijke aanpak van illegale casino's', Presentation held at the seminar *Gokken en georganiseerde criminaliteit*, 6 April 2005, Centre for Information and Research on Organised Crime, Amsterdam, Vrije Universiteit.

Temporary parliamentary committee Bouwfraude (2002), *Bouwfraude en corruptie bij ambtenaren*, Letter to parliament 28093, nr. 22. Den Haag, January 2002.

Thomas, J.J. (1999), 'Quantifying the black economy: 'Measurement without Theory' Yet Again?', *The Economic Journal*, **109** (456), 381–389.

Thony, J.F. (2002), 'Money Laundering and Terrorism Financing – An Overview', Prepared for the IMF Seminar on Current Developments in Monetary and Financial Law, Washington D.C., 7–17 May 2002.

Thoumi, F. (2003), 'The Numbers' Game: Let's All Guess the Size of the Illegal Drugs Industry!', Paper prepared for TNI seminar on The Economic Impact of the Illicit Drug Industry, December 2003.

Tinbergen, J. (1962), *Shaping the World Economy: Suggestions for an International Economic Policy*, New York: Twentieth Century Fund.

Transnational Institute (2003), 'Crime and Globalization, The Economic Impact of the Illicit Drug Industry', seminar December 2003, http://www.tni.org/crime-docs/impact.pdf

Transparency International (2003) Transparency International Corruption Perception index, http://www.transparency.org/policy_research/surveys_indices/cpi/2003.

Transparency International (2005) Transparency International Corruption Perception index, http://www.transparency.org/policy_research/ surveys_indices/cpi/2005

Truman, E.M. and P. Reuter (2004), *Chasing Dirty Money: Progress on Anti-Money Laundering*, Institute for International Economics.

Tulder, F.P. van (1985), *Criminaliteit, pakkans en politie*, Sociaal Cultureel Planbureau, Den Haag: Distributiecentrum Overheidspublikaties.

Tulder, F.P. van and B.C.J. van Velthoven (2003), 'Econometrics of crime and litigation', *Statistica Neerlandica*, **57** (3), 321–346.

Tweede Kamer der Staten-Generaal (2003), *Misbruik en oneigenlijk gebruik op het gebied van belastingen, sociale zekerheid en subsidies*, Tweede Kamer debat 17050, nr. 256. Den Haag: Sdu Uitgevers.

Tweede Kamer der Staten-Generaal (2003), *Vragen van het lid Vendrik (Groen-Links) aan de staatssecretaris van Financiën en de minister van Justitie over witwaspraktijken bij Holland Casino*, Kamervragen met antwoord 2003–2004, nr. 66, Den Haag: Sdu Uitgevers.

Unger, B., J. Ferwerda, W. de Kruijf, G. Rawlings, M. Siegel and K. Wokke (2006), 'The Amounts and the Effects of Money Laundering', Report for the Dutch Ministry of Finance, February 2006, http://www.minfin.nl/binaries/minfin/assets/pdf/old/06_011a.pdf

Unger, B. and M. Siegel (2006) *Workers' Remittances, The corridor between The Netherlands and Suriname*, Project done for the World Bank and the Dutch Ministry of Finance, September 2006, http://www.minfin.nl

United Nations (1988), *UN Convention against the Illicit Traffic in Narcotic Drugs and Psychotropic Substances*, Vienna.

United Nations (1998a), 'Social and Economics Costs of Illicit Drugs', *United Nations Chronicle*, Online Edition, **35** (2).

United Nations (1998b), *Report on Financial Havens, Banking Secrecy and Money Laundering*, http://www.imolin.org/imolin/finhaeng.html.

United Nations Development Programme (1996), *Human Development Report 1996*, New York, Oxford: Oxford University Press.

United Nations Development Programme (1999), *Human Development Report 1999*, New York, Oxford: Oxford University Press.

United Nations Interregional Crime and Justice Research Institute (2000), *International Crime Victims Survey 2000*, UNICRI.

United Nations Office on Drugs and Crime (1998), *Economic and Social Consequences of Drug Abuse and Illicit Trafficking*, UNODC, Technical Series No. 6.

United Nations Office on Drugs and Crime (1998), *Financial Havens, Banking Secrecy and Money-Laundering*, New York: United Nations.

United Nations Office on Drugs and Crime (2000), *Seventh United Nations Survey on Crime Trends and Operation of Criminal Justice System*, UNODC.

United Nations Office on Drugs and Crime (2003), *UNODC model money-laundering, proceeds of crime and terrorist financing bill*.

United Nations Office on Drugs and Crime (2004), *Drugs and Crime Trends in Europe and Beyond*, Vienna: UNDOC 29 April, 2004.

United Nations Office on Drugs and Crime (2005), *Bi-Annual Seizure Report 2004/2*, UNODC April 2005.

United Nations Office on Drugs and Crime (2006), *World Drug Report 2006*, 2 volumes, http://www.unodc.org/pdf/WDR_2006/wdr2006_volume1.pdf

United States Commerce Deparment (2001), *US International Transacions 2000*, United States Commerce Departement, Bureau of Economic Analysis.

United States Department of Justice (2002), *Department of Justice Seeks Offshore Credit Card Records*, Press Release 25 March 2002, Washington DC: Department of Justice.

United States Department of the Treasury Financial Crimes Enforcement Network (2005), *In the matter of the New York Branch of ABN AMRO Bank N.V. New York, New York: Assessment of Civil Money Penalty*, Washington DC: US Department of the Treasury.

United States Federal Reserve et al. (2005) *In the matter of ABN AMRO N.V. Amsterdam, The Netherlands, ABN AMRO BANK N.V. New York Branch, New York, New York, ABN AMRO BANK N.V. CHICAGO BRANCH, Chicago Illinois. Order of Assessment of a Civil Monetary Penalty, Monetary Payment and Order to File Reports Issued Upon Consent*, FRB Dkt. No. 05-035-CMP-FB, Washington DC: US Federal Reserve.

United States Treasury Department (2003), *The 2002 National Money Laundering Strategy*, The White House, 23 September 2001. Billing code 3195-01-P.

Uppsala Conflict Data Program (2005), *Uppsala Conflict Database*, Uppsala Universitet, Uppsala, Sweden.

Veer, A. van 't (1998), *Spelregels*, Deventer: Gouda Quint.

Visini, S. and R. Haflinger (2003), 'Switzerland', in T. Graham (ed.) (2003), *Butterworths International Guide to Money Laundering Law and Practice*, Second Edition, Butterworths.

Walker, J. (1995), 'Estimates of the Extent of Money Laundering in and through Australia', Paper Prepared for the Australian Transaction Reports and Analysis Centre, September 1995, Queanbeyan: Jonh Walker Consulting Services.

Walker, J. (1999a), 'How Big is Global Money Laundering?', *Journal of Money Laundering Control*, **3** (1).

Walker, J. (1999b), *Measuring the Extent of International Crime and Money Laundering*, Prepared for KriminálExpo, Budapest, 9 June 1999.

Walker, J. (2002), *Just How Big is Global Money Laundering?*, Sydney: Australian Institute of Criminology Seminar.

Walker, J. (2003), Lecture in Bangkok, Thailand.http://members.ozemail.com.au/~john.walker/crimetrendsanalysis/THAILAND%20MONEY%20LAUNDERING_files/frame.htm

Werf, R. van der and P. van de Ven (1996), *The Illegal Economy in the Netherlands*, Voorburg/Heerlen: Centraal Bureau voor de Statistiek.

Werf, R. van der (1997), 'Registration of illegal production in the national accounts of the Netherlands', Submitted by Statistics Netherlands and presented at the conference of European Statisticians.

Whelan, D.C. (2005), 'Organized crime and sports gambling in the USA', Presentation held at the seminar *Gokken en georganiseerde criminaliteit*, 6 April 2005, Centre for Information and Research on Organised Crime, Amsterdam, Vrije Universiteit.

WODC, Wetenschappelijk Onderzoeks en Documentatie Centrum, Scientific Research and Documentation Centre (the Netherlands), diverse annual reports.

World Trade Organization (2005), *Statistics Database*, Geneva: WTO.

Yaniv, G. (1994), 'Taxation and Dirty money laundering', *Public Finances/Public Finance*, **49** (Supplement), 40–51.

Yaniv, G. (1999), 'Tax Evasion, Risky Laundering, and Optimal Deterrence Policy', *International Tax and Public Finance*, **6** (1), 27–38.

Zanetta, H. and H. Schuh (2003), *Combating Fraud 2002, Don't give economic and financial crime a chance! The Austrian tax and customs administration at the service of the taxpayers*, Vienna: Federal Ministry of Finance.

Zdanowicz, J., S. Pak and M. Sullivan M (1999), 'Brazil-United States trade: capital flight through abnormal pricing', *The International Trade Journal*, **13** (4), 423–443.

Index